MW01630146

Chaïm Soutine
Against the Current

Chaïm Soutine at Saint Guirec, ca. 1932–1935
Photographer unknown

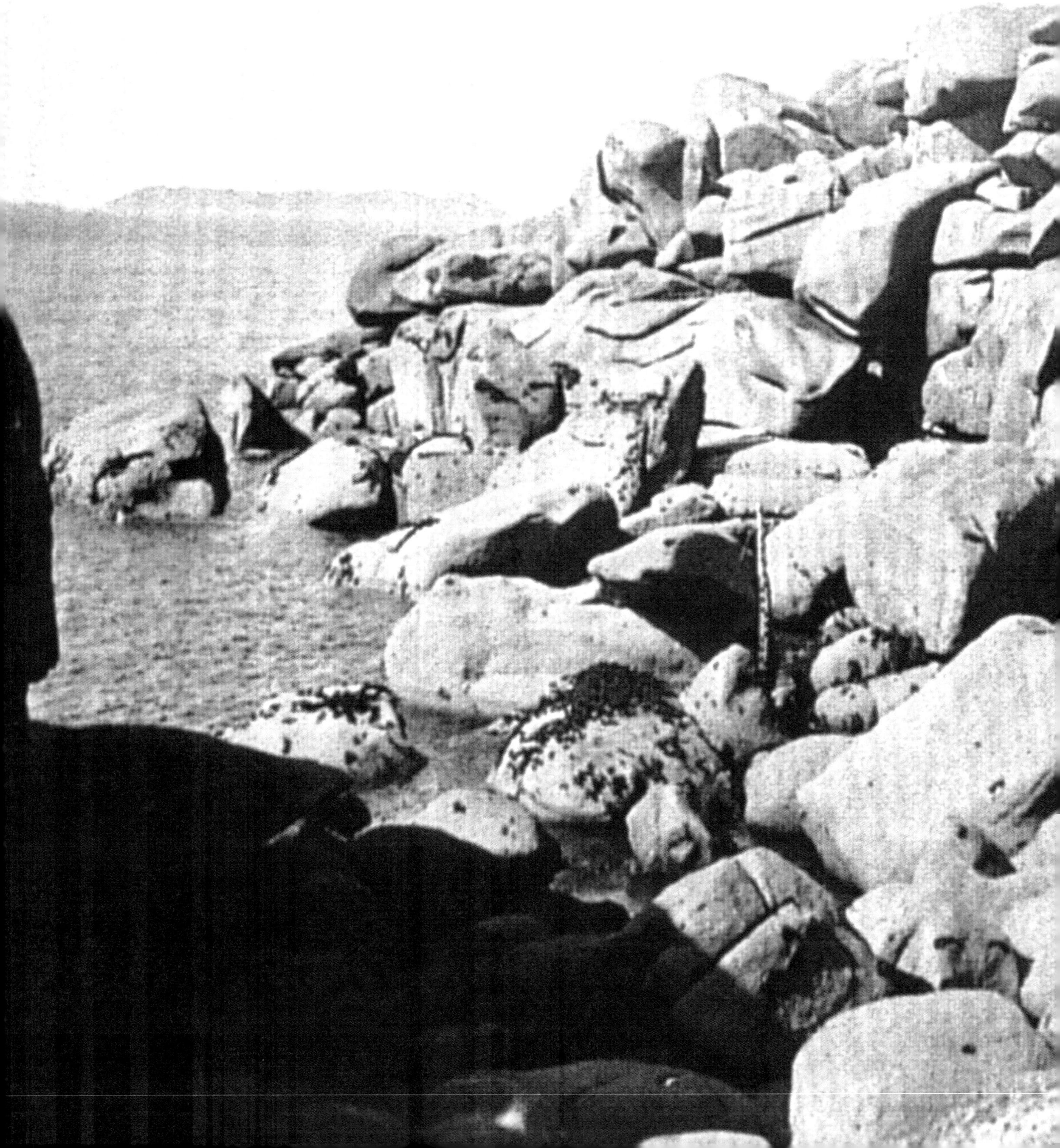

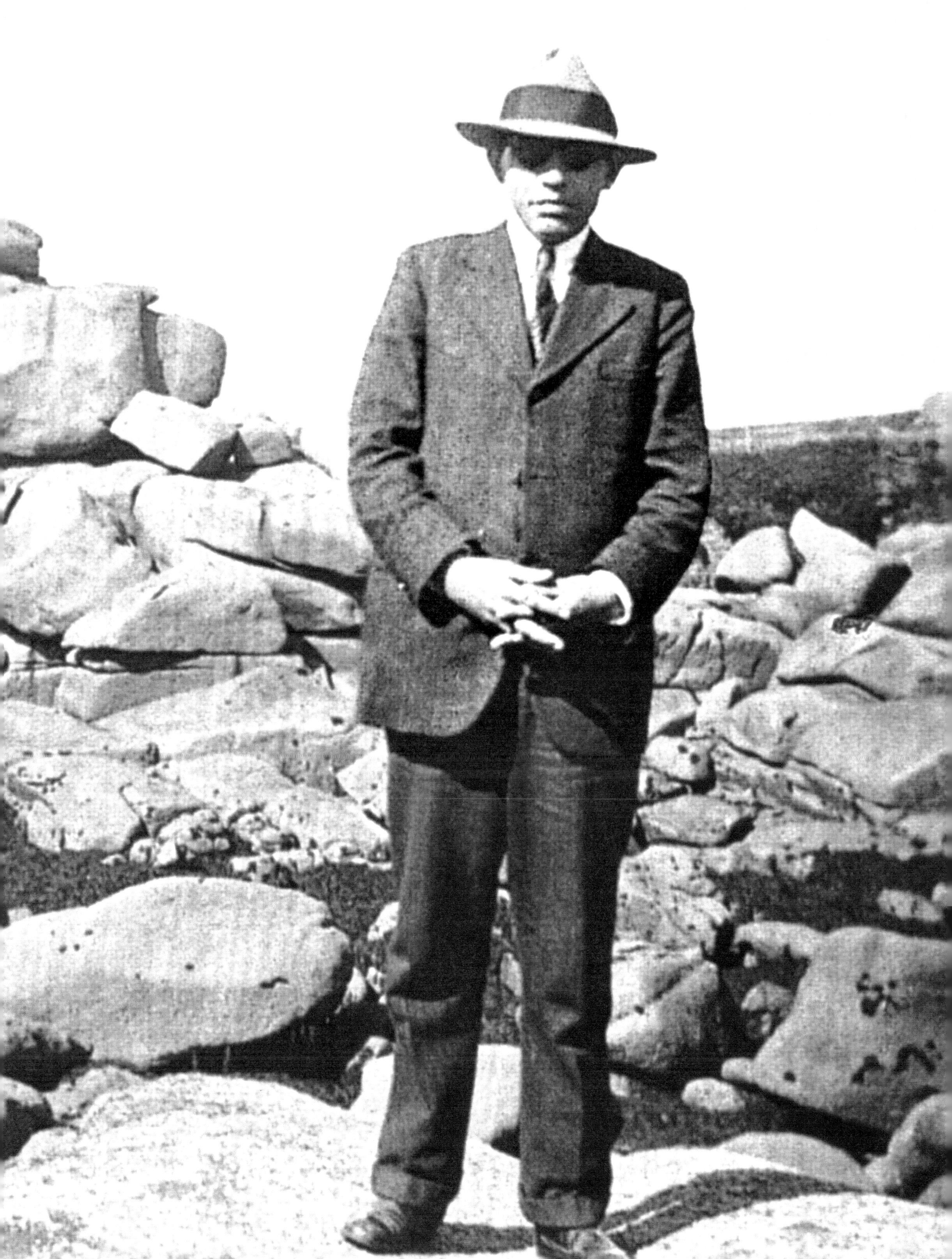

Edited by Susanne Gaensheimer and Susanne Meyer-Büser

This exhibition is a collaboration between Kunstsammlung Nordrhein-Westfalen, Louisiana Museum of Modern Art, Humlebæk, and Kunstmuseum Bern.

Chaïm Soutine. Against the Current
K20 Kunstsammlung Nordrhein-Westfalen, Düsseldorf, Germany
September 2, 2023, to January 14, 2024
Louisiana Museum of Modern Art, Humlebæk, Denmark
February 9 to July 14, 2024
Kunstmuseum Bern, Switzerland
August 16 to December 1, 2024

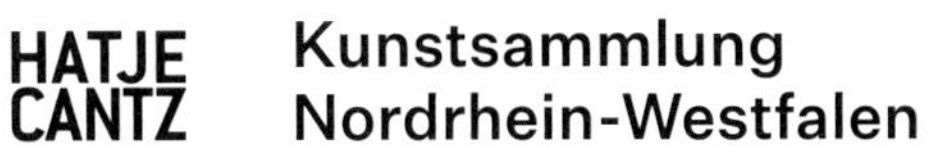

Chaïm Soutine

Against the Current

Lenders to the Exhibition

We would like to express our sincere gratitude to the
following museums, institutions, and private lenders
who have significantly contributed to the success
of this exhibition with their generous support.

ALBERTINA, Vienna
Buffalo AKG Art Museum, Buffalo
Centre Pompidou, Paris, Musée national d'Art
moderne / Centre de création industrielle
The Cleveland Museum of Art, Cleveland
The Courtauld Gallery, London
David Lévy, Modern & Postwar Art, Brussels
Galerie Larock-Granoff, Paris
Galerie Thomas, Munich
The Israel Museum, Jerusalem
Kunsthaus Zürich
Kunstmuseum Bern
Kunstmuseum Luzern, Lucerne
Kunstsammlung Nordrhein-Westfalen, Düsseldorf
The Lewis Collection, London
Los Angeles County Museum of Art, Los Angeles
MAH Musée d'Art et d'histoire, Geneva
Minneapolis Institute of Art, Minneapolis
Musée Calvet, Avignon
Musée d'Art moderne de Paris
Musée de Grenoble
Musée de l'Orangerie, Paris
Musée des Beaux-Arts, La Chaux-de-Fonds
Musée Unterlinden, Colmar
Museum Folkwang, Essen
The Museum of Modern Art, New York
National Galleries of Scotland, Edinburgh
National Gallery of Art, Washington, DC
The Norton Simon Foundation, Pasadena
Petit Palais, Geneva
Princeton University Art Museum, Princeton
Private Collection, Houston
Saint Louis Art Museum, Saint Louis
SMB Staatliche Museen zu Berlin, Nationalgalerie
SMK Statens Museum for Kunst, Copenhagen
Staatsgalerie Stuttgart
Stiftung Im Obersteg, Basel
Tate
Von der Heydt-Museum Wuppertal

We also extend our thanks to those lenders who wish
to remain anonymous.

Contents

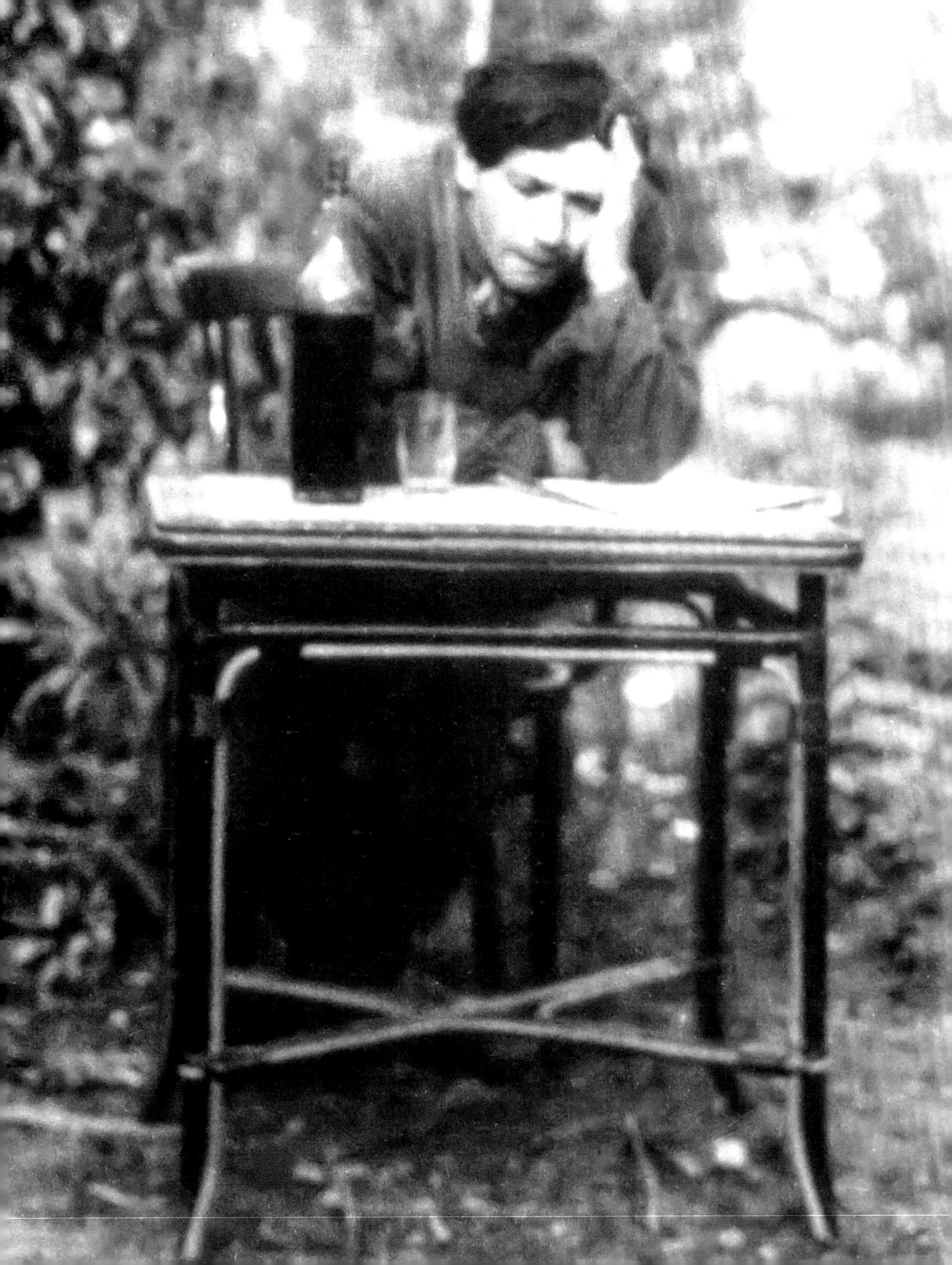

Chaïm Soutine— "An Artist's Artist"

Although in France, North America, and Switzerland, it is almost taken for granted that Chaïm Soutine (1893–1943) is one of the central figures of modernism, he has as yet rarely been exhibited in other countries, and his work is represented in very few public collections. The last comprehensive museum exhibition in Germany took place more than forty years ago (1981) at the Westfälisches Landesmuseum in Münster. Apart from the Kunstsammlung Nordrhein-Westfalen, only a few other German museums have works by Soutine in their collections—the Staatsgalerie Stuttgart, the Von der Heydt-Museum Wuppertal, the Neue Nationalgalerie in Berlin, and the Museum unter Tage in Bochum house one painting each. Three works from a private collection are on long-term loan to the Museum Folkwang in Essen. In Denmark, thus far, there has never been a Soutine exhibition, and his only known work in a public collection there hangs in the Statens Museum for Kunst in Copenhagen. In Switzerland, the situation is different. Thanks to the collecting activities of numerous private individuals, there are some major holdings, such as the Emil Bührle Collection at the Kunsthaus Zürich, the Stiftung Im Obersteg at the Kunstmuseum Basel, and the Kunstmuseum Luzern in Lucerne. Thanks to a generous gift from the art dealer Georges Frédéric Keller in 1981, the Kunstmuseum Bern owns six works by Soutine from different periods of his career. For the Kunstsammlung Nordrhein-Westfalen, the former director Armin Zweite acquired the painting *Still Life with Pheasant* (ca. 1919; see [10]) in 1997. It was an important purchase at a time when prices for the artist's works were already high. It remains the only work by Soutine in the Kunstsammlung, but it served as the starting point for considering an exhibition on this particular artist in collaboration with the Louisiana Museum of Modern Art and the Kunstmuseum Bern.

Chaïm Soutine grew up in a shtetl near Minsk in present-day Belarus. He was the tenth of eleven children. Hunger and discrimination marked his childhood. Nevertheless, he managed to begin taking painting lessons at the age of fourteen, first in Minsk, then at the Vilnius Academy of Fine Arts in the Lithuanian region of the Russian Empire, and from 1913, when he was twenty years old, in Paris, France. The French metropolis became his surrogate home, but Soutine remained an outsider, initially unable to master the language and unfamiliar with the social conventions. The poverty that had dominated his daily life since his youth seemed once again to catch up with him in Paris, making it difficult for him to take part in social life. This did not change when, in 1922/23, the American art collector Albert C. Barnes purchased fifty-two paintings by the hitherto completely unknown expressionist painter and Soutine's financial situation improved over night.

Soutine's paintings are explosions of color and, despite the many adverse circumstances, declarations of love for life and for people who, like him, find themselves on the lowest rung of society. Bellhops, chambermaids, cooks, altar boys, and choristers were his models. With them, as with his paintings of tottering landscapes and slaughtered animals, he captures the attitude toward life of an entire era—a generation scarred by war, social ills, and the relentless clash of religious and political worldviews. The figures and motifs remain deeply moving because their vulnerability expresses the existential anxieties of our time. A major theme of the exhibition, *Chaïm Soutine. Against the Current*, is also emigration and the permanent uprooting of people that results from it. This phenomenon, both individual and societal, spans the globe to the present day, when rootlessness has become an unchanging feature of modern life in the twenty-first century.

Soutine has never been very well known to the general public of Germany or Denmark. Among the circles of international artists in the twentieth century, however, he was highly esteemed, and the study of his work and person is repeatedly cited as an origin and impulse for the artistic creativity and designs of others. Soutine is what is known today as an "artist's artist." After the Second World War, in the fifties and sixties, it was primarily the representatives of Abstract Expressionism, the artist group CoBrA, and the School of London who chose Soutine as a model of inspiration. Willem de Kooning (1904–1997, NL/US), Jackson Pollock (1912–1956, US), and above all Francis Bacon (1909–1992, UK) are his most famous admirers. In recent decades, Soutine's influence has been explored and widely confirmed in several major exhibitions in France and across North America.

Even today, Soutine's name comes up unusually often when contemporary artists are asked about key figures in their creative biographies. Although his paintings were created some one hundred years ago, they seem to hold a fascinating and enduring appeal. The present exhibition seeks to unravel this mystery. All the more so because, in our museums, which are rooted in modernism and art after the Second World War, we are interested at the same time in developing the careers of young international artists and working with them on contemporary social issues. One of the central themes of this exhibition is therefore the question of Soutine's continued relevance. In order to build a bridge from the modernist period to the present, the Louisiana Channel has produced a film of interviews for the exhibition that explores the question of why the fascination with the work and the person of this particular artist continues unabated to this day. Dana Schutz (1976, US), Amy Sillman (1955, US), Emma Talbot (1969, UK), Leidy Churchman (1979, US), Thomas Hirschhorn (1957, CH/FR), Chantal Joffe (1969, US/UK), and Imran Qureshi (1972, PK) tell us how Soutine has influenced their own development and what fascinates them as artists about him and his uncompromising painting.

This retrospective, with some sixty paintings, invites the viewer not only to look at partial aspects of his oeuvre, but rather to gain a differentiated overview of Soutine's multifaceted work as a painter. We hope that the exhibition will reach a wide and new audience and that Soutine will take the place in the public imagination that he deserves as a major representative of modernism. We would like to thank the numerous international museums and private lenders who have entrusted us with their works for the duration of the show across three venues, thus enabling us to realize this wonderful exhibition. In particular, we would like to thank Claire Bernardi, Director of the Musée de l'Orangerie in Paris, for her extraordinary generosity in providing numerous loans. We are also grateful to Xavier Rey, Director of the Centre Pompidou, and Brigitte Léal, its former Deputy Director, as well as Fabrice Hergott, Director of the Musée d'Art moderne de Paris, and Chief Curator Sophie Krebs. Special thanks also go to Henriette Mentha and Géraldine Meyer, Curators of the Stiftung Im Obersteg at the Kunstmuseum Basel.

The Freunde der Kunstsammlung Nordrhein-Westfalen e.V. generously supported the exhibition at the Kunstsammlung Nordrhein-Westfalen, for which we are grateful. We would also like to take this opportunity to thank the Cultural Foundation of the German Federal States expressly for its support of this exhibition project in Düsseldorf. The Kunstmuseum Bern is particularly grateful to the Canton of Bern for its valuable support.

Last but not least, we would like to thank the curators of the exhibition: Susanne Meyer-Büser of the Kunstsammlung Nordrhein-Westfalen, who developed the idea of a Soutine exhibition almost five years ago and pushed for its realization, as well as Kirsten Degel of the Louisiana Museum of Modern Art and Marta Dziewańska of the Kunstmuseum Bern. With a great deal of energy and in open and creative collaboration, these three curators selected the loans, adapted the exhibition to the requirements of their three very different museums, and realized it in a highly professional manner.

Susanne Gaensheimer, Kunstsammlung Nordrhein-Westfalen, Düsseldorf
Poul Erik Tøjner, Louisiana Museum of Modern Art, Humlebæk
Nina Zimmer, Kunstmuseum Bern

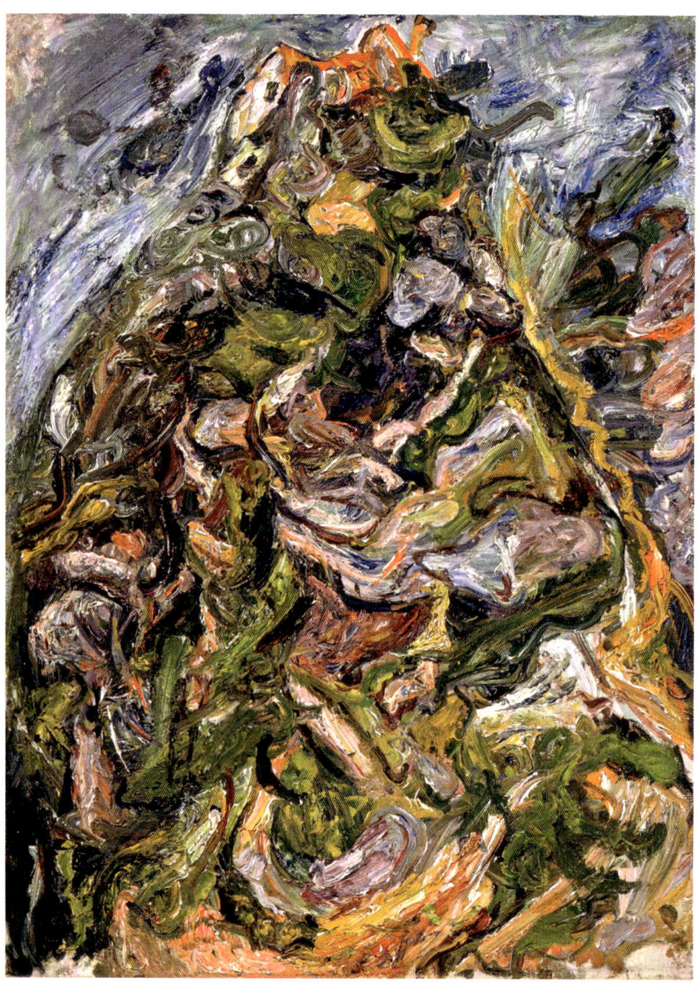

"I see the hill with a house on top, but below, and to the left, I find a hook-nosed witch, a handkerchief tied around her head, holding the collar of a squatting dragon. But the beast's right side is defined by a dark area which now appears to be a curling-horned steer, drastically foreshortened, rising up to the farmhouse, while below, guarding his eyes with his forearm, a man tumbles backward into the sea. A few minutes later, I might have difficulty in finding some of these forms again. Perhaps the landscape will return, with all its roads, banks of trees, coils of earth, and flying clouds. But the very manipulation of pigment has pried the subject from nature into the personal sensation of terror, violence—and paint. Such a picture repays hours of examination, for it is fitted together as deftly as any Cubist portrait."[1]

Thomas B. Hess, 1951

1
La Colline de Céret, ca. 1921
(*Hill at Céret*)
Los Angeles County Museum of Art

1   Thomas B. Hess, *Abstract Painting*
(New York: Viking, 1951), pp. 69–70.

Exciting, Moving, Poignant— The Paintings of Chaïm Soutine

What is it that makes this outsider and maverick stand out from the myriad of artists who lived in Paris during the nineteen-twenties? What makes him so special? What is the source of fascination that still emanates from the person and his work? Is it the intense, complex paintings that leave such a lasting impression? Is it the emotional fragility of his existence, which clung to him throughout his life like an unloved garment? Or the eternal otherness and sense of never-quite-belonging—to a religion or culture, to a group of friends, to like-minded people in the art world? His contemporaries described Soutine as a shy loner with unusual quirks and habits who trusted very few people. He seemed to be restlessly driven and frequently changed his lodgings. During his early years in Paris, he was almost completely destitute, starving and sleeping at the place of a different friend almost every night. Even later, around 1923, when he was successful, he changed his apartment and studio several times a year. After 1930, as an accomplished artist, he even sought out accommodations in the villas of his collectors and patrons.

Soutine as a person is very difficult to grasp, if only because he saw so little value in leaving anything to posterity in writing. There are no notes, no diary, and only a few postcards and letters. There are also only a small number of drawings and sketches, which shed light on his working methods. Photographs that give an impression of his person and his milieu are equally rare. They mostly date from the period after 1923, showing the artist expensively dressed in suits, which do not seem to fit his character very well and served as a protective barrier against the outside world. The few concrete biographical facts are supported only by isolated documents, which is why many scholarly studies are based on the re-ports of friends and collectors that, all the same, often contradict each other and frequently appear distorted and affected. The detailed biography prepared by Catherine Frèrejean for this catalog underscores how difficult it is to gain a clear picture from the confusing array of facts.

The juxtaposition of radicalism and sensitivity, as well as Soutine's extreme painting style, is certainly to be considered among the reasons for his lasting appeal. Another lies in the unusual approach and choice of subjects and motifs that linger in our memory. The still lifes with animal carcasses, for example, tell of the artist's hunger, but also of the suffering of creatures in a general and existential sense. In her essay, "The Discovery of Chaïm Soutine," Susanne Meyer-Büser examines the at times unsettling, but always touching portraits that Soutine painted of people he encountered on the street and also in the service of wealthy high society: cooks, confectioners, and hotel employees. From 1919 to 1928, Soutine devoted himself intensively to the genre of portraiture. With their asymmetrical facial features and oversized white and red uniforms, the sitters often seem like caricatures of their professions. *The Pastry Chef (Baker Boy)* (ca. 1919) and a large number of further works were discovered and acquired for a handsome fee by the American art collector Albert C. Barnes in the winter of 1922/23, making Soutine, who had previously been virtually unknown, famous overnight. The author examines the special role played by one particular portrait in the painter's career and how the story of Soutine's discovery, which sounds more like a fantastic fairy tale, established his unique position within the Parisian art scene.

In her contribution to this catalog, Marta Dziewańska explores the reasons for the enduring fascination with Soutine's painting. Her essay, "The Fury of a Brushstroke," examines why Soutine's painting continues to move us today and how contemporary anxieties and despair are reflected and expressed in his pictures. Her starting point is the landscape paintings created in Céret from 1919 to 1922 and in Cagnes-sur-Mer from 1923 to 1925. In the views of hills, mountains, town squares, and streets, perspectives collapse in on themselves. Every sense of stability and orientation is lost in these works of intense painting; the plunging lines carrying off the viewer.

During the First World War and in the decade that followed, Paris was a focal point for many artists, writers, performers, and the like from Eastern Europe. Soutine was one of them. The tenth of eleven children, he grew up in an Orthodox Jewish family in Smilavičy, in present-day Belarus. His childhood was marked by privation and arduous toil. At the age of fourteen, he defied the Jewish prohibition against the creation of images by taking painting lessons in Minsk. When he painted an Orthodox Jewish man from his shtetl, he came up against strict adherents of Orthodox doctrine and was brutally assaulted. With the damages his mother received through civil action for his injuries, he left home and moved first to Vilnius in 1910 and then to Paris in 1913 to further his artistic education. In her essay, "Soutine, Between Two Worlds," Pascale Samuel explores the artist's Jewish roots and looks at the history and culture of Soutine's native region. Using the metropolis of Paris as an example, she provides insight into the situation of artists who emigrated from Eastern Europe and shows how critically their works were received by the French public in the period between the two world wars.

Soutine's most important years in Paris coincided with a period of political and social reconstruction. After the First World War, French society undertook a search for its cultural identity. The immigration of Eastern European Jews was met with widespread hostility in Paris. Anti-Semitism reached a peak in the twenties and early thirties. This also affected Soutine, who first lived in La Ruche, a dilapidated studio complex in passage de Dantzig, where he made the acquaintance of Alexander Archipenko, Marc Chagall, Ossip Zadkine, Moïse Kisling, and Jacques Lipchitz, all of whom were immigrants like himself. In her essay, "Soutine and the École de Paris," Sophie Krebs explores the extent to which French art criticism in the twenties served the anti-Semitic and xeno-phobic currents of the time. She reveals the paradox of the Parisian art scene, which was at once the site of cosmopolitan and revolutionary currents as well as nationalist ideologies. In her examination of the early reception and publications of Soutine's art, she outlines the anti-Semitic and anti-foreign tendencies evident in them.

Claire Bernardi's essay, "In Art's 'Big Bowl of Soup'—Soutine's Legacy," builds a bridge across the art of the twentieth century. She shows that, within the context of modernism, Soutine forged an individual path very early on between abstraction and figuration. While Soutine's independent nature and idiosyncrasies made him an outlier of modernism during his lifetime, after his death he was increasingly seen as a precursor of Abstract Expressionism and the School of London. Subsequent generations of painters revered him and invoked him as a role model and source of inspiration. These included Willem de Kooning, Jackson Pollock, Jean Dubuffet, and especially Francis Bacon. Later, they were joined by Georg Baselitz, Marlene Dumas, Amy Sillman, Anish Kapoor, and still others. In the contemporary world of painting, for example, Dana Schutz, Nicole Eisenman, Cecily Brown, and Leidy Churchman all make reference to Soutine.

In addition to our sincere thanks to the participating authors for their insightful contributions to this catalog, we would like to express our special gratitude to Hatje Cantz for their professional cooperation in the production of the publication. In particular, we would like to thank Angelika Thill, project manager at Hatje Cantz, as well as the producer, Kati Klaeske, and especially the copy editors Iris Seemann and José Enrique Macián for their keen insights and careful work with the texts. We would also like to thank Gérard Goodrow and R. J. Wheelwright for their faithful translations from German and French, as well as the graphics team at Bureau Mathias Beyer in Cologne for the handsome design of the catalog.

We would like to express our special thanks to the exhibition assistants: Catherine Frèrejean, who worked tirelessly and with great dedication for the Kunstsammlung Nordrhein-Westfalen; Louis Nitze, who supported the realization of the exhibition at the Louisiana Museum of Modern Art; as well as Livia Wermuth and Anne-Christine Strobel who provided curatorial assistance at the Kunstmuseum Bern.

A project of this magnitude and quality could not have been realized without the dedicated and energetic commitment of the entire team at each museum. We would therefore like to express our sincerest thanks to all the colleagues involved at the three museums, who have once again contributed with the utmost, reliable professionalism in making a wonderful exhibition project find its way to the public.

Susanne Meyer-Büser, Kunstsammlung Nordrhein-Westfalen, Düsseldorf
Kirsten Degel, Louisiana Museum of Modern Art, Humlebæk
Marta Dziewańska, Kunstmuseum Bern

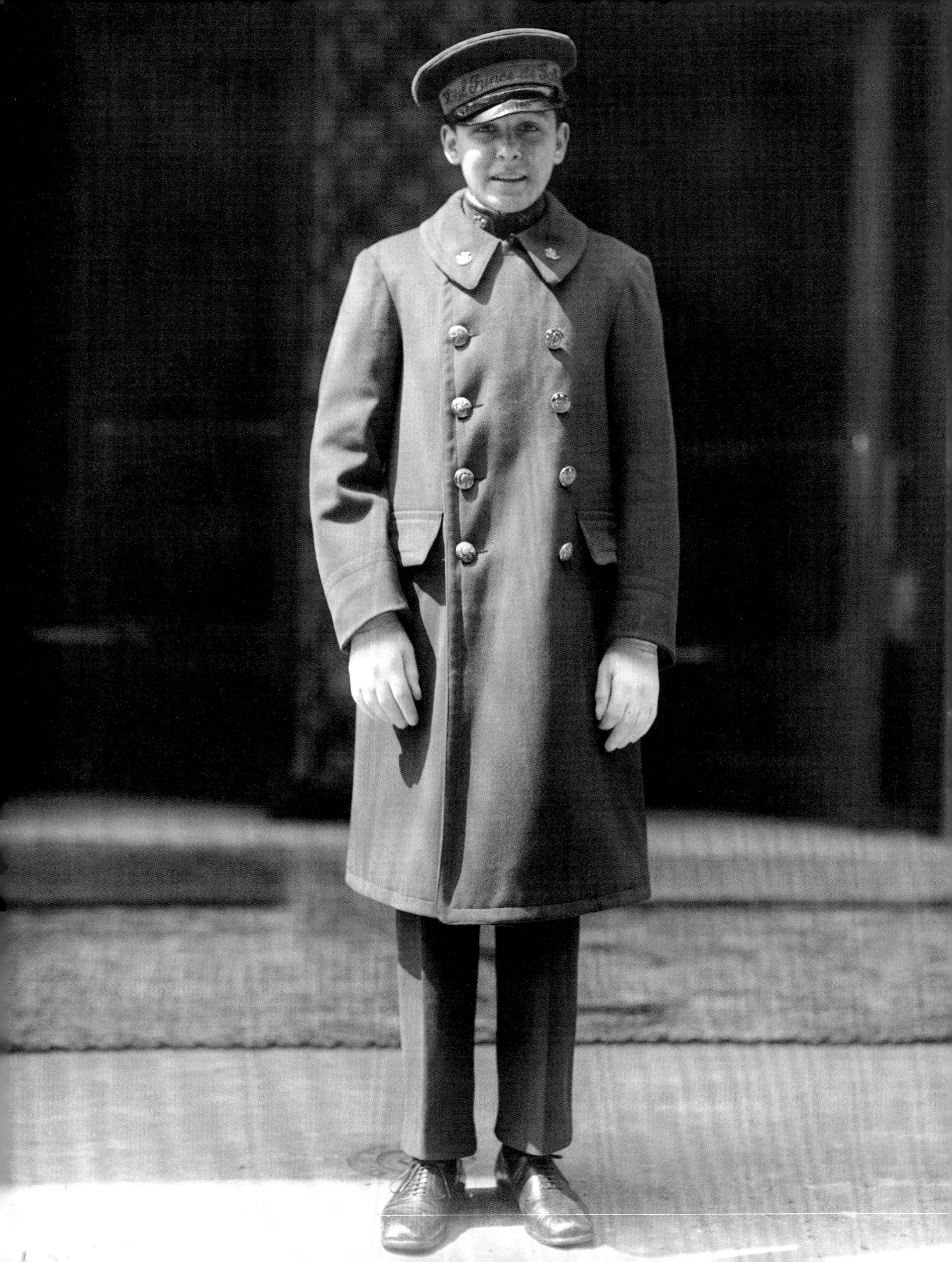

The Discovery of Chaïm Soutine

Susanne Meyer-Büser

It was in postwar Paris, in December 1922, that an unknown and destitute painter drew the attention of the American art collector Albert C. Barnes. What followed was a sensation in the art world and became the stuff of legend. Overnight, a penniless Jewish immigrant from present-day Belarus became a celebrated star of the Parisian art scene. For the then twenty-nine-year-old Chaïm Soutine, this encounter was the turning point in his life and would forever transform his artistic output.

Of the thirty or so portraits, which Soutine had created up to that point, of people both young and old dressed in the work clothes they wore as uniforms, the painting *The Pastry Chef (Baker Boy)* (ca. 1919; fig. 1) is by far the most important for the artist. It was this work first and foremost that made him famous in one fell swoop. The story that Barnes also acquired fifty-one other works by Soutine in the winter of 1922/23 spread like wildfire, acquiring enormous symbolic power, and not only in art circles—the fairy tale of the forgotten artist and his paintings suddenly recognized for their true meaning and worth.

Perhaps in another time and place, this story might not have attracted so much attention, but it took place in France just after the catastrophe that was the First World War, at a time when the country was regrouping in the midst of an economic crisis and as conflicting groups and interests struggled to renew the national identity. Restorative forces from the fields of politics and culture had proclaimed the *rappel à l'ordre* so that the diverse international artistic influences could be mastered by concentrating on French values. It was at this moment that a painter from Eastern Europe, of all people, recalled the wavering tradition of artistic models and pillars of *la grande nation*. For Soutine himself, this was a profound caesura in his life and the starting point for his portrait series of cooks, bellhops, and altar boys.

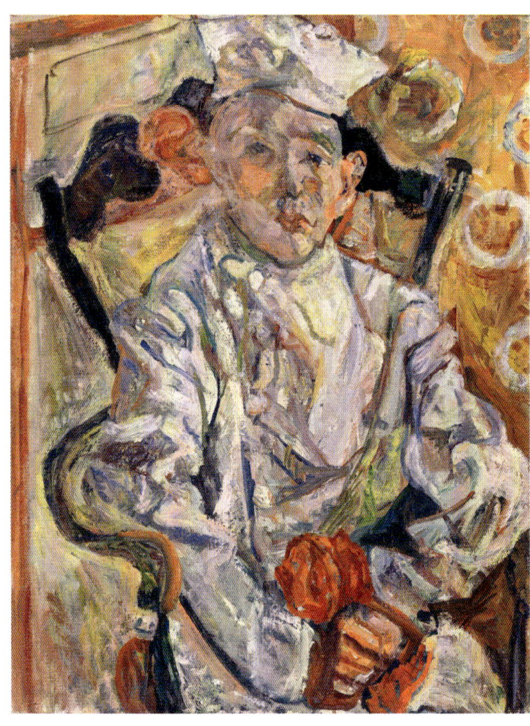

1
Le Pâtissier, ca. 1919
(*The Pastry Chef [Baker Boy]*)
Barnes Foundation, Philadelphia

The Pastry Chef—The Key Work

The Pastry Chef (Baker Boy) was painted in Céret around 1919, at a time when Soutine was living alone and in seclusion, studying the works of Paul Cézanne and, especially, Vincent van Gogh. In both *The Pastry Chef (Baker Boy)* and *Woman Seated in an Armchair* (fig. 2), painted at the same time, Soutine was probably inspired by Van Gogh's work *La Berceuse* (1889; fig. 3). Van Gogh had painted five different versions of the portrait, whose title may be translated as "the lullaby," during his time in Arles. It shows the motherly Augustine Roulin rocking a cradle by means of a cord held in her hands. Van Gogh is said to have painted the scene with the intention of offering comfort to the lonely of the world. The painting thus opens up a world of emotions that, it can be assumed, touched Soutine deeply.

But unlike Vincent van Gogh, who painted *La Berceuse* with an emphasis on simplicity and a flat use of color, Soutine painted his portrait of a seated woman and particularly *The Pastry Chef (Baker Boy)* fully in the style of French Impressionist *peinture claire* ("light painting"). The white of the pastrycook's jacket is thus composed of many small brushstrokes of mixed tones from the surrounding canvas. Violet, pink, yellow, blue, and brown are the dominant colors. The brushwork is lively and contrasts with the serenity exuded by the young pastrycook. It is the first in a series of portraits of people in work uniform. The white jacket worn by confectioners and cooks was used to protect their own clothing, but also as an outward sign of cleanliness and hygiene in the handling of food and work surfaces. The pastrycook, however, seems to swim in his oversized work clothes. It bunches together in countless folds, and the sleeves are too long. A white toque sits like a crown on his round head, which protrudes directly from his clothes. If only it were not for this distortion and the deformation of the young face, as well as the oversized red ear. It is unsettling and causes the viewer to pause because it contradicts the anatomically possible. Its shape

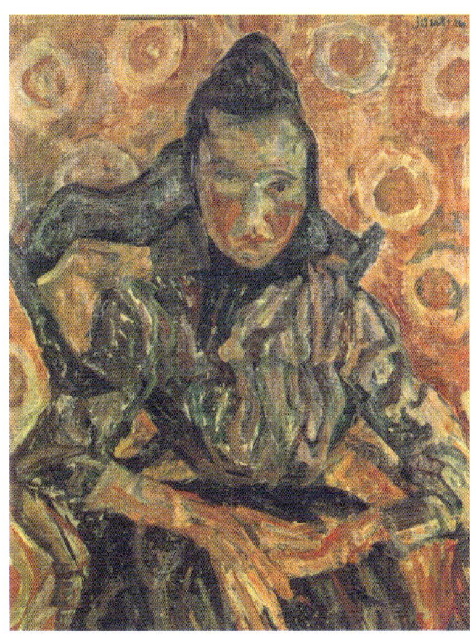

2
Femme assise dans un fauteuil, ca. 1919
(*Woman Seated in an Armchair*)
Private Collection

echoes that of the chair, which itself resembles a throne, and the wallpaper in the background. Its frontal view, the angled position, and the red color, which evokes a "tweaked ear" (i.e., chastisement) are disconcerting. The ear is the most obvious indicator that the work goes far beyond a simple genre painting of a pastrycook.

Another recurring moment of irritation in Soutine's portraits is caused by the disparate, uneven pairs of eyes, which seem to fixate on the viewer or to look just past them. Often, one eye is higher than the other, whereby one may be hidden as if behind a veil, while the other is clear and focused. In *The Pastry Chef (Baker Boy)*, the latter echoes the defiantly curved mouth and the fist that protrudes with unusual realism from the fabric of the jacket. This subtle mixture of emotions, of repression and resistance, can be found in many of Soutine's portraits and still resonates with many viewers today.[1]

3
Vincent van Gogh
La Berceuse, 1889
(*La Berceuse [Woman Rocking a Cradle]*)
The Metropolitan Museum of Art, New York

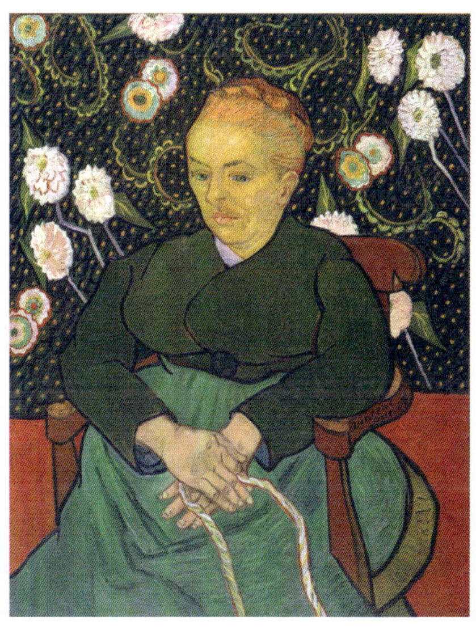

19

The American Millionaire and the Painter from the Shtetl

To what extent the social and psychological dimensions of *The Pastry Chef (Baker Boy)* were of importance to Albert C. Barnes and encouraged him to acquire it is not clear from source material. Different accounts exist of how the art collector discovered the portrait of the pastrycook and how the first meeting between the millionaire and the "peintre maudit"[2] took place in the winter of 1922/23. According to one version, Barnes found the painting in a corner of the dealer Léopold Zborowski's showroom, dirty and torn;[3] according to another, it was hanging in a restaurant; according to yet another, the work was first shown to him by his own art dealer Paul Guillaume, who had previously acquired it. In any case, Barnes, enraptured by the painting's style and charm, is said to have exclaimed, "Mais c'est une pêche!"[4] and demanded to know the name of the work's author. His chauffeur eventually found Soutine, filthy and ragged on a park bench, and took him to Barnes, who had him bathed and ordered clothes for him from an English tailor. He later recalled this with some irony: "Ah! So, this is Soutine. Good. A boor! I'll never forgive myself for having been such an idiot as to trouble myself with him."[5] To get him off the street, Barnes rented the artist a studio. All the versions of the story in circulation emphasize the contrast between the pure, fine painting and the painter's miserable condition—and thus highlight the splintered cultural conditions of postwar France.

In addition to the accounts of peers and contemporaries, Paul Guillaume's articles in particular helped attract attention in the Parisian art scene to Soutine in the months that followed. As early as January 1923, the influential art dealer reported in *Les Arts à Paris* on the discovery of the unknown outsider, Soutine, as well as on his patron's exquisite sense and nose for art.[6] This and other articles were instrumental in drawing the attention of the French and American art markets to both Soutine and Barnes's collecting activities.

In fact, the sale of *The Pastry Chef (Baker Boy)* had an immediate positive effect on the artist's financial situation, even though the price paid for this work, and the fifty-one others, was more than modest by today's standards.[7] However, the personal and social recognition it brought Soutine must have been of inestimable value to him.

For almost ten years, Soutine had lived in particularly miserable conditions and almost exclusively among other immigrants from Eastern Europe. Due to difficulties in his ability to speak and read French and his socialization within a narrow Jewish Eastern European cultural milieu, it was not easy for him to integrate into urban cosmopolitan Parisian society. Furthermore, there had been no public recognition of his art up to that point.

Born in a shtetl near Minsk, Soutine had come to Paris in the summer of 1913, on the eve of the First World War, with his artist friend Michel Kikoïne. Together with Pinchus Krémègne, who was already living in Paris, the three had attended the Vilnius Academy of Fine Arts. Like many young artists emigrating from Eastern Europe at the time, they intended to make their home in the art capital. Upon his arrival, Soutine was penniless and only fluent in Yiddish. He first lived in the dilapidated studio complex La Ruche,[8] and from 1916 in a studio in the Cité Falguière. Both places provided refuge for immigrants, but also for derelict and forlorn people of all kinds. In these early years, Soutine earned money by doing odd jobs. As in his homeland, poverty, hunger, and deprivation were the order of the day. Published sources contain numerous reports of Soutine's precarious physical and mental state during these years, including the unbearable condition of his lodgings. In addition, there were also certain habits and tics that strained his ability to be around others. Immediately after his arrival, Soutine enrolled in the summer of 1913 in an academic painting course in the studio of Fernand Cormon at the École des Beaux-Arts. In the mornings, the newcomers from abroad received instruction in the techniques and peculiarities of French painting; and in the afternoons, they were free to study ancient and, especially, French art at the Louvre.[9]

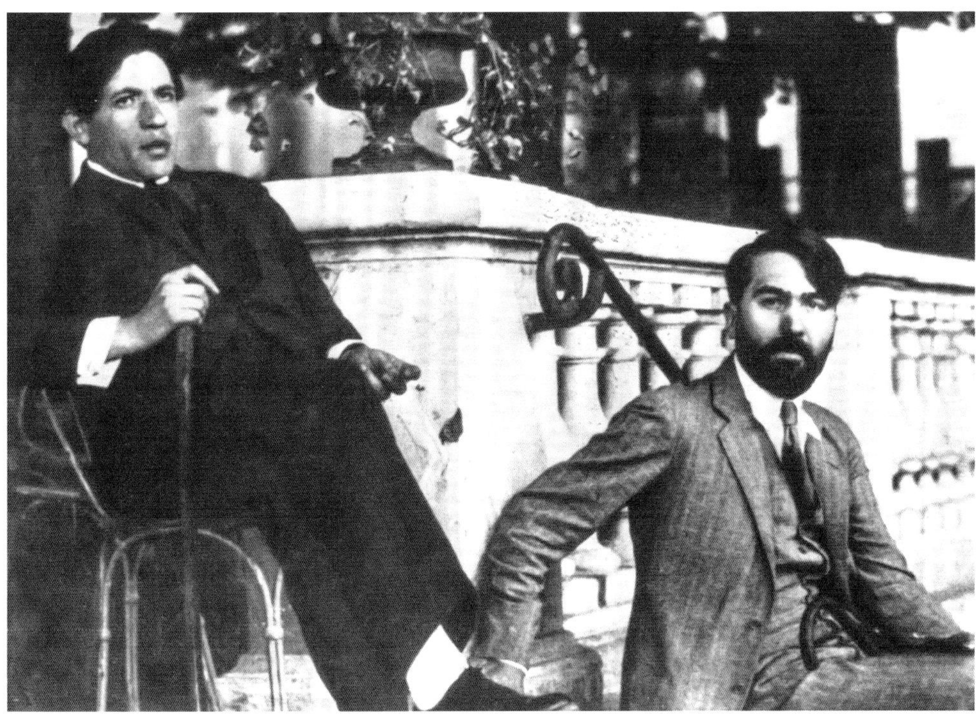

4
Chaïm Soutine and Léopold Zborowski, ca. 1930
Photographer unknown

In 1915, the sculptor Jacques Lipchitz, a friend of Soutine's, introduced him to Amedeo Modigliani.[10] The Italian painter, who came from a Jewish bourgeois, liberal background, had lived in Paris since 1906 and was represented by the art dealers Paul Guillaume and Léopold Zborowski. Although Modigliani and Soutine were very different in temperament and appearance,[11] they developed a close friendship. Ten years his senior, Modigliani, a successful painter, was convinced of Soutine's talent and persuaded Zborowski to promote him (fig. 4). As an artist of the gallery, Soutine was paid five francs a day from 1919 onward—a very small sum, even at the time. Through Modigliani, Soutine's horizons broadened considerably, and he came into contact with contemporary movements such as Cubism, Surrealism, and similar trends. This new, stimulating environment, however, had no visible influence on his own art. Like his friend Modigliani, Soutine did not join any of the many artistic groups and movements. He visited the Louvre, immersed himself in the study of the art of past centuries, and continued to follow his own individual path.

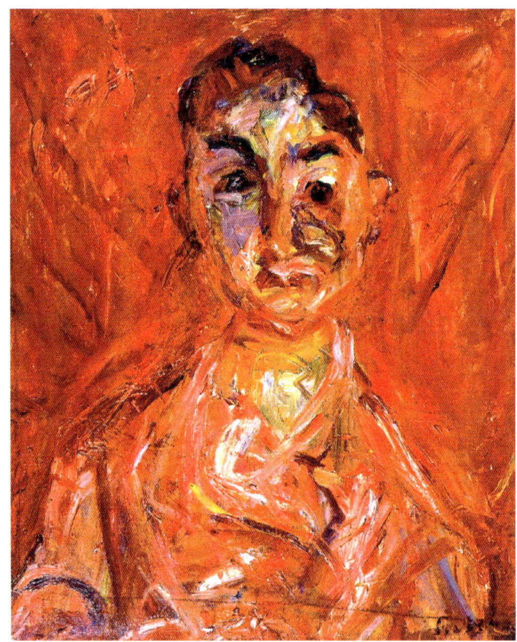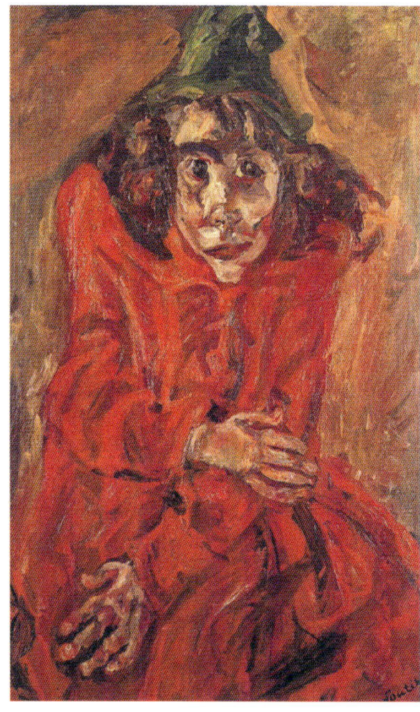

Céret—People on the Streets and on the Margins of Society

In 1919, Zborowski sent Soutine to paint in Céret, a legendary commune in the French Pyrenees, where Henri Matisse and the Cubists Pablo Picasso, Georges Braque, and Juan Gris had had their artistic breakthroughs a few years earlier. The decision to send Soutine from bustling Paris to the mountain village was probably made with the intention of helping him develop as a painter. Or perhaps the art dealer was simply conceding to his wife's insistence that she would no longer tolerate the "unkempt" young artist around her.[12]

Soutine spent nearly three years withdrawn in the small town near the Spanish border. These years indeed proved to be a period of considerable artistic development, during which Soutine greatly expanded his means of expression and the intensity of his painting. In this so-called Céret period, he produced some two hundred paintings by the end of 1922, mostly landscapes, but also a number of important portraits. Since virtually no works survive from the period between 1913 and 1917—Soutine himself took great pains to destroy the works of his early career—his representations of people are only known from 1917 onward.

In Céret, Soutine found the models for his portraits in the neighborhood and on the street. They were people who, like himself, were not tied to a fixed domestic or professional arrangement and had time to spare for sittings. Perhaps this explains the large number of portraits of children, such as *Child with a Toy* (ca. 1919; see [12]); adolescents, such as *Butcher Boy* (ca. 1919/20; fig. 5); and the elderly, as in the series of praying men (1919–1922). He also painted a large number of portraits of the mentally ill, such as *The Mad Woman* (ca. 1919; fig. 6) and *Village Idiot* (1920; see [15]). It is possible that Soutine felt a special affinity for people from the lower classes of society because he, too, had the status of an outsider in the village community.

What these portraits from the Céret period have in common is that they are limited to a few compositional schemes. They are mostly seated persons in half-length or three-quarter length portraits. The face is turned toward the viewer, the hands lie on the lap, and the surroundings are kept neutral. In some pictures, the red background is quite striking. Soutine had obtained a curtain from the local butcher, who used it to protect meat. In Céret, the color red became a special means of expression for Soutine. In *Butcher Boy*, the color of the face and that of the background merge in a veritable excess. Here, the theme of bloody flesh, which Soutine took up in many variations, dominates the whole painting by means of the brushstrokes and intensity of color, so that it approaches an all-over painting. The blending of structures in the figure represented and in the surrounding space also occurs in the series of praying men. As earlier in the landscapes, Soutine uses angular forms with sharp edges to create very lively, moving surfaces in these portraits. People and landscapes defy stasis and seem to lean unrestrained to the right.

By depicting the physical forms and facial features of the mostly unknown models in an unbeautified, asymmetrically deformed and distorted manner, Soutine not only gives them unmistakable personalities, but also creates a sense of proximity and evokes a degree of recognition with the subjects. The crooked noses, uneven eyes, and oversized red ears of the young models seem like the lesions and scars of a wounded life and set off a disturbing spiral of thoughts, as in the painting *Child with a Toy*.

New Self-Confidence—Pastrycooks, Bellhops, Waiters, and Altar Boys

The portrait of a pastrycook (*The Pastry Chef (Baker Boy)*) was painted around 1919 and formed part of the series of portraits of people from Céret. It was, however, only with the work's successful sale three years later that Soutine turned more intensively to the pictorial genre of cooks and confectioners. From 1925 onward, the series of bellhops, valets, waiters, and altar boys followed. *The Pastry Chef (Baker Boy)* is not only a turning point in Soutine's career, but also the beginning of a long series of portraits of "ordinary people in working uniform." Soutine thus focused on the milieu of the destitute and all those who lived at the bottom of the social ladder.

It is impossible to say whether Soutine would have continued to devote himself so intensively to this pictorial genre had it not been for his incisive, fateful encounter with Albert C. Barnes. The truth is that Barnes became aware of Soutine primarily because *The Pastry Chef (Baker Boy)* was in the tradition of the French Impressionists. When Barnes came to Paris, he was looking for young talent to add to his collection of related Impressionist works. In a sense, then, Soutine owed the triumph of his pastrycook to his successful assimilation of the traditions of French painting. And not wanting this success to end, after the sale of *The Pastry Chef (Baker Boy)*, Soutine painted seven more works depicting cooks, chefs, kitchen assistants, confectioners, and their apprentices. *Pastrycook of Cagnes* (ca. 1922/23; fig. 7) and *The Little Pastrycook* (1922/23; see [18]) were painted immediately afterward.

Both works were acquired by Paul Guillaume in 1926 and 1930, respectively, after the success of *The Pastry Chef (Baker Boy)* had convinced him that the market demanded more of this type of subject.[13]

In her 2017 essay, Karen Serres very plausibly pointed out that Soutine's turn to the subject of young cooks, and later small altar boys, served a genre motif from the nineteenth century that was very popular in French society.[14] Postcards and paintings produced in large numbers depict farcical scenes in which young cooks and sacristans engage in mischievous pranks. The scenes amused the public because the boys' behavior runs counter to the role models of their professions and the "adult" uniforms they wear (fig. 8).

The improved social status that the sale of *The Pastry Chef (Baker Boy)* brought Soutine was clearly reflected in his works. Still during the winter of 1922/23, Soutine began a new phase in his painting that lasted until about 1925. It is known as the Cagnes period, named after the town of Cagnes-sur-Mer in the South of France, near Nice, where Soutine stayed intermittently at the time. The basic compositional structure of the portraits remained largely unchanged, with the subjects seated in the center as half-length or three-quarter length portraits facing the viewer. The background, however, became increasingly more neutral. In *Pastrycook of Cagnes*, the visual choice of motif is most clearly related to the artist's own earlier model: the large ears, the gaze, and the pose are similar to *The Pastry Chef (Baker Boy)*. The brushwork, however, is different,

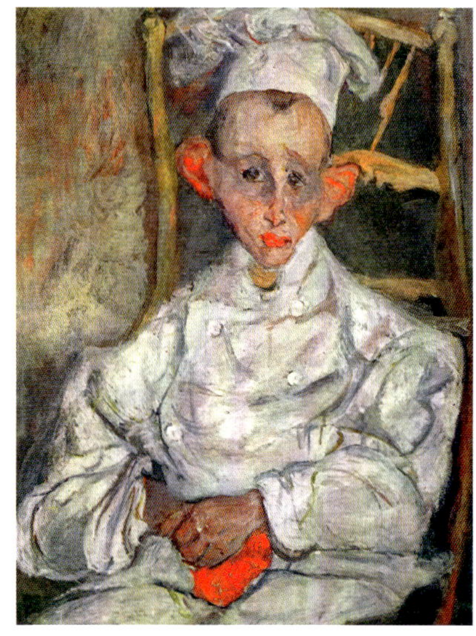

7
Le Pâtissier de Cagnes
ca. 1922/23
(*Pastrycook of Cagnes*)
Private Collection

more fluid and curved. The white of the jacket, still composed of a variety of colors, becomes brighter and more focused. It is said that in Céret, Soutine lived in a cheap barn and could not pay his models.[15] In Cagnes-sur-Mer, however, he was now able to dine out in restaurants. It is likely that this is also where he found the models for his cooks. Parallel to the development in his landscape paintings, the formal language in his portraits became more self-contained and curvilinear from 1923 onward. It is striking that in *The Little Pastrycook*, the sitter's shoulders are no longer sloping, but instead curve upward. The legs are spread wide across the bottom of the picture plane, and the whole pose of the pastrycook is expansive, extending beyond the edges of the canvas. The curves echo the pastrycook's toque, which resembles a crown or perhaps a foolscap.

The new self-confidence exuded by the sitters is particularly noteworthy. Although *The Pastry Chef (Baker Boy)* and *Pastrycook of Cagnes* were also inspired by historical portraits of rulers—in particular, Soutine admired Jean Fouquet's half-length portrait of Charles VII (1440/1460)—these portraits were characterized by a passivity on the part of the sitters. Since *The Little Pastrycook*, however, the cooks and kitchen assistants usually maintain eye contact. And the spread legs, although a dominant pose, are by no means to be understood as quotations of lordly poise. Rather, it is the self-confident and subtly provocative posture of impudent street youths that Soutine picks up on here. Such irritation is only heightened more by the fact that the little pastrycook is barely visibly snarling.[16]

From 1925 onward, Soutine spent most of his time in Paris. Since his paintings had been fetching considerable prices since 1924, his financial resources had increased to the point that he could afford to frequent exclusive hotels, bars, and restaurants. Photographs from this period show him wearing hats, white shirts, and tailored suits (fig. 4). The confectioners and cooks found themselves replaced in a new series by bellhops, doormen, valets, and waiters. These images of mostly young men reflect Soutine's changing social environment. They are people in historicized, often ill-fitting uniforms, representatives of the hotels and nightclubs the artist now frequented.

The change from white jacket to red livery also corresponded to Soutine's artistic reorientation. Whereas during his early studies at the Louvre he had been inspired by Jean Fouquet, Jacopo Tintoretto, El Greco, Jean-Auguste-Dominique Ingres, and Gustave Courbet, the paintings of Rembrandt van Rijn now became his sources for ideas and creative inspiration. Rembrandt's *Slaughtered Ox* (1655) in particular inspired Soutine to take up this motif in ten different variations (see [48], [49], [52]). Soutine sought and found in the depiction of the slaughtered beasts a metaphor for existential suffering, and at the same time, he immersed himself in the challenge of composing a large surface in countless shades of red. The problem of color over a broad area had already been the artistic subject matter in his series of pastrycooks. There, Soutine had made the non-color white shine in many vibrant shades. Now, in his depictions of slaughtered bovine and the parallel series of bellhops, he turned to heavily evocative shades of red, making its powerful, even violent presence—often in combination with white—his new main theme.

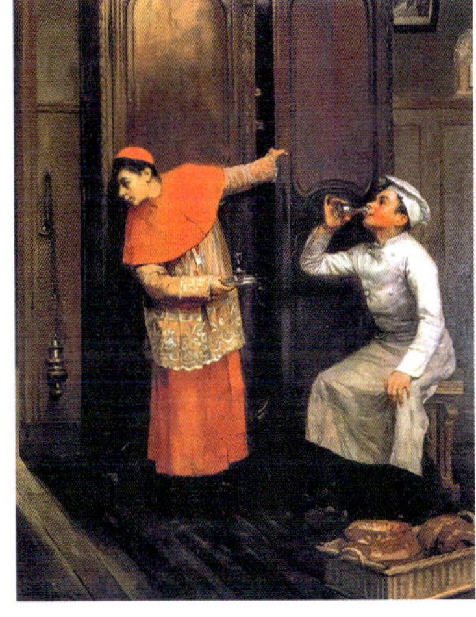

8
Paul-Charles Chocarne-Moreau
Une Libation spirituelle, 1893
(*A Spiritual Libation*)
Whereabouts unknown

From a social point of view, Soutine was one of the few artists in France during the twenties who used the medium of painting to depict people from the lower classes. Comparable approaches at the time can only be found in paintings of the Neue Sachlichkeit (New Objectivity), where blue-collar workers and members of the so-called demimonde were depicted. The portraits of hotel and restaurant employees, however, are no more marked by explicit social criticism than the earlier portraits of pastrycooks and altar boys. Rather, Soutine identified with these figures because they reflected something of himself. They are marked by inner conflict and ambivalent emotions; they oscillate between pride and defiance, regal bearing and provocative proletarian aplomb; but they are also marked by the toils and burdens of their professions and their position at the bottom of the social hierarchy (fig. 9).

Not quite fitting into a role, feeling alienated, constrained, and confined was surely an underlying feeling that Soutine himself knew only too well. The artist, who clearly enjoyed his sudden success, seemed to be well aware that he, too, placed his labor at the service of higher society and was dependent upon it. It stands to reason, then, as Barnaby Wright has argued in his essay on Soutine's portraiture,[17] that Soutine was repeatedly drawn to these people on the margins of society because he saw something of himself in them—an outsider who placed himself at the service of higher society but did not really fit into the prescribed roles and molds.

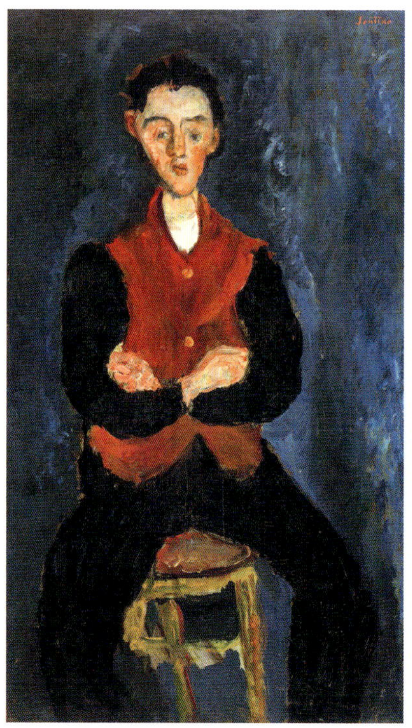

9
Le Valet de chambre
ca. 1927
(*The Valet*)
Private Collection

1 Incidentally, *The Pastry Chef (Baker Boy)* is the only portrait in the series of workers in uniform for which it is possible to reliably reconstruct who sat for Soutine. It was the seventeen-year-old Rémi Zocchetto, who was then employed in Céret as an apprentice at the Hôtel Garetta: see Karen Serres, "Modern Workers: Soutine's Sitters in Context," in *Soutine's Portraits: Cooks, Waiters and Bellboys*, ed. Karen Serres and Barnaby Wright, exh. cat. Courtauld Gallery, London 2017/18 (London: Paul Holberton, 2018), pp. 47–71, here p. 57.

2 "Soutine, Pascin, Utrillo and Modigliani—they have been grouped together as though violence of temper and proneness to trouble constituted a school of art. In France they are called *les peintres maudits*—painters under a curse." Monroe Wheeler, "Soutine," in *Soutine*, by Monroe Wheeler, exh. cat. Museum of Modern Art, New York 1950/51; Cleveland Museum of Art 1951 (New York: Museum of Modern Art, 1950), pp. 31–111, here p. 31.

3 David Sylvester, *"The Mysteries of Nature within the Mysteries of Paint,"* in C. *Soutine: 1893–1943*, ed. Ernst-Gerhard Güse, exh. cat. Westfälisches Landesmuseum, Münster 1981/82; Kunsthalle Tübingen 1982; Hayward Gallery, London (Arts Council of Great Britain) 1982; Kunstmuseum Luzern, Lucerne 1982 (London: Arts Council of Great Britain, 1982), pp. 33–47, here p. 35.

4 Paul Guillaume, "Soutine," *Les Arts à Paris*, no. 7 (January 1923): pp. 5–6, here p. 6.

5 Soutine told Chana Orloff about this remark: Chana Orloff, "Mon ami Soutine," *Evidences*, no. 21 (November 1951), pp. 17–21, here p. 18. A slightly altered version, quoted here, is found in Esti Dunow, "Chaim Soutine: Leben und Werk," in *Chaim Soutine: Ein französischer Expressionist*, ed. Tobias G. Natter, exh. cat. Jüdische Museum Wien, Vienna 2000 (Vienna: Jüdisches Museum, 2000), pp. 11–38, here p. 25.

6 Paul Guillaume, "Le Docteur Barnes," *Les Arts à Paris*, no. 7 (January 1923), p. 2, see Esti Dunow, "Chaim Soutine, 1893–1943" (PhD diss., New York University, 1981; privately published, 1990), p. 53.

7 Henriette Mentha, "Karl Im Obersteg, an Early Collector of Chaïm Soutine" in *Soutine und die Moderne/Soutine and Modernism*, ed. Nina Zimmer, exh. cat. Kunstmuseum Basel 2008 (Cologne: DuMont, 2008), pp. 99–114, here p. 103. Barnes is believed to have acquired the works by Soutine in the winter of 1922/23 for around 30 to 50 francs each. Immediately afterward, the prices rose to 3,000 to 5,000 francs, and as early as 1926 were fetching prices of 10,000 to 22,000 francs at an auction at the Hôtel Drouot in Paris.

8 During the time when Soutine lived in La Ruche, Krémègne, Kikoïne, Jehudo Epstein, and Léon Indenbaum were among a group of Jewish artists there. Marc Chagall left La Ruche at the beginning of the First World War and settled for a time in Russia.

9 Sophie Krebs, "Soutine—A Case Apart," in *Soutine und die Moderne/Soutine and Modernism*, pp. 39–62, here p. 40.

10 Jacques Lipchitz, as told to Dorothy Seckler, "I Remember Modigliani," *ARTnews* 49, no. 10, February 1951, pp. 26–28, https://www.artnews.com/art-news/retrospective/archives-jacques-lipchitz-remembers-amedeo-modigliani-1951-9505; see Dunow, "Chaim Soutine: Leben und Werk," p. 19.

11 Maurice Vlaminck, "Souvenir de Modigliani," *L'Art vivant* 1, no. 21, November 1, 1925, pp. 1–2; see Dunow, "Chaim Soutine: Leben und Werk," p. 19.

12 At the Zborowskis' home, "Modigliani would come to dinner and bring Soutine, much to the annoyance of Anna [Zborowski]. Soutine was just too dirty, smelly, and pathetic for her. One day Modigliani painted a portrait of Soutine on a door in the apartment. When Zborowski complained, Modigliani replied, 'Someday you will be able to sell the door for its weight in gold.' 'But until then,' Anna said angrily, 'we have to live with that portrait.'" Pierre Sichel, *Modigliani: A Biography of Amedeo Modigliani* (New York: Dutton, 1967), pp. 360–361; quoted in Billy Klüver and Julie Martin, *Kiki's Paris: Artist and Lovers 1900–1930* (New York: Harry N. Abrams, 1994), p. 80.

13 See Barnaby Wright, "Soutine's Misfits," introduction to exh. cat. *Soutine's Portraits: Cooks, Waiters and Bellboys*, pp. 15–46, here p. 30.

14 Serres, "Modern Workers," pp. 58–59.

15 Rémi Zocchetto, for example, reported, "Soutine promised him ten sous a sitting, but he never had ten sous, and after six sittings offered him a painting instead. 'I was a fool to refuse,'" he admitted; quoted in Peter Stone, "Soutine at Céret," *Art and Artists* 5, no. 1 (April 1970): pp. 54–57, here p. 56; see Serres, "Modern Workers," p. 57.

16 Karen Serres and Barnaby Wright, Cat. 3, in exh. cat. *Soutine's Portraits: Cooks, Waiters and Bellboys*, p. 102.

17 Wright, "Soutine's Misfits," pp. 21, 44.

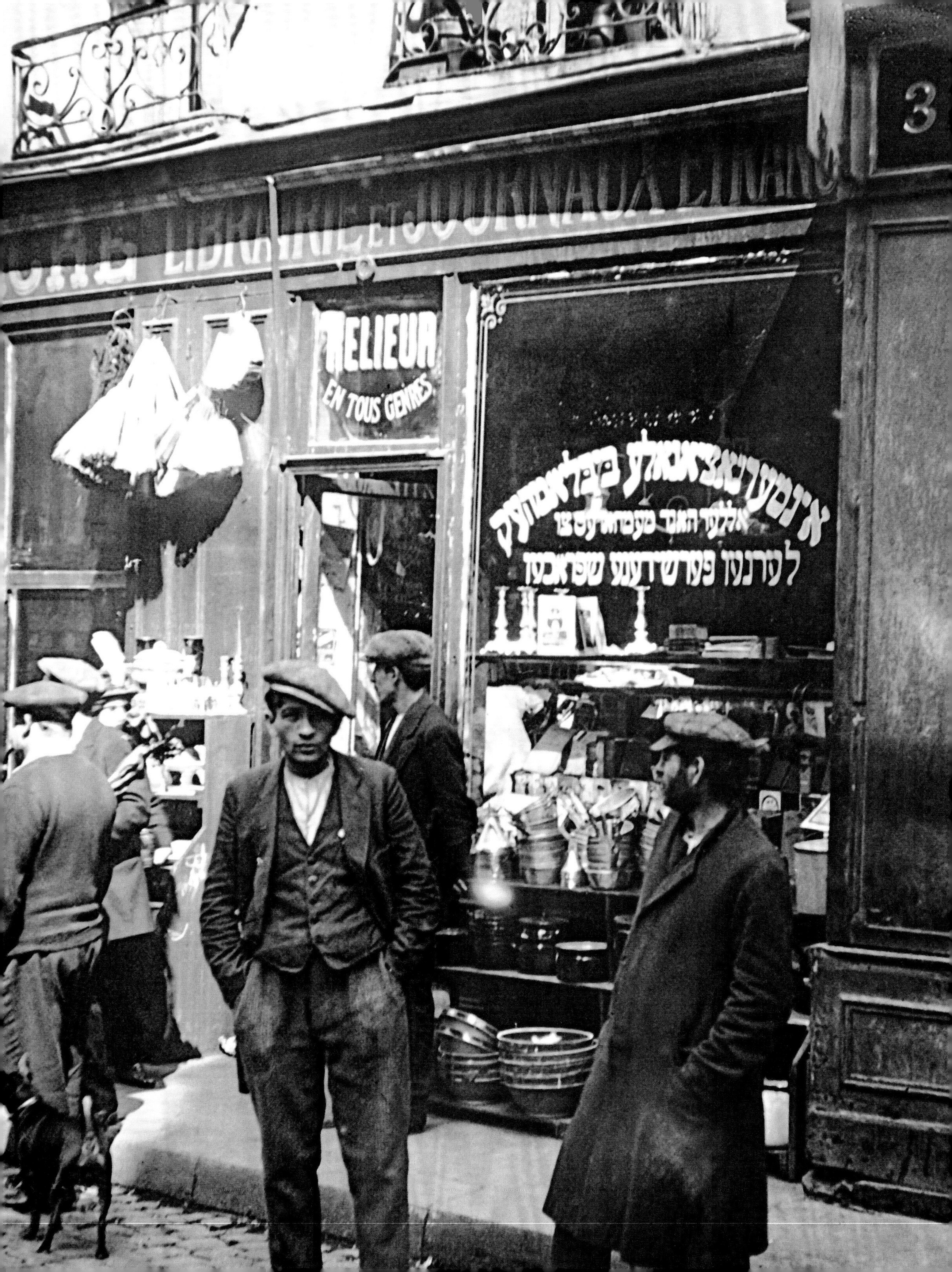
LIBRAIRIE ET JOURNAUX ÉTRAN
RELIEUR
EN TOUS GENRES
אין דעם גרויסאלט פאלישאלק
אללער האנד מעבחוולעסצו
ל טרנטה פארשידענע שפראבן
3

Soutine, Between Two Worlds

Pascale Samuel

"What is certain is that Soutine is a hero of legend; he breaks the framework of personal destiny to become something of an event. The very beginning of his turbulent life foreshadows its tragic end."[1]

Emil Szittya, 1955

The bookshop Librairie Speiser
Paris, ca. 1920
Projections Molteni
Musée d'Art et d'histoire du
Judaïsme, Paris

Chaïm Soutine: a name, a man, himself an embodiment of the fate of Jewish artists arriving in Paris from all over the world at the turn of the twentieth century, those who from the mid-twenties were referred to by critics as the École de Paris (School of Paris). There are a number of clichés attached to his name that are worth re-examining. Had he really escaped a tragic destiny? Had he come from the ghetto as French critics of the interwar period imagined? Why did he become the incarnation of the Jewish artist, although we know no work by him that has a Jewish theme?

Eluding the clichés that surround Soutine is not an easy task, though. The artist himself hardly spoke and virtually never wrote—and the few letters that survive are prosaic in content and laconic in style.[2] Unlike Marc Chagall or Ossip Zadkine, he did not leave an autobiography or diary to posterity. Nor did he express himself on the subject of his art, and in the absence of direct sources, historians have only the testimonies of his friends and relatives. Those who knew him, such as the critics Waldemar George and Emil Szittya, described him as a timid-looking man, a wandering soul from the Jewish ghetto, a victim in his childhood of both a traditionalist religious community and the discriminatory policies of the czars. George, originally from Poland, and Szittya, from Hungary, shared a common exile with Soutine, but they confined him to the caricature of painting's "Wandering Jew."

The absence of primary written sources complicates any attempt at accessing Soutine's biography and, with it, the relationship of his work to Ashkenazi Jewish culture.[3] It makes it hard to synthesize the tradition of "the lives of the artists," built on their singularity, with a broader historical perspective, and particularly one that focuses on the migrations at the very beginning of the twentieth century. Here, Soutine is not "a hero of legend"[4] but one individual among many—one among many caught up in a vast population movement involving more than a million people between 1901 and 1914.[5] Little used, the testimonies of these émigrés, written in Yiddish, are today among the sources at our disposal.[6] So, by returning to the history and culture of the region Soutine came from, we will try to locate him in the broader context that pushed Jewish artists to leave the Russian Empire at the beginning of the twentieth century. This will let us shed light on his youth, comparing it with that of artists from the neighboring province around Vitebsk (such as his contemporaries, the aforementioned Marc Chagall and Ossip Zadkine) and to focus on a transitional generation that sought to use art to extract itself from its traditional upbringing. This will highlight the specific reasons that pushed Jewish artists to move to Paris to become creators in their own right.

Soutine's recognition within the Parisian art scene, like that of some of the Jewish artists of his generation, will be the final focus of this text. Soutine often changed studios, and the successive addresses map his gradual progress from his arrival in Paris to commercial success—and that, tarnished by the anti-Semitism expressed in the press of the twenties and thirties—which transformed him from the figure of the "Wandering Jew" of his beginnings into the incarnation of the "cosmopolitan artist."

From Smilavičy to Paris

Soutine was born in 1893[7] in Smilavičy, a town of four thousand inhabitants in what is now Belarus. Unlike many other emigrants, he always kept the name given to him after birth, *Chaïm* (meaning "life" in Hebrew), which linked him forever to the Jewish culture of Eastern Europe.

Until 1917, this territory on the western fringe of the Russian Empire, from the south of Latvia to the Black Sea, corresponded to the Pale of Settlement where the empire's Jews were forced to reside. Created by Catherine the Great, the region was twice the size of France and included lands conquered by Russia from 1791. It covered most of present-day Lithuania, Belarus, Poland, Moldova, and Ukraine. The Jewish population was numerous (around twenty percent, depending on the region), their settlement dating back to the fourteenth century, and their economic and cultural activities of great importance. In the lands of present-day Belarus, the Litvak culture[8] and the religious movement of Hasidism[9] developed concurrently. Litvak Judaism was shaped by the *Haskalah* (Jewish Enlightenment), which strove for the integration of Jews into European society by promoting education based on the sciences, philosophy, and literature. Hasidism is a mystical current within Judaism originating in present-day Ukraine focused on piety. Thus, Jewish life in the Pale of Settlement cannot be seen as having been homogeneous.

Smilaviču was what is called in Yiddish a *shtetl*, a Jewish town—the privileged site of Jewish life in Eastern Europe. There were open relations with neighboring communities, but here Jews lived in a familiar intimacy cemented by daily religious rituals, Torah study, and a use of Yiddish.

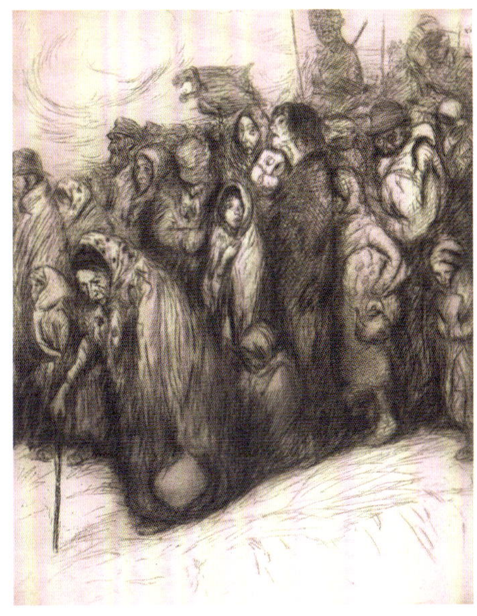

1
Abel Pann
Expulsion, 1915–1917
Musée d'Art et d'histoire
du Judaïsme, Paris

The situation in the Pale deteriorated in 1881/82 with a first wave of pogroms, and then with the Kishinev pogroms of 1903 and 1905, which were supported by czarist troops. A climate was thus established of "'dry' pogroms, violence was no longer necessary, for anti-Semitism was now cloaked in legality."[10] In 1887, secondary education was subjected to a *numerus clausus* in order to close certain professions to Jews: the proportion of Jewish students could not exceed ten percent in the Pale of Settlement, five percent outside the region, and three percent in Moscow, St. Petersburg, and Kyiv.[11] It is therefore easy to understand the resulting Jewish mass emigration: 800,000 between 1881 and 1900 and 1.3 million between 1901 and 1914.[12] It is estimated that seventeen percent of Russia's Jewish population emigrated between 1881 and 1914 (fig. 1).[13]

In this context, what did the desire to become an artist mean for the eighth son[14] of a poor cobbler in a shtetl where Hasidic culture dominated? Critic Waldemar George, in the first monograph on Soutine,[15] reports that as a youth Soutine was badly beaten by the sons of a venerable old man with a long white beard, whose portrait he was said to have painted without permission. Is it true that the inhabitants of Smilavičy had a superstitious fear of images, as Emil Szittya writes,[16] and that they applied the biblical prohibition to the letter,[17] although it is the making of idols that is strictly prohibited by the Ten Commandments? This taboo is not found in Chagall[18] or Zadkine, and their memoirs do not lend credence to this stereotypical image of the misunderstood and rejected artist. On the contrary, they report having been supported by their parents in their artistic apprenticeship and having received a secular education, in addition to the traditional religious education of the *cheder*.[19] One can thus assume that the Hasidic influence in Smilavičy was stronger than in a city of some 100,000 inhabitants like Vitebsk.

Hersh Fenster, a Yiddish-speaking journalist from Poland who lived in France beginning in 1922, wrote of Soutine: "At home his habit of drawing is considered a useless thing, a calamity. His father would rather see him become a rabbi."[20]

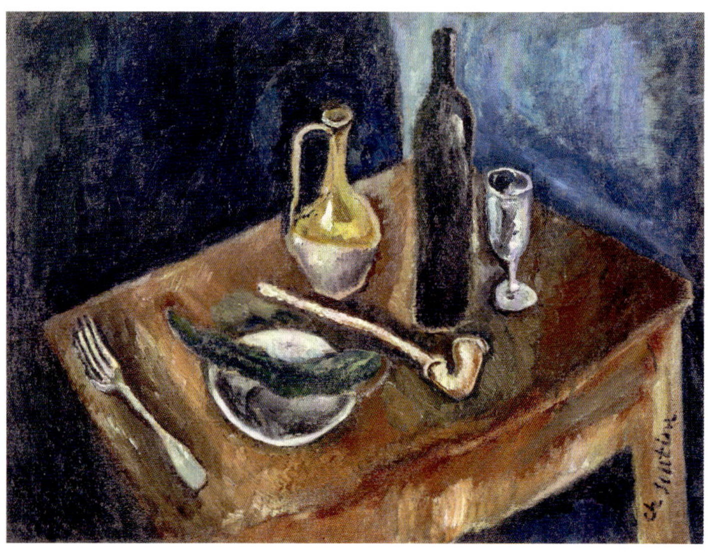

2
Nature morte à la pipe, 1916
(*Still Life with Pipe*)
Centre Pompidou / Musée d'Art
moderne de Troyes

This highlights not so much the community's rejection of art as its lack of interest in it. Fenster reports that after the beating Soutine sustained, widely seen as having been disproportionate, Soutine's parents received financial compensation that allowed them to send their son to Minsk.[21] It was there that Soutine met Michel Kikoïne in the studio of Jacob Kruger, who ran a drawing school. This was the beginning of an apprenticeship that would continue in 1910 at the Vilnius Academy of Fine Arts. Vilnius, with its 200,000 inhabitants, was also then an important center of Jewish cultural and religious life.[22] However, for Soutine, as for his associates Michel Kikoïne and Pinchus Krémègne, Paris was the necessary and desired next step, the dream goal of their lives as artists. Such a one-way ticket was the shared destiny of some 100,000 Russian Jews who chose to leave the Pale for France between 1880 and 1925.[23]

Soutine arrived in Paris in 1913. He followed, more or less, the same uneasy route that Chagall had undertaken two years before, spending several days in fourth class railroad carriages crossing the 2,000 km that separate Vilnius from Paris.

Artists who arrived in Paris at the beginning of the twentieth century found the metropolis fizzing with energy and new forms of expression that enabled them to blossom and emancipate themselves socially and culturally. For Jews, France also radiated the image of a hospitable country. As the Yiddish saying "Lebn vi Got in Frankraykh" (Happy as God in France) reminds us, it was only in 1791 during the French Revolution that Jews were first granted full citizenship,[24] opening access to all sectors of political, economic, and cultural life. For those who had experienced segregation and discrimination in their country of origin, France offered an incomparably better life. Emil Szittya says of Soutine, as of himself, "it was in France that, for the first time, he had the sensation of no longer being a 'Jew' but a 'man' like the others ... One was no longer treated as a pariah but simply as a man who had not yet had his chance."[25] Hence they felt grateful to their adopted country for its hospitality and chose to stay when war was declared in 1914, enlisting in the Foreign Legion in large numbers. Soutine was among them, but he was discharged because of his poor health.

From La Ruche to Villa Seurat—From Anonymity to Fame

When he arrived in Paris, Soutine joined Pinchus Krémègne at La Ruche ("The Beehive").[26] The central building had begun life as a pavilion of the 1900 Paris Exposition. This metal and brick structure, without running water or other creature comforts, was relocated to the edge of the 15th arrondissement near the abattoirs of Vaugirard.

As the studios were cheap, the colony attracted mainly foreigners of modest origin. There were many Jewish artists from Eastern Europe among them: these included Marc Chagall, Henri Epstein, Léon Indenbaum, Jacques Lipchitz, Ossip Zadkine, Pinchus Krémègne, Michel Kikoïne, and Chaïm Soutine. They came from Warsaw, Kraków, Lodz, Odessa, or Vilnius, and Yiddish was their mother tongue and their lingua franca.[27] La Ruche, which Zadkine compared to a "sinister Brie cheese," was to act as a bridge between the Jewish world they had left and the Parisian life they were joining.[28] As soon as they could, all these artists would leave this hive to find a more comfortable working environment (fig. 2).

In 1912, Jewish artists at La Ruche launched the journal *Makhmadim*,[29] designed to "treat with the Jewish style in the plastic arts." This publication, devoid of text and whose Hebrew title means "delights, pleasures," was the first periodical entirely dedicated to Jewish art. As Marek Szwarc writes, *Makhmadim* "was to be our homeland and follow us everywhere, like the tent follows the nomads that we were."[30] Soutine did not participate in this journal, nor in the reflections on the elaboration of a specifically Jewish art through religiously inspired iconography or subjects related to Jewish life in the shtetl. Had he been struck by what historian Arthur A. Cohen has called "an undeniable loss of Jewish self-consciousness," a forgetting of his roots?[31] Be that as it may, Soutine's own search took him elsewhere.

For fifteen years Soutine led a wretched existence. Unlike other artists such as Chagall, who received a small stipend from his patron Maxim Vinaver, Soutine was destitute. In Paris, Soutine had multiple, changing addresses. It was hard for him to settle down, above all because he had no money. He ultimately left La Ruche for the Cité Falguière (fig. 3).

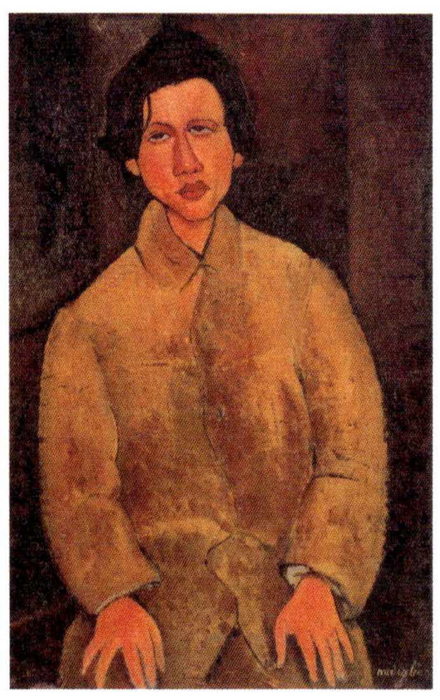

The interwar period, however, brought critical and commercial success to some of these artists, especially Soutine, who became famous overnight after fifty-two of his works were bought by the American collector and philanthropist Albert C. Barnes in the winter of 1922/23. He became "a star that rises in the firmament of modern painting, his canvases, which a year ago could not find a buyer, now sell for ten thousand francs or more, with their price increasing every day."[32]

This unforeseen success was not well received by critics. In his article for *L'Ère nouvelle* of November 29, 1923, Louis Vauxcelles denounced more than ever "the monopolization of the appellation *Art de France* by artists born abroad . . . by Slavs such as Monsieur Soutine . . . This Barnes has every right to buy works by Soutine. To be sure, or even those by Kikoïne, Krémègne, and all the rubbish churned out by the Little Entente. The important thing is that across the ocean these bizarre, foreign creations are not mistaken for French art."

The sudden visibility of Jewish artists, in a milieu where critics and dealers of Jewish extraction were already active, may have led to the belief in the twenties in the existence of a "Jewish School," arousing a virulent rejection at a time when political anti-Semitism was being expressed in the public arena. The articles published in the extreme right-wing press bore unambiguous titles: "That so many painters are strange is unfortunate . . . but that there are so many foreigners among them is even more so."

Yet things took on a new dimension in 1924 with the decision of the Salon des Indépendants to present works according to nationality. This caused a scandal that lasted over many months, and numerous artists refused to exhibit there.

Then, in 1925, a lively anti-Semitic polemic took shape in the *Mercure de France* under the title "Does Jewish Painting Exist?" All the clichés were trotted out: the absence of Jewish painters in the Louvre, the proliferation of the name Lévy at exhibitions, and the denunciation of "Jewish mercantilism." It was also in 1925, in opposition to the jingoism and xenophobia of the term "École française" (French School), that the expression "École de Paris" (School of Paris) was popularized in the writings of André Warnod.[33] The writer thus designated the group of foreign artists who had arrived in the capital at the beginning of the twentieth century and praised their contribution to the French art scene. These artists do not belong to any "school" per se, they do not share a style, but they are linked through a common history and ideal.[34]

It was also to defend themselves, and to assert their origin without having to be ashamed of it, that Éditions Le Triangle initiated its monograph series *Artistes juifs* (Jewish Artists) in 1927 with titles published in French and in Yiddish. Such an initiative, which partnered Jewish artists with famous critics, remains un-precedented in France. It testifies to the presence of many Yiddish speakers

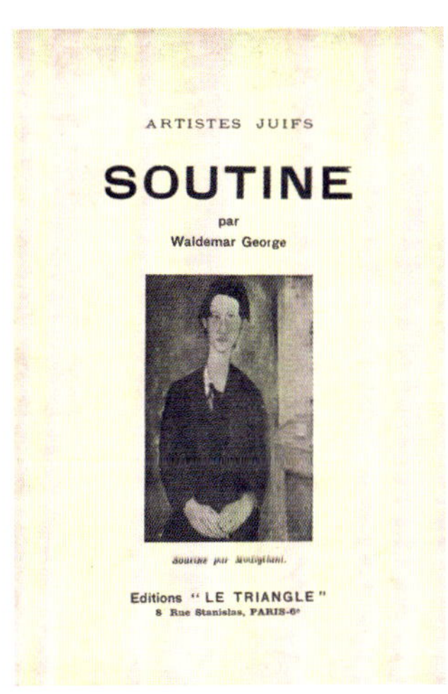

4
Waldemar George, *Soutine*
Éditions Le Triangle, Paris 1928
Musée d'Art et d'histoire du Judaïsme, Paris

in the field and to the publisher's desire to have a European-wide distribution. It must nevertheless also be seen within the context of the development of Zionism—coming a decade after the Balfour Declaration, which supported the establishment of a "national home for the Jewish people" in Palestine—and of the search for a new national art. It was in this collection that the first mono-graph on Soutine was published in 1928 by Waldemar George (fig. 4).

Some people had detested Soutine when he was destitute and wore filthy, tattered clothes. Then he became a successful artist, took up residence at the Villa Seurat, and in spite of himself, personified the figure of the cosmopolitan artist (fig. 5). He painted Chartres Cathedral, altar boys, and young pastrycooks, but in the eyes of some critics he remained a foreign artist.

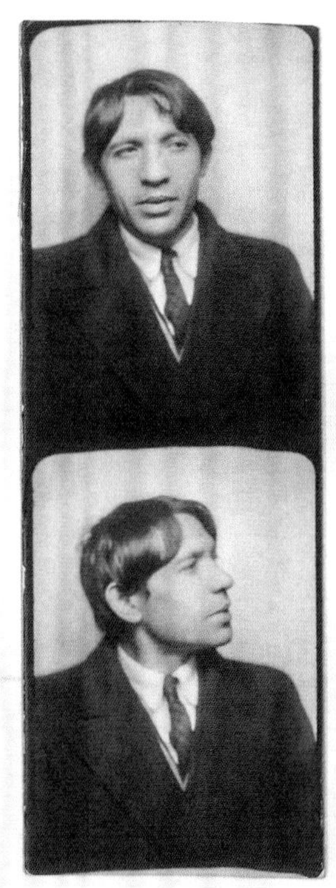

5
Passport photo of Soutine, ca. 1928/29
Photo: Pierre E. Richard

The Dream Becomes a Nightmare

In 1940, German occupation sounded the death knell for the École de Paris. On October 4, to completely outline the "status of Jews" set down the day before, the Vichy government enacted a law on "foreign nationals of the Jewish race," which ordered their internment in "specially designated camps" or their assignment to "house arrest," forcing artists to flee or else go into hiding. Soutine, stateless, was registered in October 1940 as a Russian refugee under number 35702 by the Bureau des Affaires juives (Bureau of Jewish Affairs). From then on, he was liable to be arrested at any moment and began a semi-clandestine existence. For Soutine, as for most foreign Jews, the dream of a better life in France turned into a nightmare. He felt hounded, and his health deteriorated as his ulcer left him no respite.

The dynamic of the first École de Paris was thus interrupted by the death, undercover life, or exile of its artists, but also by the destruction, theft, or dispossession of their works. However, few people really grasped the situation at the time, as did the journalist Hersh Fenster, who later published *Undzere farpaynikte kinstler* (Our martyred artists) in 1951. In it, he describes in Yiddish the lives of eighty-four Jewish artists active on the Parisian art scene who were deported, perished from ill-treatment or from a lack of proper medical care, like Soutine, who died at the age of forty-nine.

1   Emil Szittya, *Soutine et son temps* (Lausanne: La Bibliothèque des Arts, 1955; reissued, Paris: Éditions du Canoë, 2023), p. 9.

2   In 1964, Harvard University was able to acquire one of the most important collections of Soutine's correspondence: thirty-seven letters from Soutine to Henri Sérouya (1895–1968), a renowned scholar of the Kabbalah.

3   The term Ashkenazi refers to Jews from Central and Eastern Europe.

4   Szittya, *Soutine et son temps*, p. 9.

5   Nancy L. Green, *The Pletzl of Paris: Jewish Immigrant Workers in the Belle Epoque* (New York: Holmes & Meier, 1986), p. 12. She estimates that 1.3 million Jewish men and women left the Russian Empire between 1901 and 1914.

6   Noah Pryłucki, Etel Tzukerman, and Nochum Gelfand, "The Yiddish Life of Chaim Soutine (1893–1943): New Materials," introd. and trans. Ofer Dynes, *In geveb: A Journal of Yiddish Studies* (April 2020), https://ingeveb.org/texts-and-translations/life-of-soutine.

7   According to sources, he was born in either 1893 or 1894. Soutine also maintained this ambiguity.

8   The term Litvaks refers to the Jewish population of the former Grand Duchy of Lithuania, which in the sixteenth century included what is now Lithuania, part of Poland, and Belarus. Vilnius, the "Jerusalem of the North," was the intellectual center. At the end of the nineteenth century, the condition of the Jewish communities in present-day Belarus and Poland was greatly improved, allowing the younger generation to attend secondary school and gain access to Russian culture. Litvaks, also known as Lithuanian Jews, developed a cultural and artistic life, open to both the world and modernity. Many of the heirs of this Litvak world, such as Emmanuel Levinas, Golda Meir, and Marc Chagall, have left their mark on the history of the twentieth century.

9   Hasidism is a mystical current within Judaism that arose during the eighteenth century. It is one of two movements within Orthodox Judaism.

10 Green, *The Pletzl of Paris*, p. 10.

11 Green, p. 11.

12 Green, p. 12.

13 See Liebman Hersch, "Jewish Migrations During the Last Hundred Years," in *The Jewish People Past and Present*, 4 vols. (New York: Jewish Encyclopedic Handbooks, 1955), vol. 1, pp. 407–430.

14 According to some sources he was the tenth child.

15 Waldemar George, *Soutine,* Artistes juifs (Paris: Éditions Le Triangle, 1928).

16 Szittya, *Soutine et son temps*, p. 18.

17 "Thou shalt not make unto thee any graven image, or any likeness *of any thing* that *is* in heaven above, or that *is* in the earth beneath, or that *is* in the water under the earth" (Exodus 20:4).

18 Marc Chagall, *Mon Univers: Autobiographie* (Quebec: Fides, 2017). The transcript in Yiddish (1925) is preserved at the YIVO Institute for Jewish Research, New York, and was translated into French by Chantal Ringuet and Pierre Anctill.

19 A *cheder* is a Jewish primary school where Hebrew and the rudiments of Judaism are taught. Traditionally all Jewish boys attended such schools, even those from the most modest origins.

20 Hersh Fenster, *Undzere farpaynikte kinstler* [Our martyred artists] (Paris: H. Fenster, 1951); translated into French as *Nos artistes martyrs* (Paris: Musée d'Art et d'histoire du Judaïsme [mahJ]; Paris: Hazan, 2021).

21 Smilavičy is approximately 30 km from Minsk.

22 In 1910, the Jews of Vilnius represented almost a third of the city's population.

23 Green, *The Pletzl of Paris*, p. 27.

24 The decree of September 27, 1791, recognized for the first time in modern history the full citizenship of the Jews.

25 Szittya, *Soutine et son temps*, p. 23.

26 La Ruche is an artists' residence founded in 1902 by the sculptor Alfred Boucher. At that time, it consisted of about a hundred studios. La Ruche still exists at its historical address in passage de Dantzig, in the 15th arrondissement of Paris.

27 Yiddish is a language derived from High German, with an element of Hebrew and Slavic vocabulary, written in the Hebrew alphabet. Since the Middle Ages, it has been the lingua franca of Jews from Alsace to the far reaches of Eastern Europe. Before 1940, Yiddish was spoken by two-thirds of the world's Jews, or eleven million people.

28 Ossip Zadkine, *Le Maillet et le Ciseau: Souvenirs de ma vie* (Paris: Albin Michel, 1968), p. 53.

29 The founder artists were Joseph Chaikov, Marek Szwarc, Isaac Lichtenstein, and Henri Epstein.

30 Marek Szwarc and Eugenia Markowa, "Un artiste est né" (unpublished, 1954), p. 312; the typescript is kept at the Musée d'Art et d'histoire du Judaïsme, Paris.

31 Arthur A. Cohen, "From Eastern Europe to Paris and Beyond," in Kenneth E. Silver and Romy Golan, *The Circle of Montparnasse: Jewish Artists in Paris, 1905–1945* (New York: Universe Books, 1985), pp. 60–79, here p. 66.

32 René Gimpel, in an entry made on April 6, 1926, in *Journal d'un collectionneur* (Paris: Calmann-Levy, 1963). Four years later, Gimpel was to buy a Soutine from Zborowski for 36,000 francs.

33 Other sources cite Roger Allard as the original author of the term.

34 The 2021 exhibition *Chagall, Modigliani, Soutine. . . Paris as a School, 1905–1940* at the Musée d'Art et d'histoire du Judaïsme in Paris traced the development of some forty Jewish artists who arrived in Paris before 1914.

Chaïm Soutine—Works

[1]
Still Life with Herrings, 1915/16
Oil on canvas
64.5 × 48.6 cm
Galerie Larock-Granoff, Paris

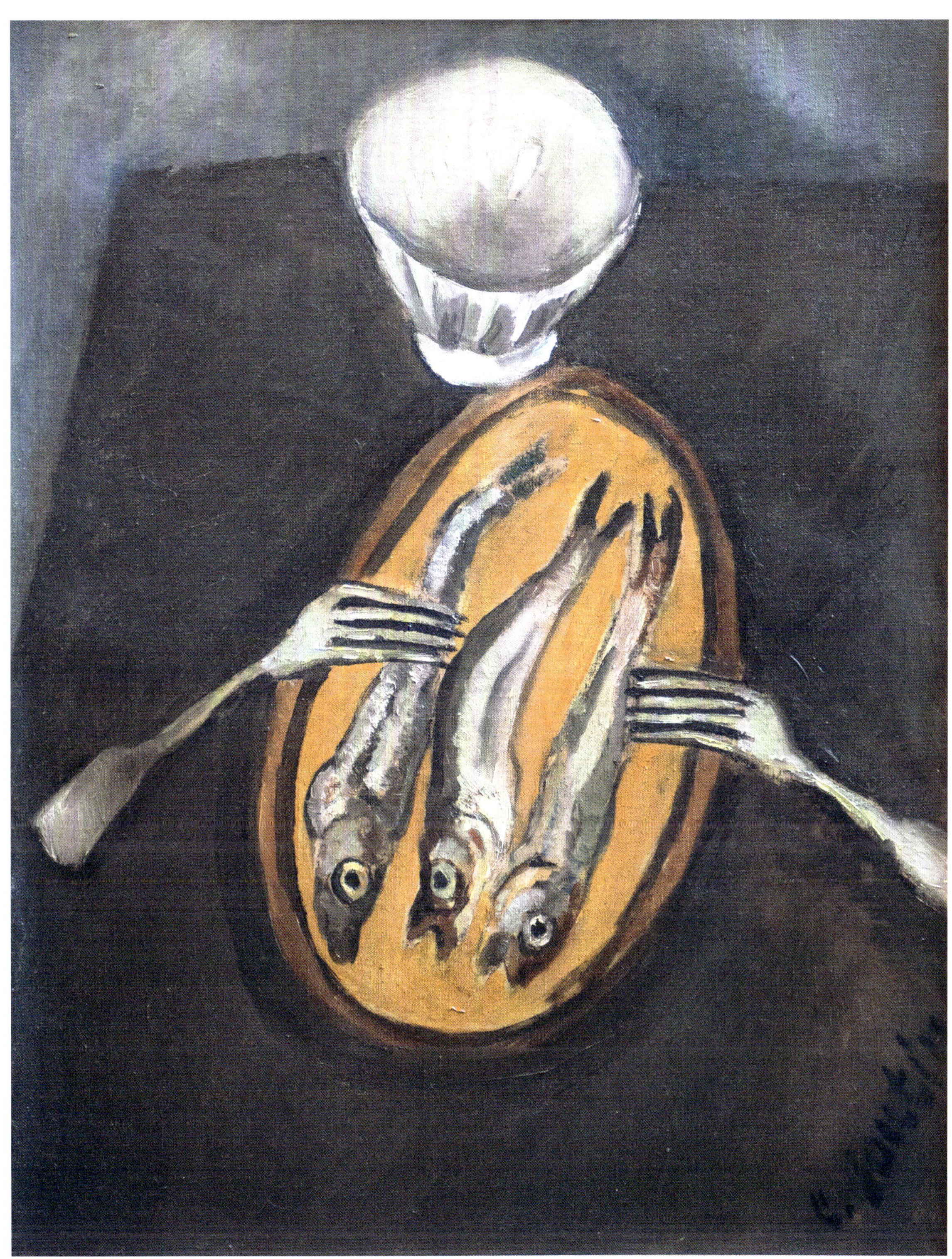

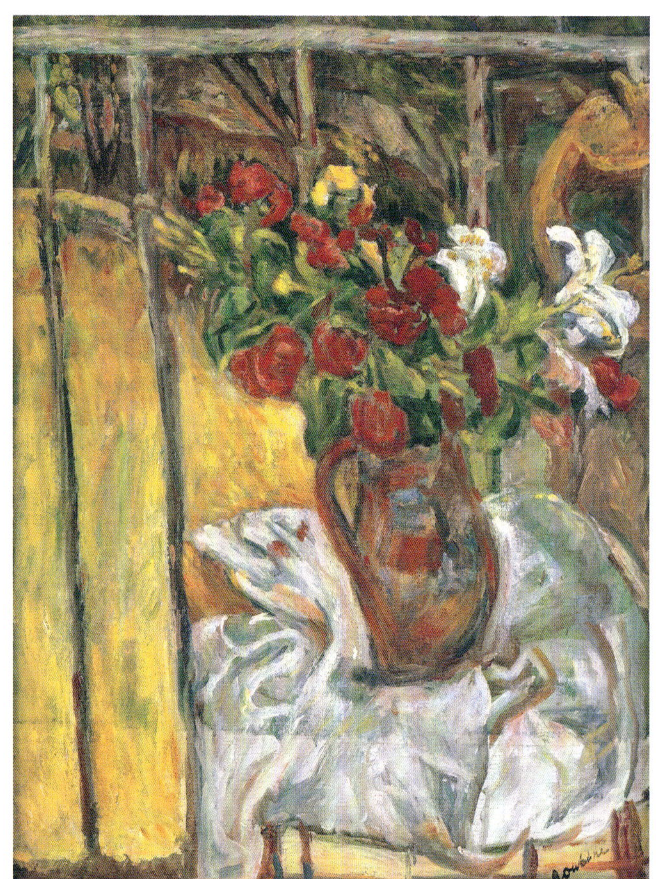

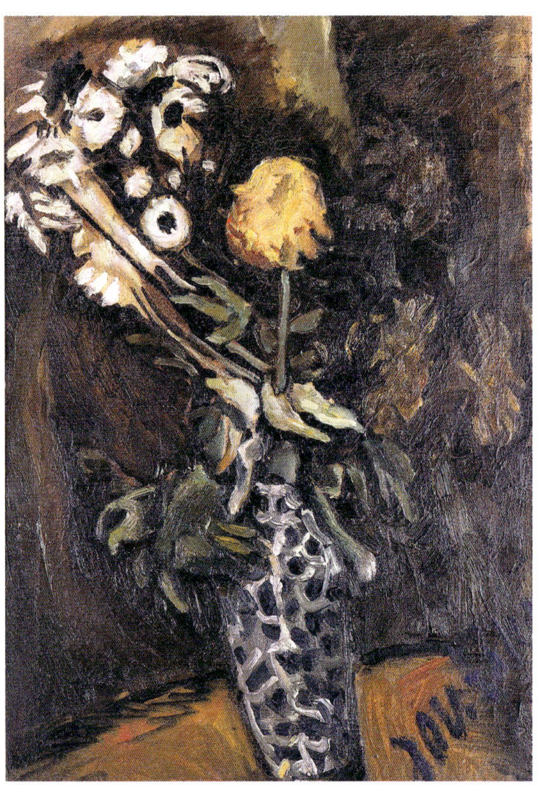

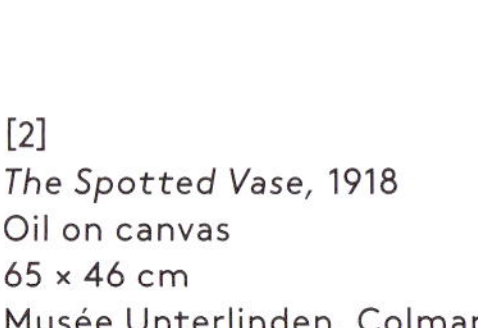

[2]
The Spotted Vase, 1918
Oil on canvas
65 × 46 cm
Musée Unterlinden, Colmar

[3]
Bouquet of Flowers on a Balcony, 1916
Oil on canvas
65.3 × 50.5 cm
Association des Amis du Petit Palais, Geneva

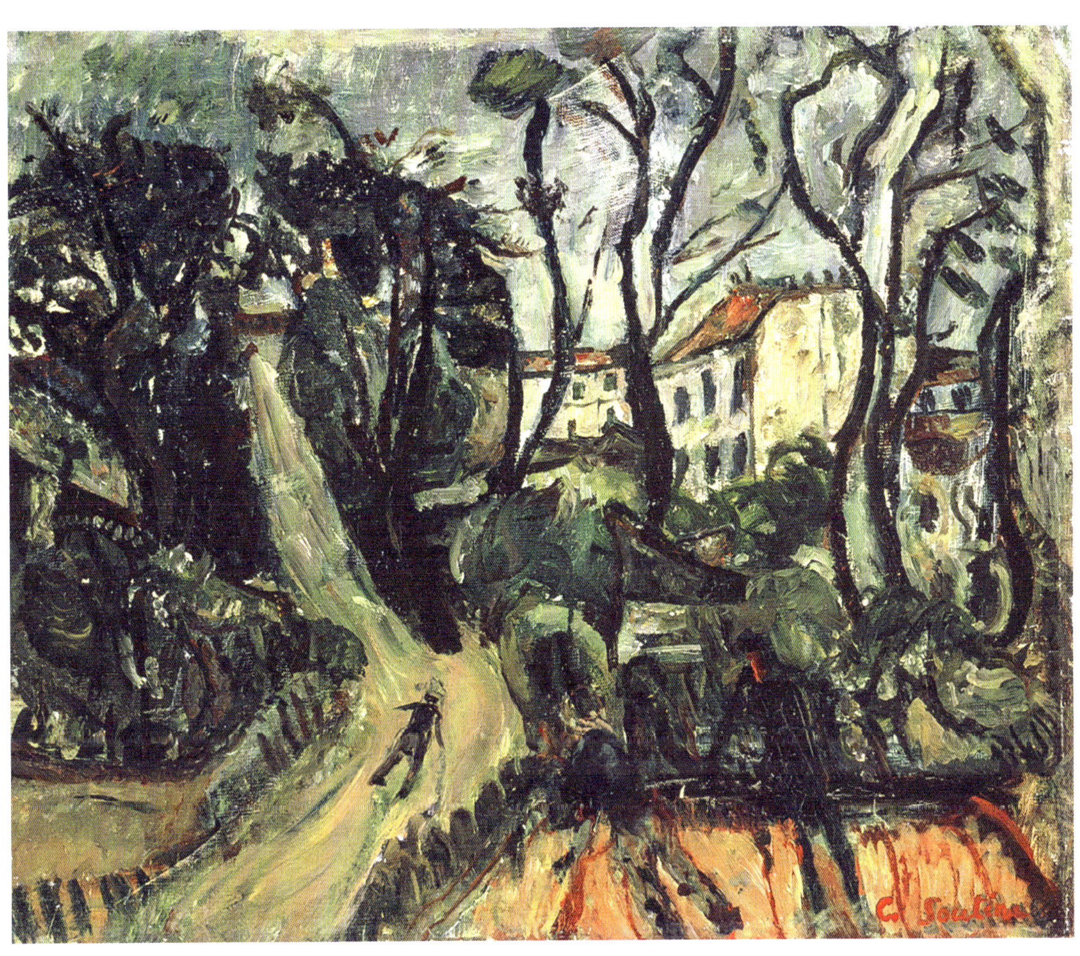

[4]
Landscape with Houses, 1918
Oil on canvas
67.5 × 79 cm
Kunstmuseum Luzern, Lucerne

[5]
Self-Portrait, ca. 1918
Oil on canvas
54.6 × 45.7 cm
Princeton University Art Museum

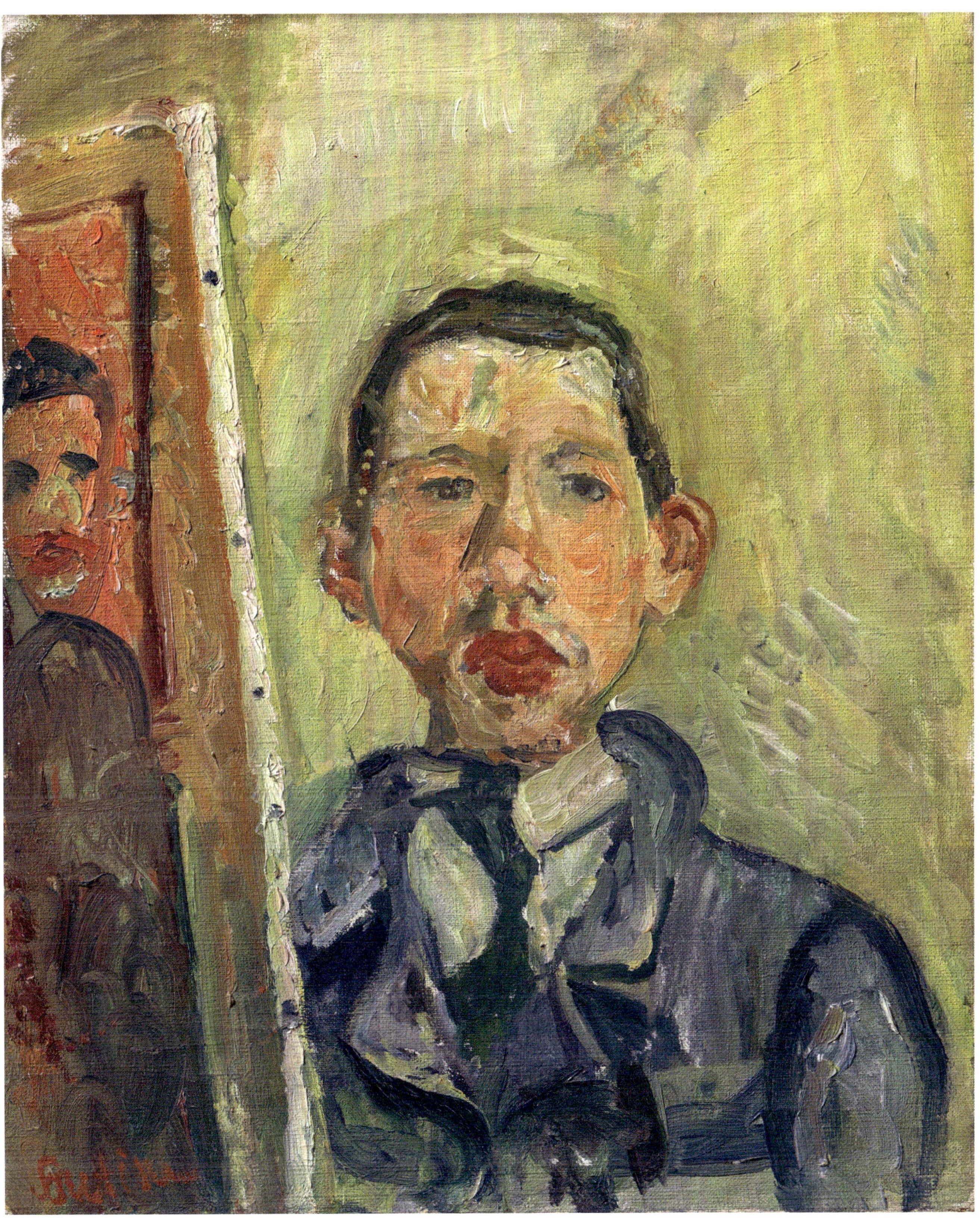

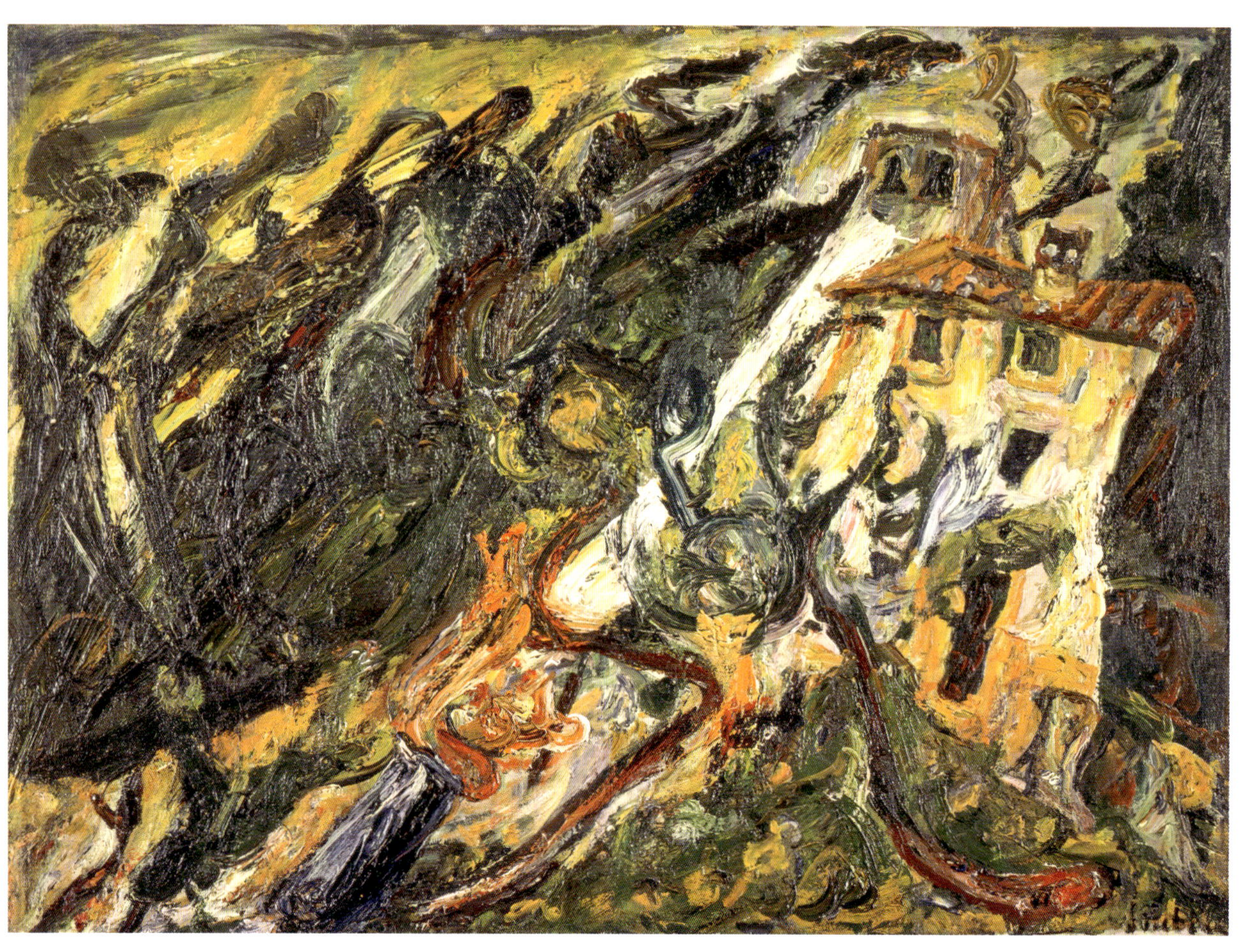

[6]
Le Mas Passe-Temps, Céret, 1920/21
Oil on canvas
62.8 × 86.3 cm
National Galleries Scotland, Edinburgh

[7]
Houses, 1920/21
Oil on canvas
58 × 92 cm
Musée de l'Orangerie, Paris

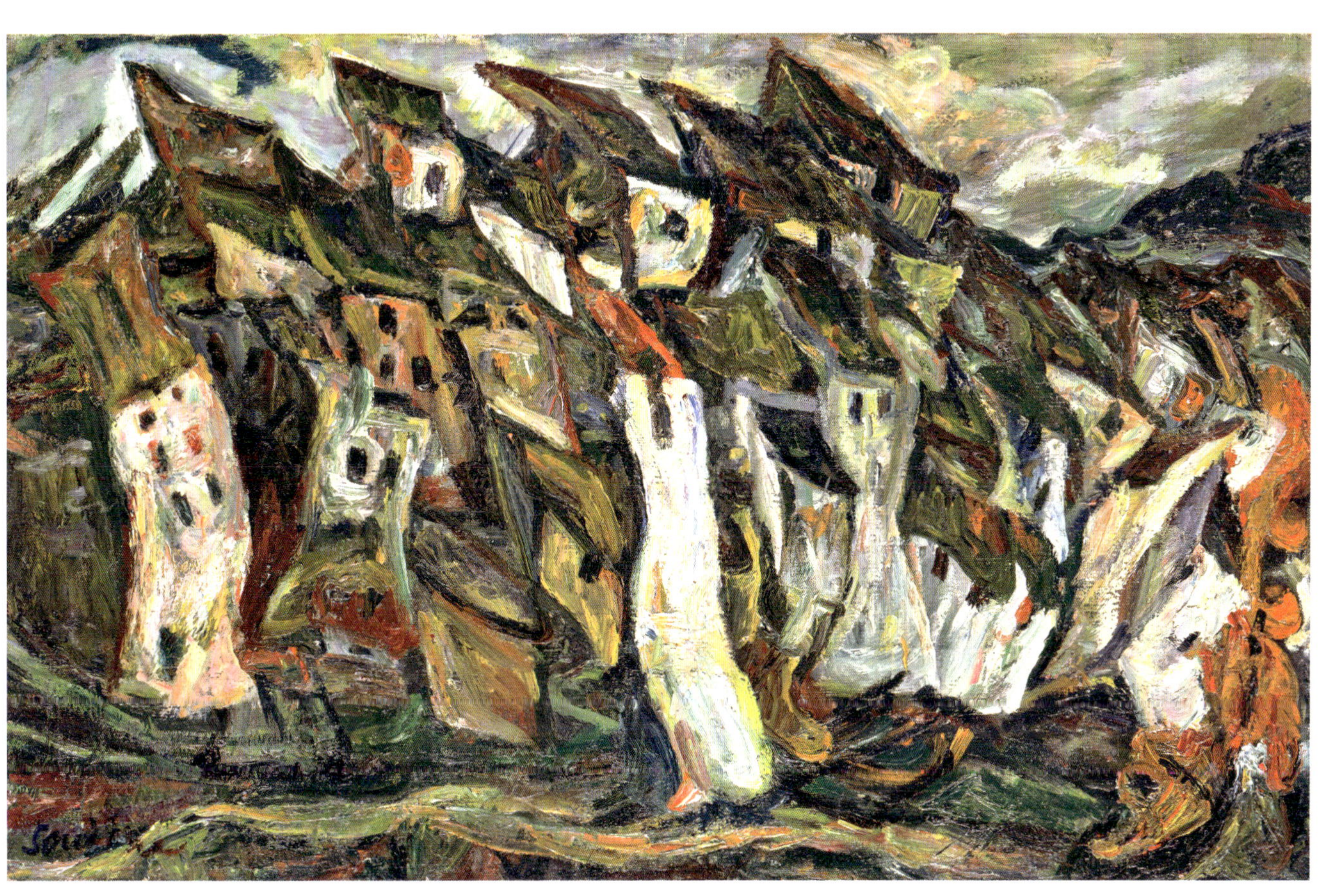

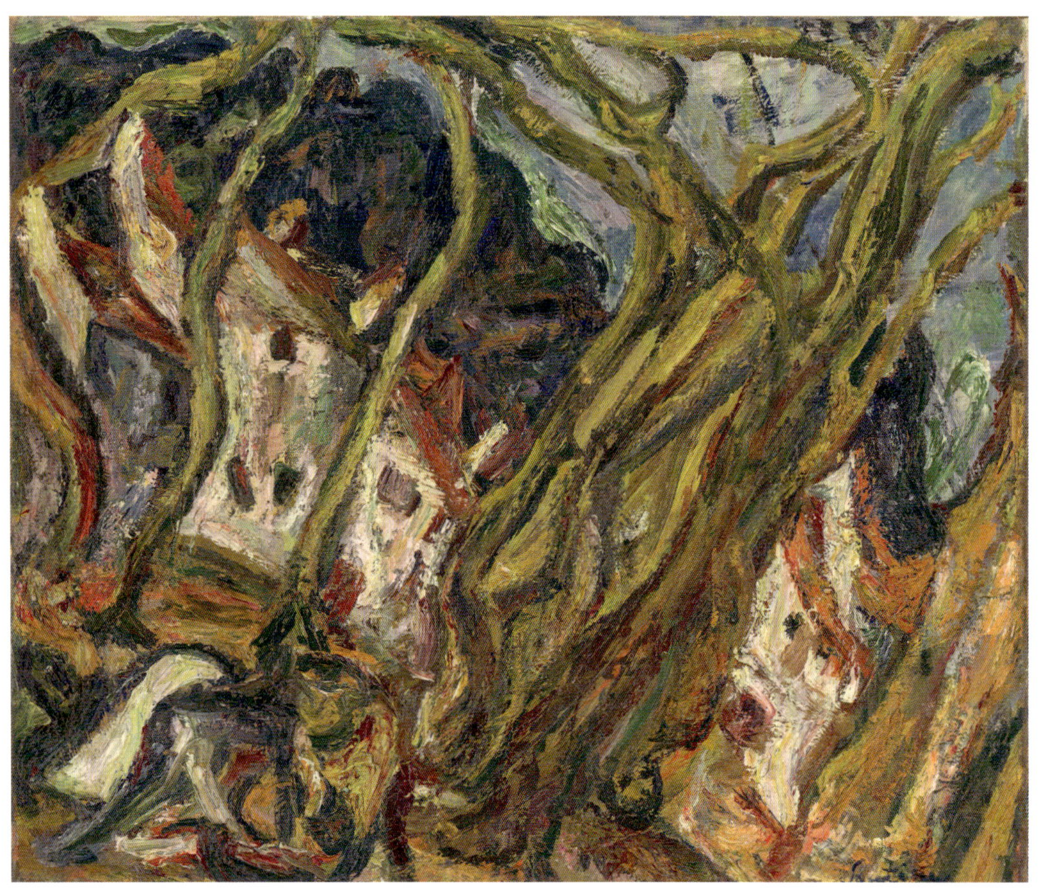

[8]
The Plane Trees of Céret, Place de la Liberté, 1920/21
Oil on canvas
60 × 73 cm
Von der Heydt-Museum, Wuppertal

[9]
Village Square at Céret, 1920
Oil on canvas
76 × 94 cm
The Israel Museum, Jerusalem

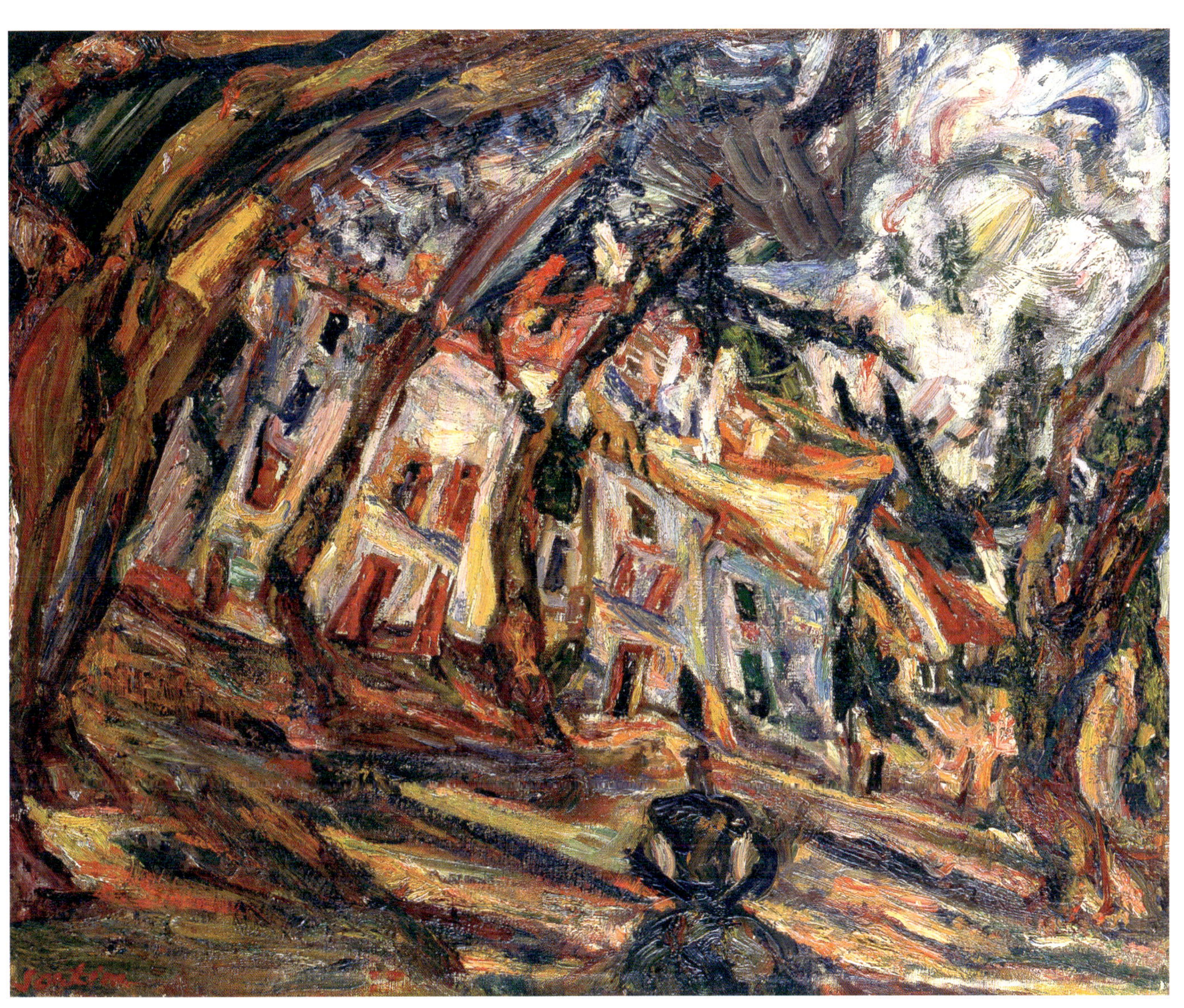

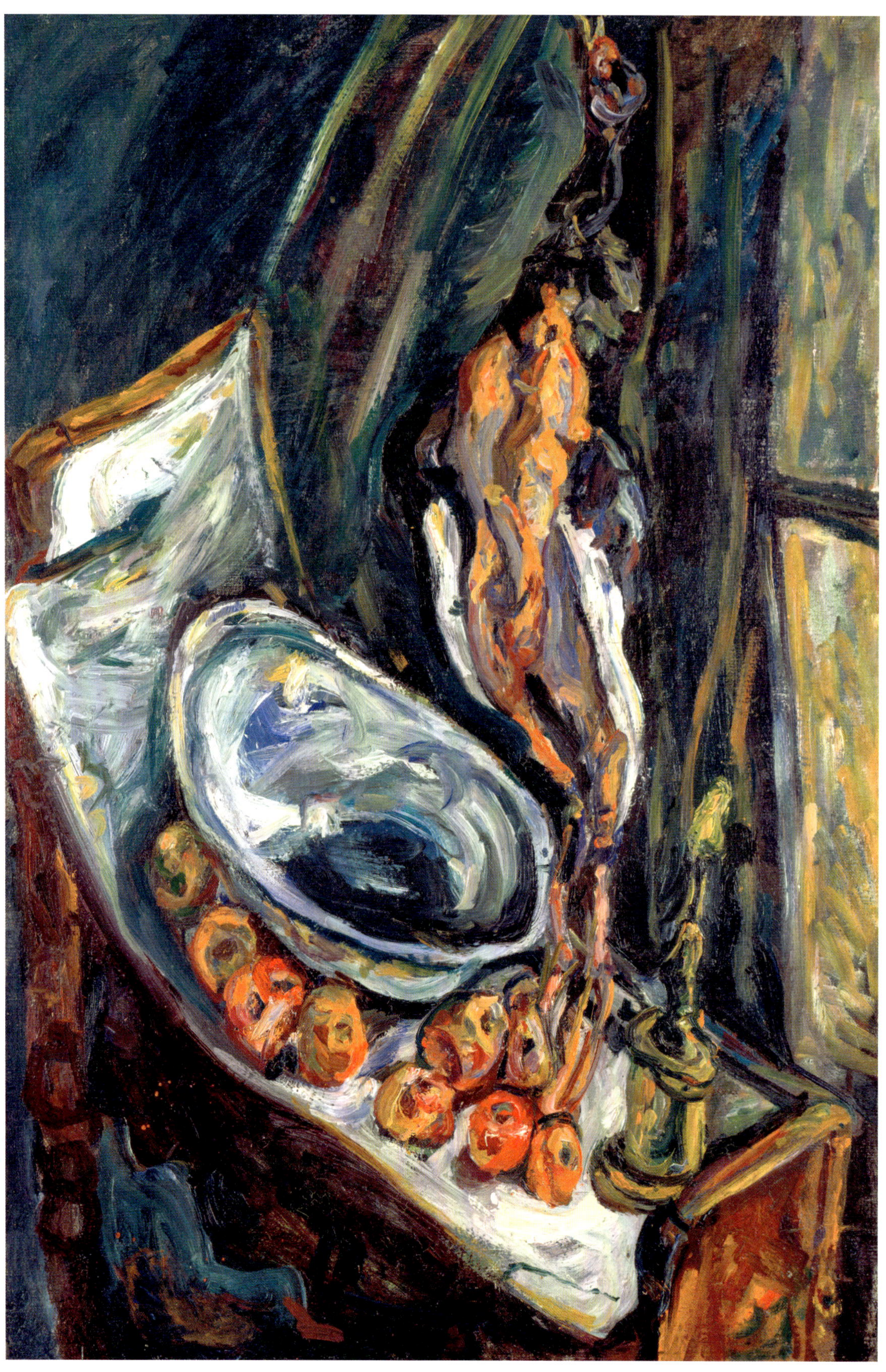

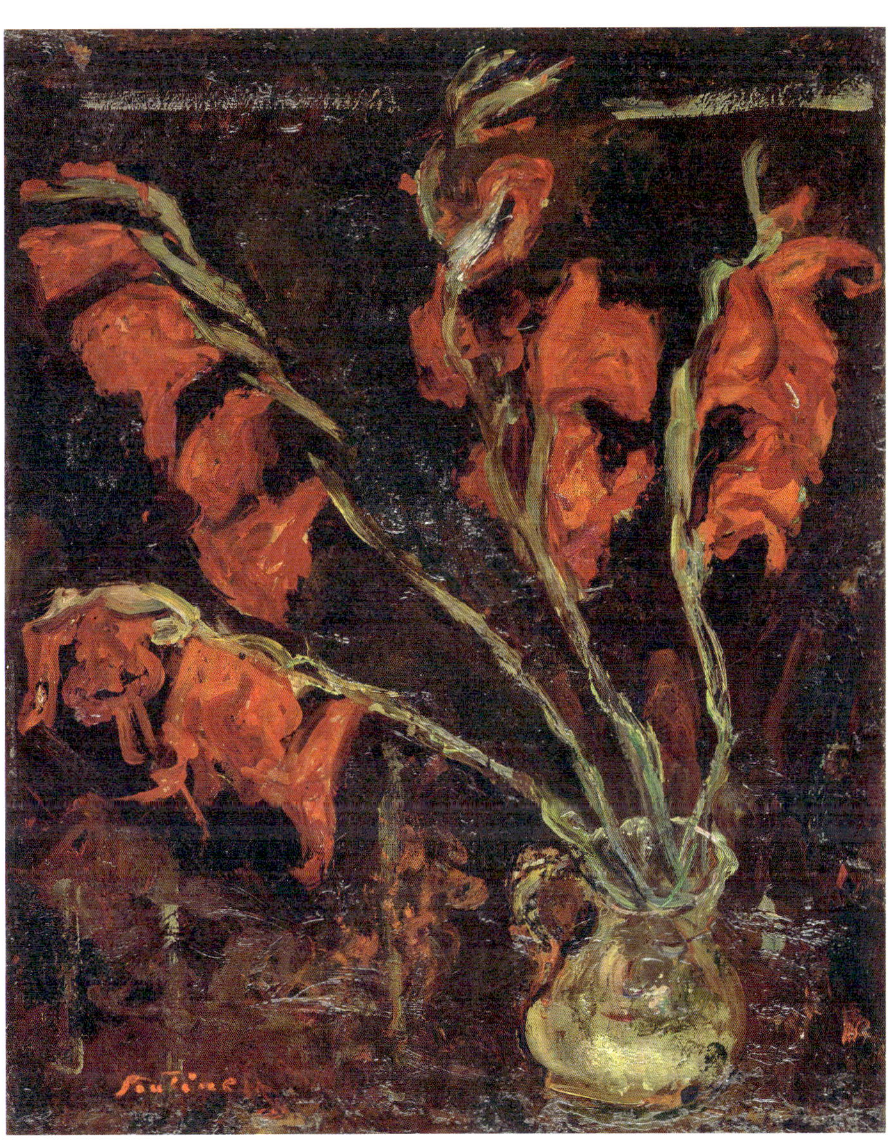

[10]
Still Life with Pheasant, ca. 1919
Oil on canvas
92 × 60.5 cm
Kunstsammlung Nordrhein-Westfalen, Düsseldorf

[11]
Gladiolas, 1919
Oil on canvas
56 × 46 cm
Musée de l'Orangerie, Paris

[12]
Child with a Toy, ca. 1919
Oil on canvas
81 × 64.5 cm
Stiftung Im Obersteg
Depositum im Kunstmuseum Basel 2004

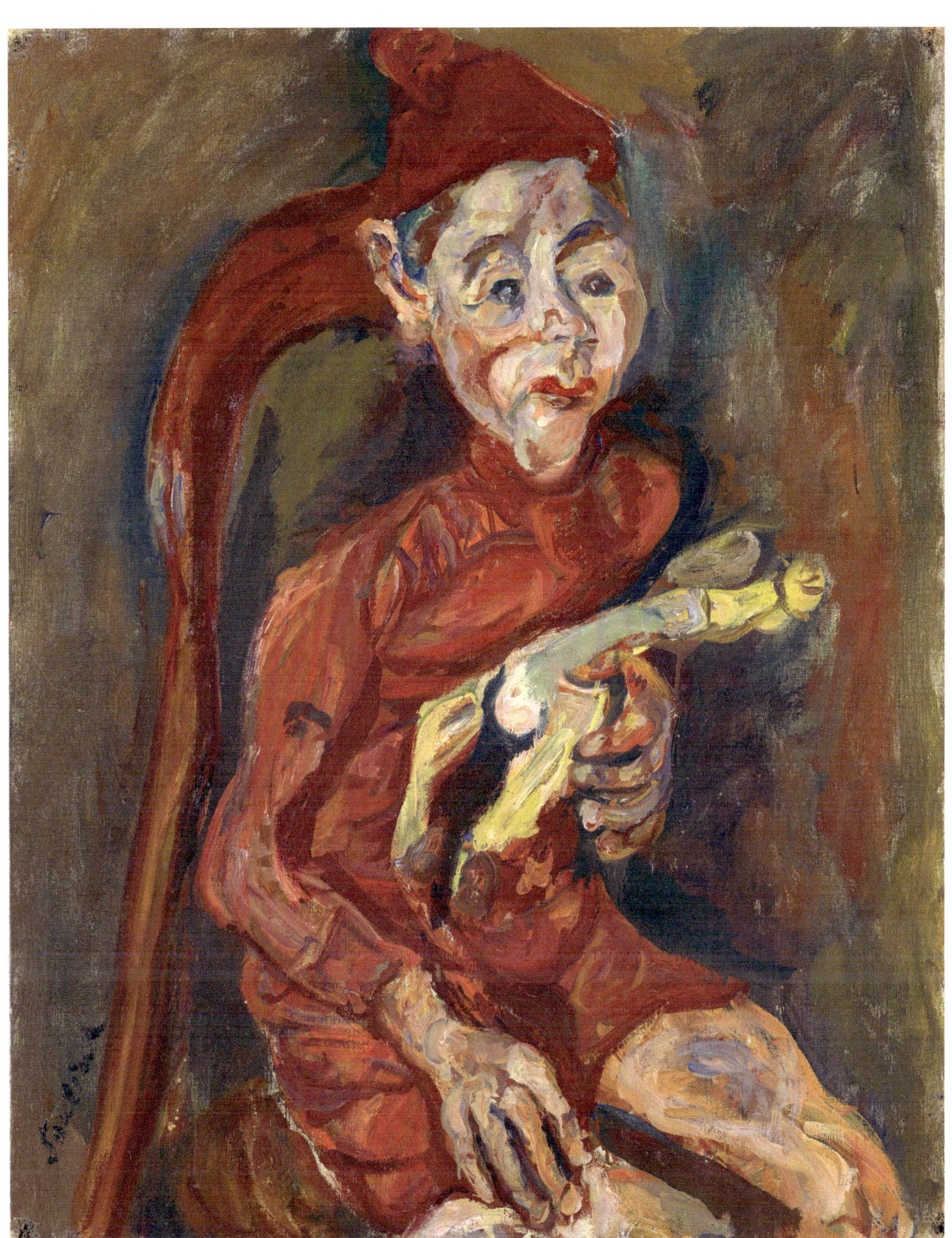

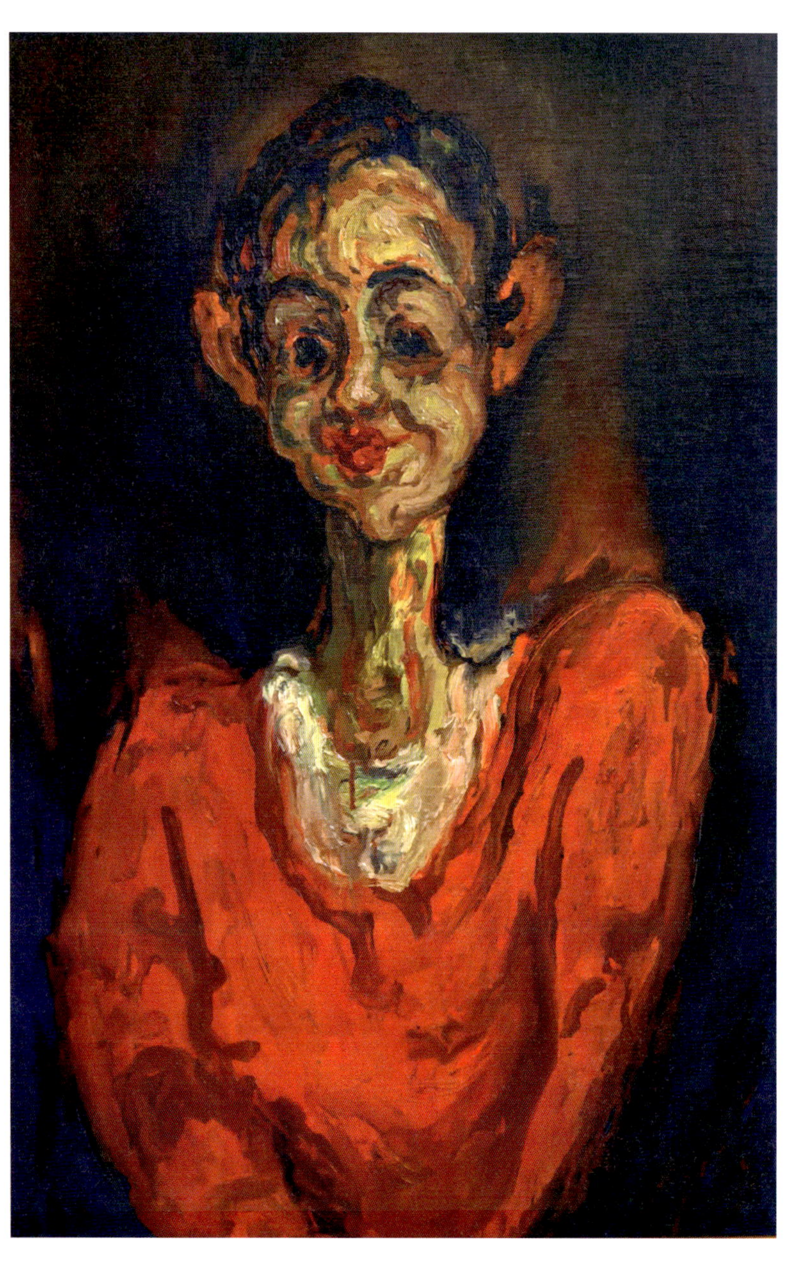

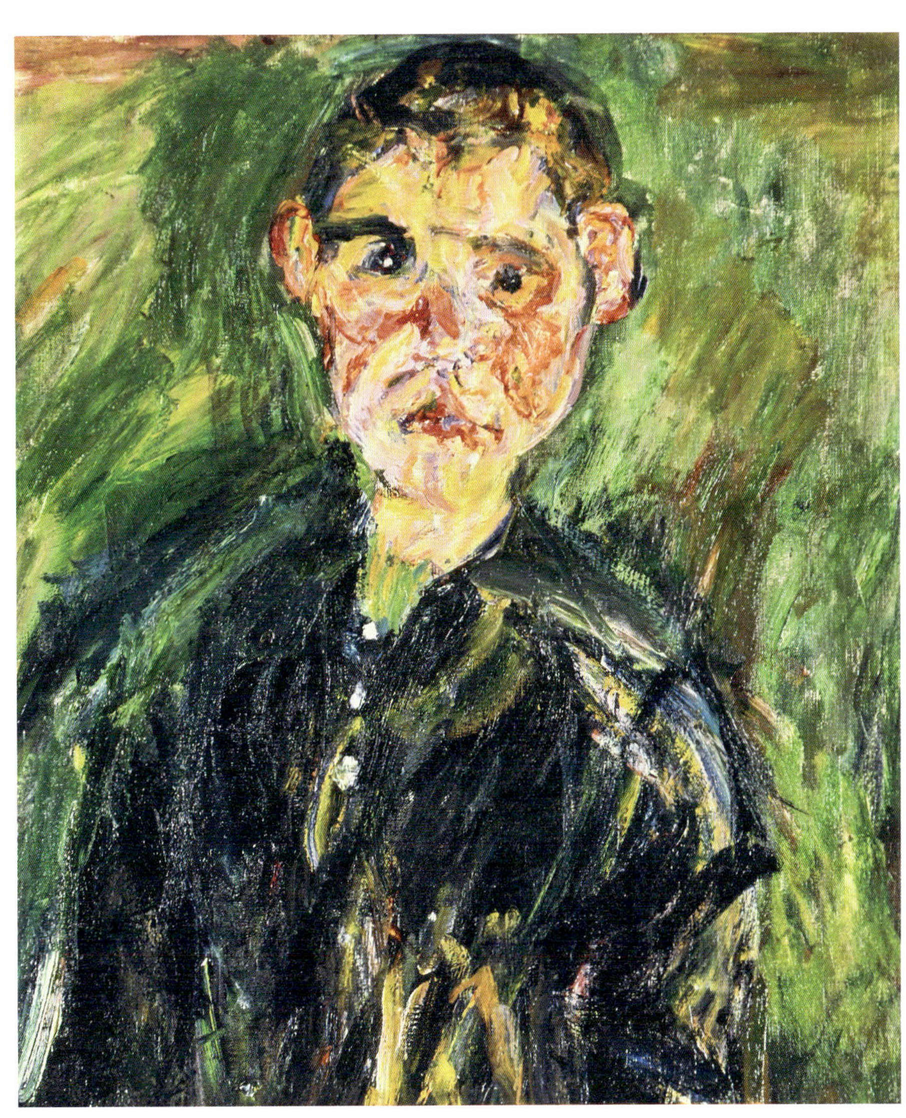

[13]
The Old Girl, ca. 1920
Oil on canvas
71.5 × 54 cm
MAH Musée d'Art et d'histoire, Geneva

[14]
Peasant Boy, 1919/20
Oil on canvas
64 × 55.2 cm
The Lewis Collection, London

[15]
Village Idiot, 1920
Oil on canvas
92 × 65 cm
Musée Calvet, Avignon

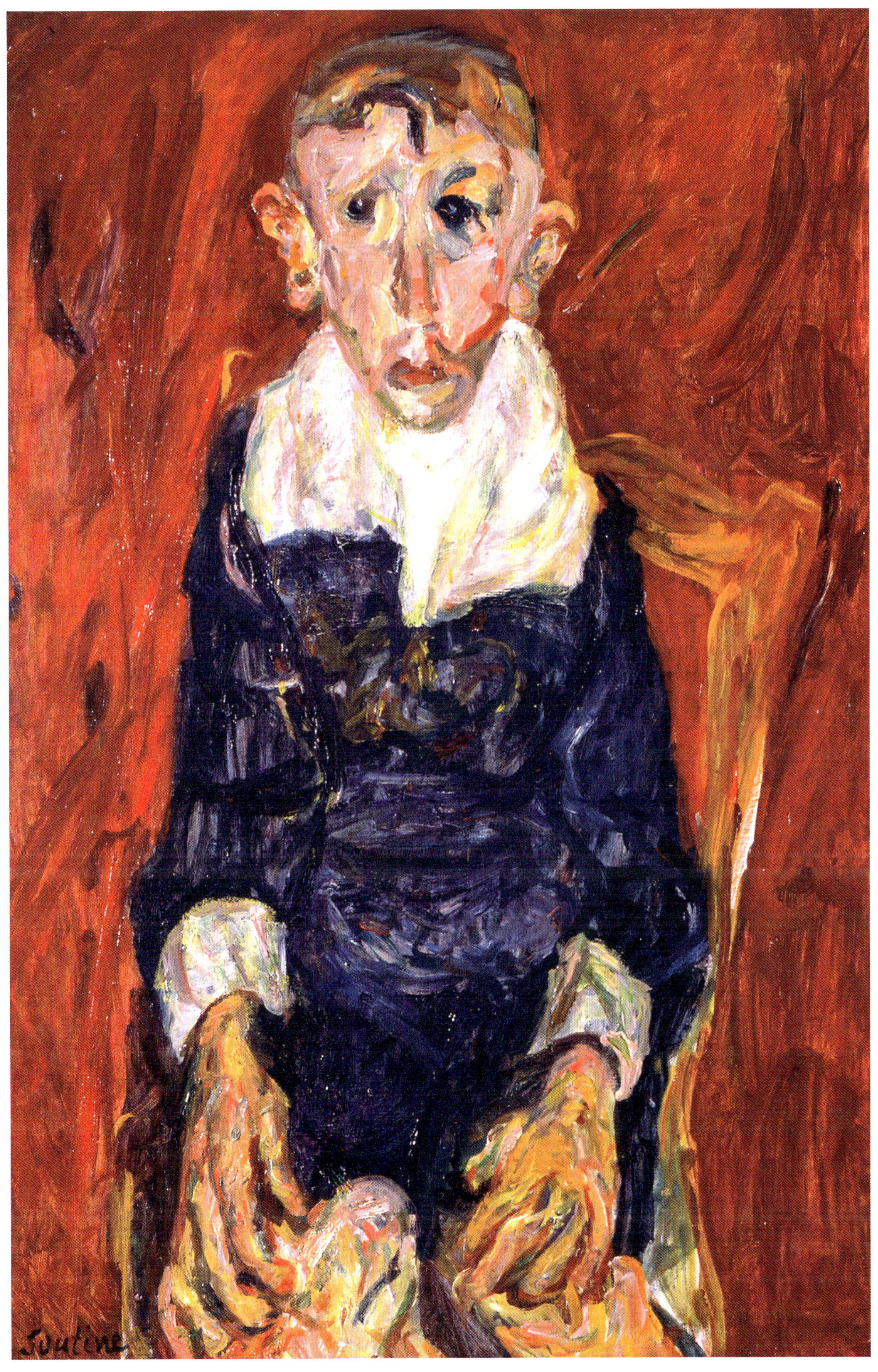
Soutine

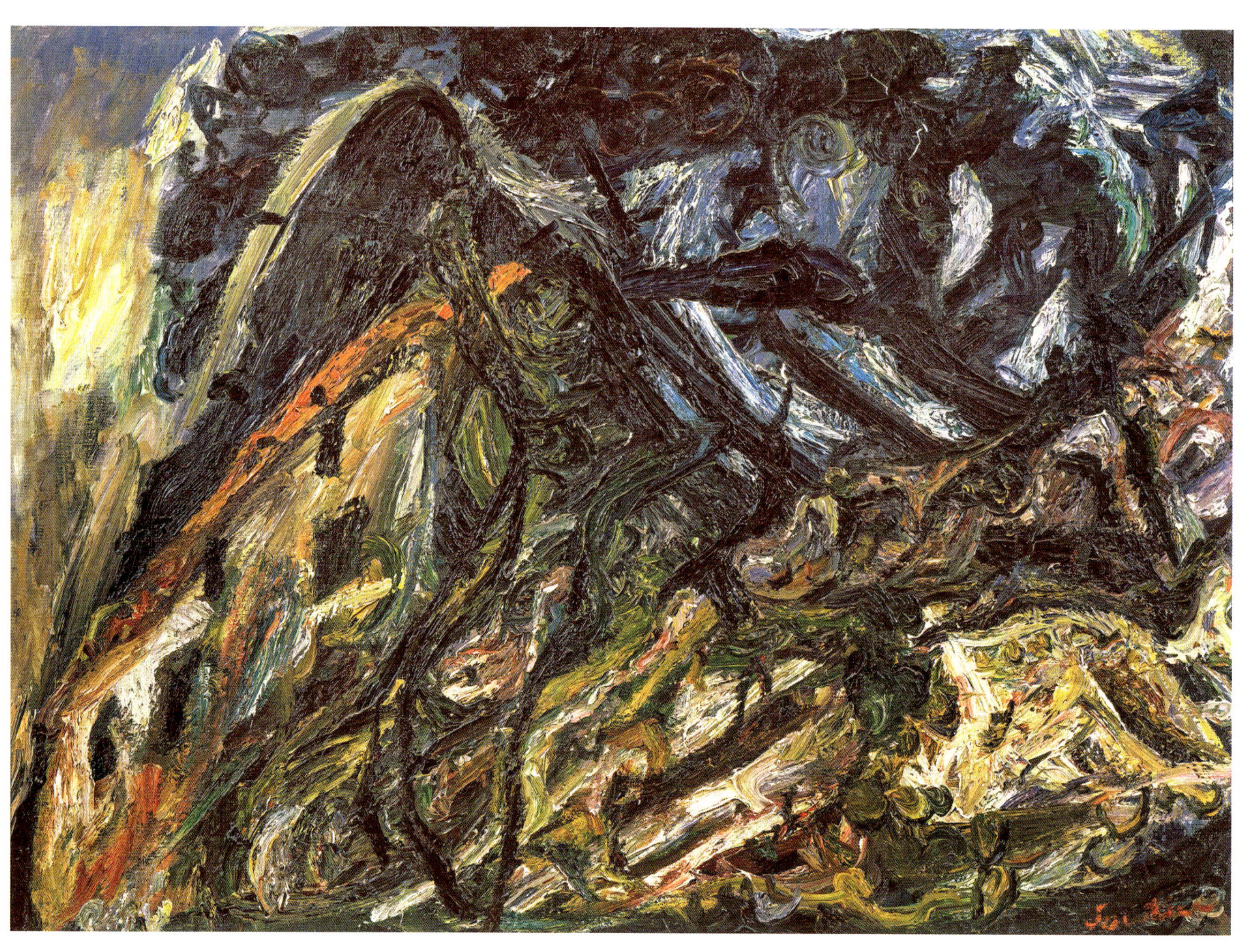

[16]
Landscape at Céret, ca. 1920/21
Oil on canvas
55.9 × 83.8 cm
Tate

[17]
Hill at Céret, ca. 1921
Oil on canvas
74.3 × 54.9 cm
Los Angeles County Museum of Art

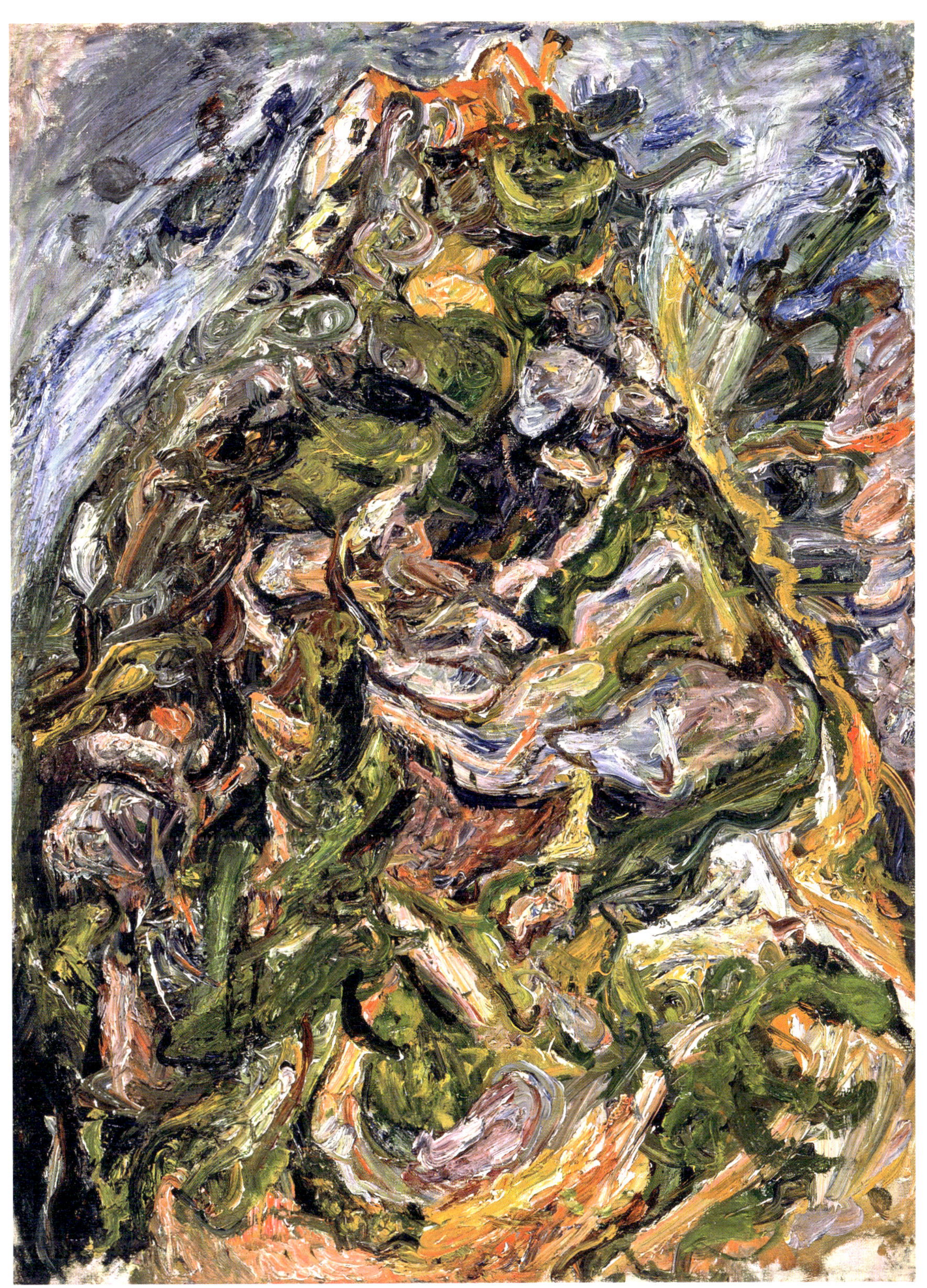

[18]
The Little Pastrycook, 1922/23
Oil on canvas
73 × 54 cm
Musée de l'Orangerie, Paris

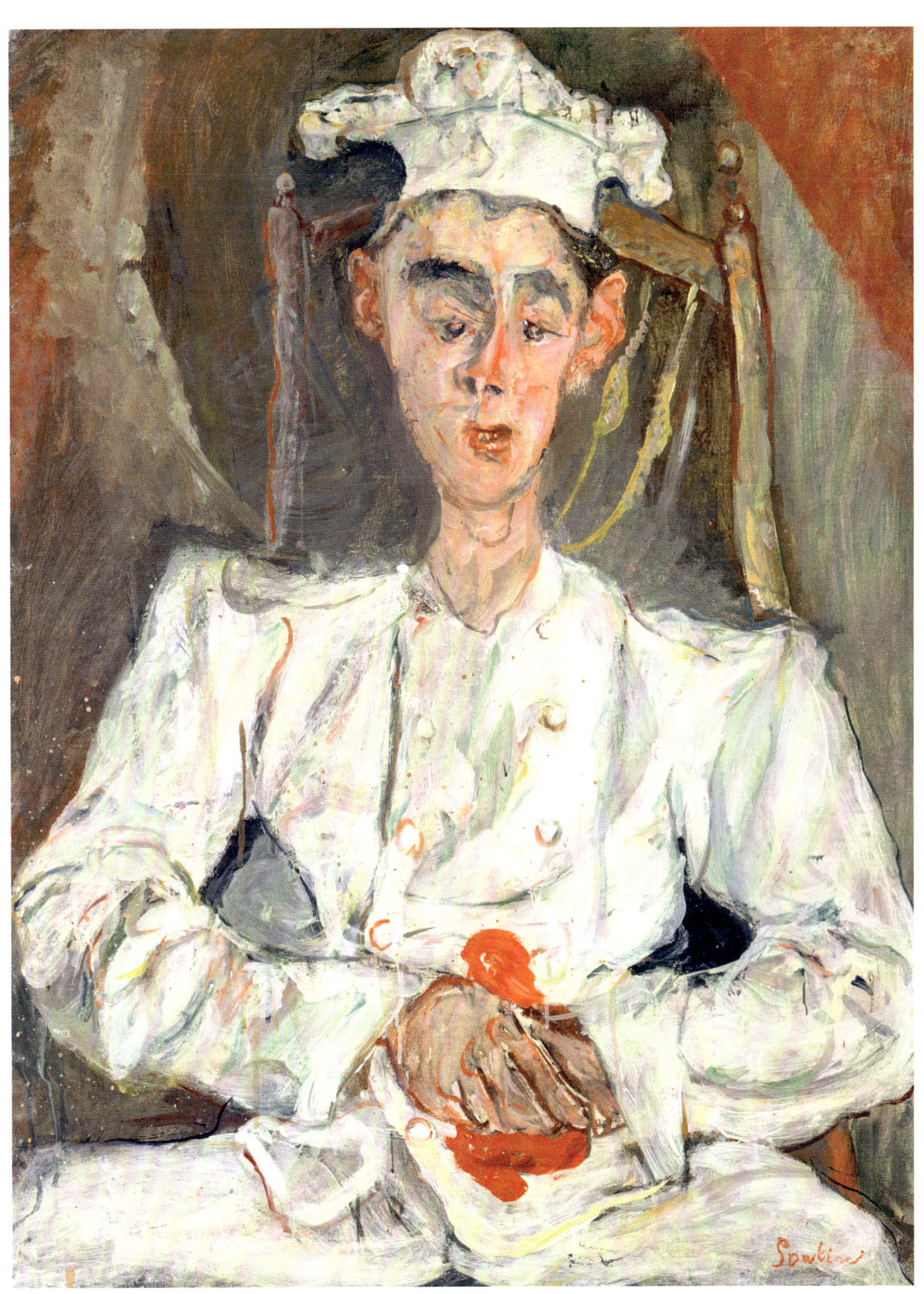

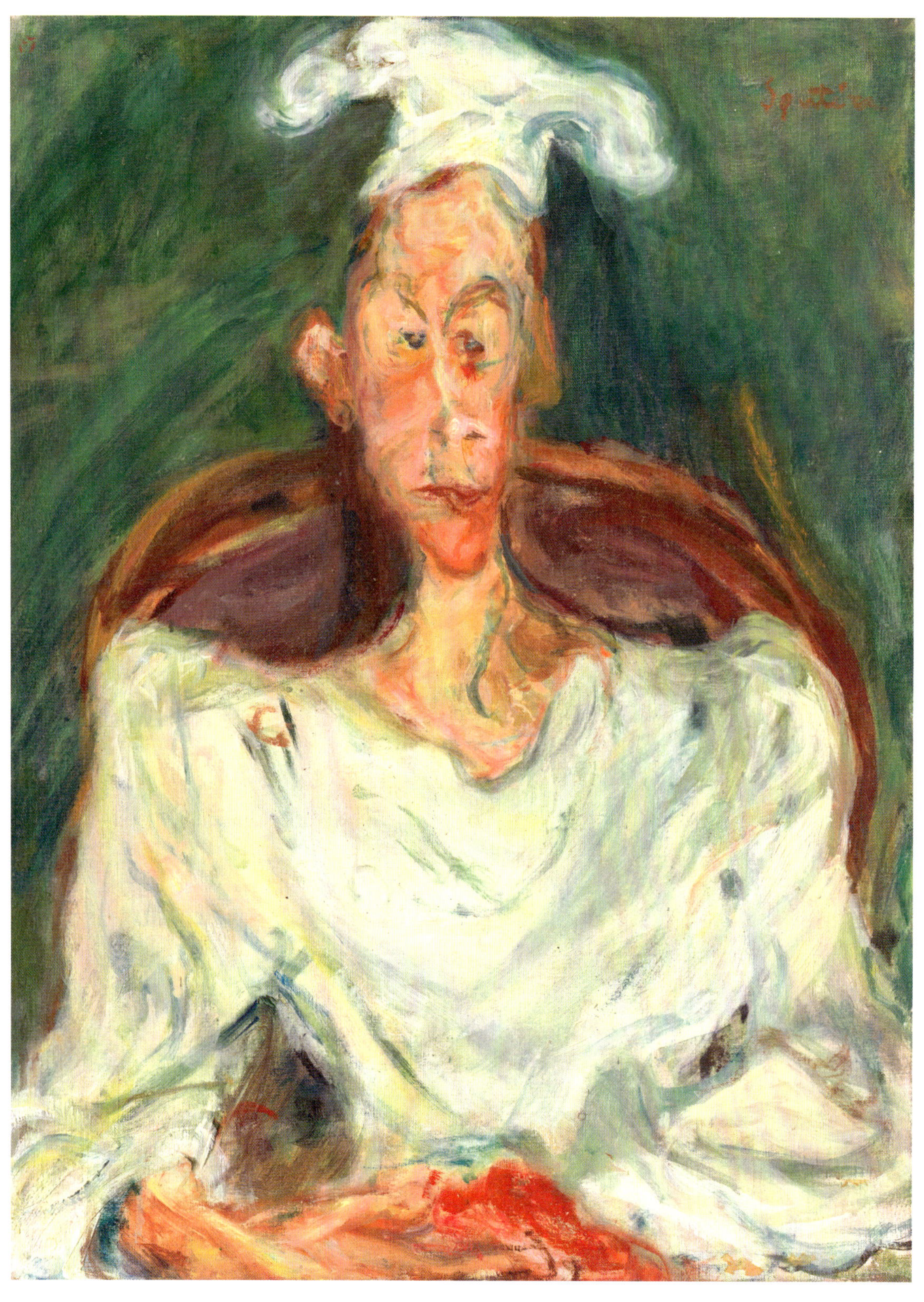

[19]
Pastry Chef, ca. 1923
Oil on canvas
64.5 × 48.3 cm
National Gallery of Art, Washington, DC

[20]
Cook of Cagnes, ca. 1924
Oil on canvas
61 × 51 cm
Kunstmuseum Bern

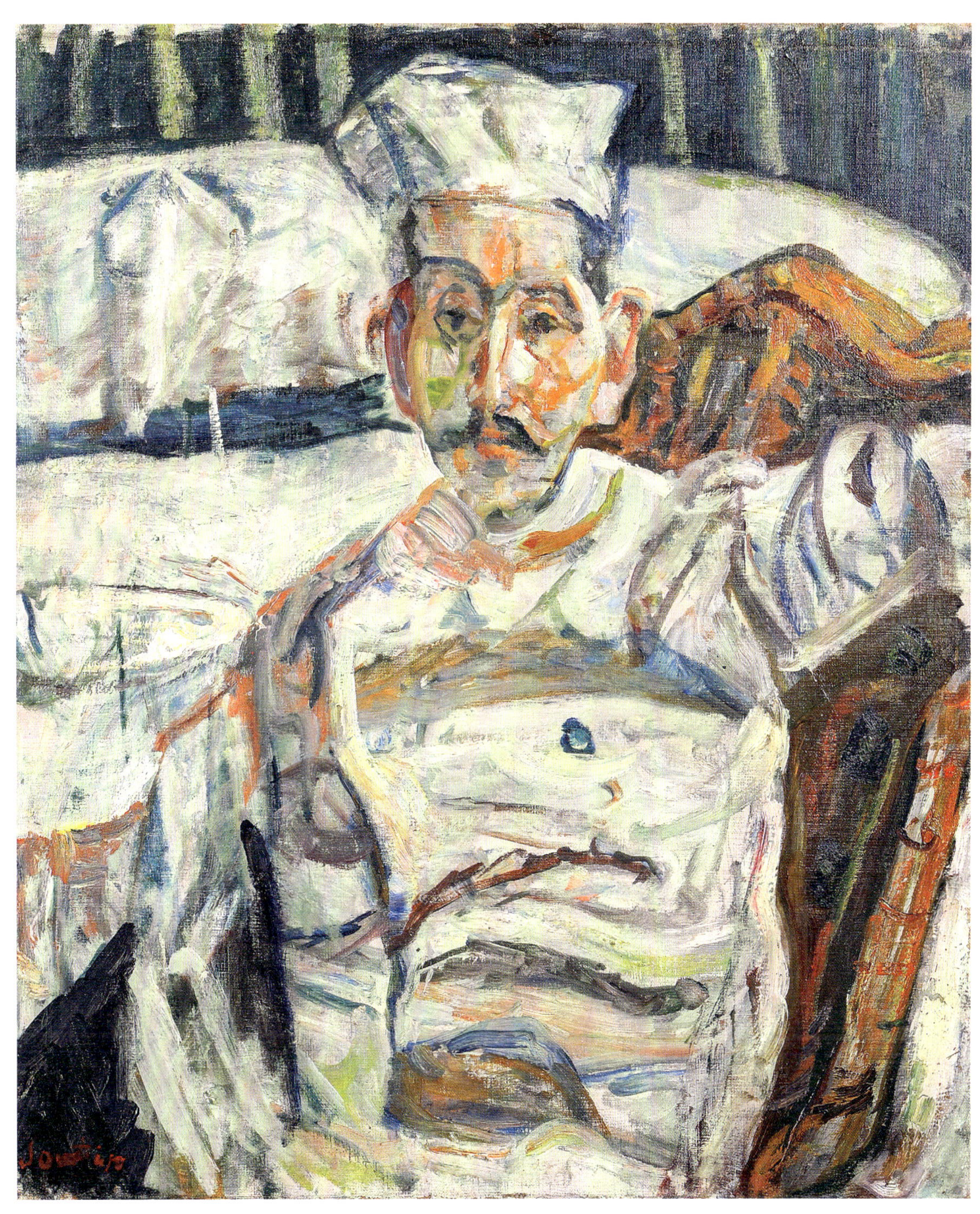
Soutine

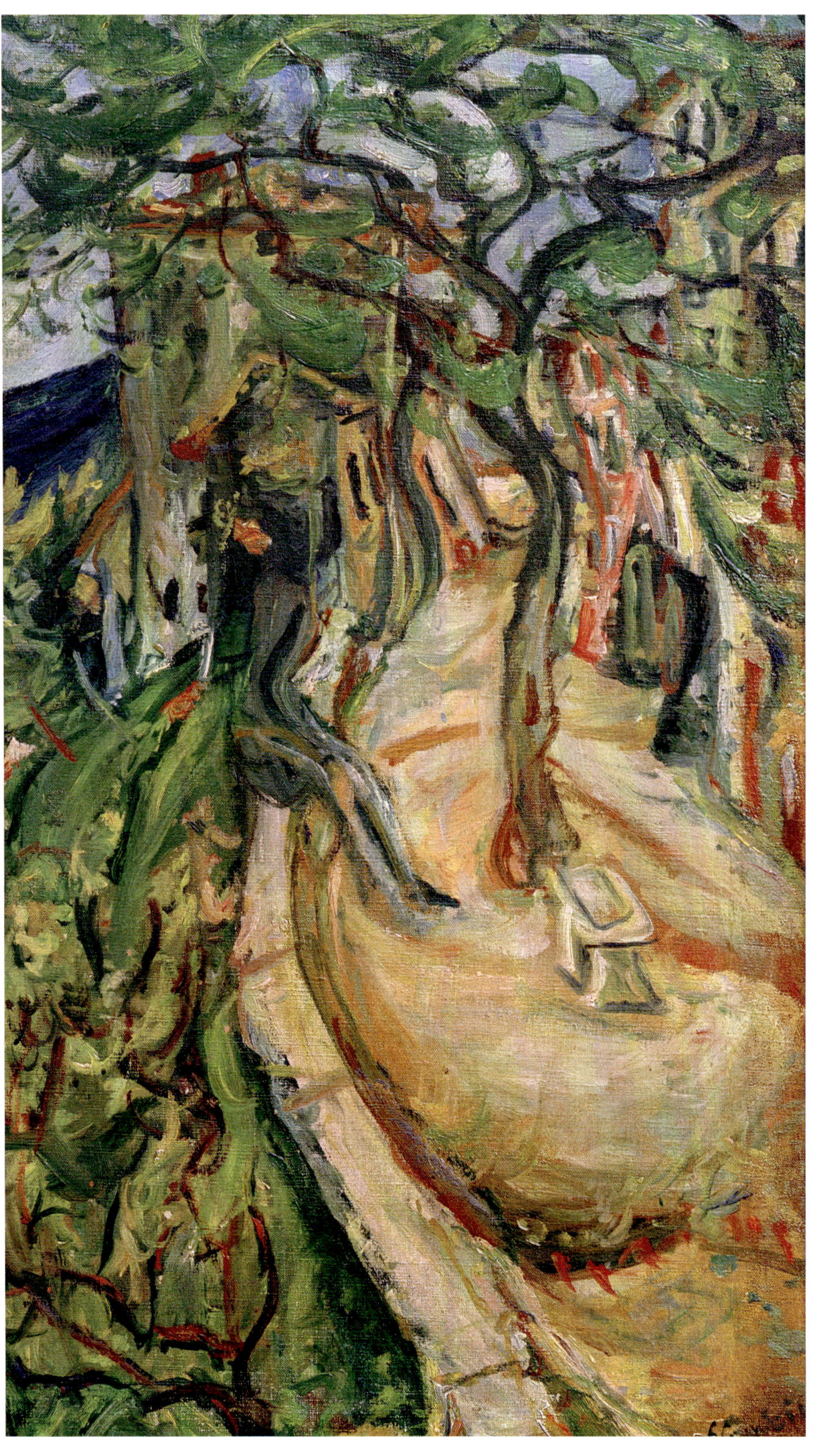

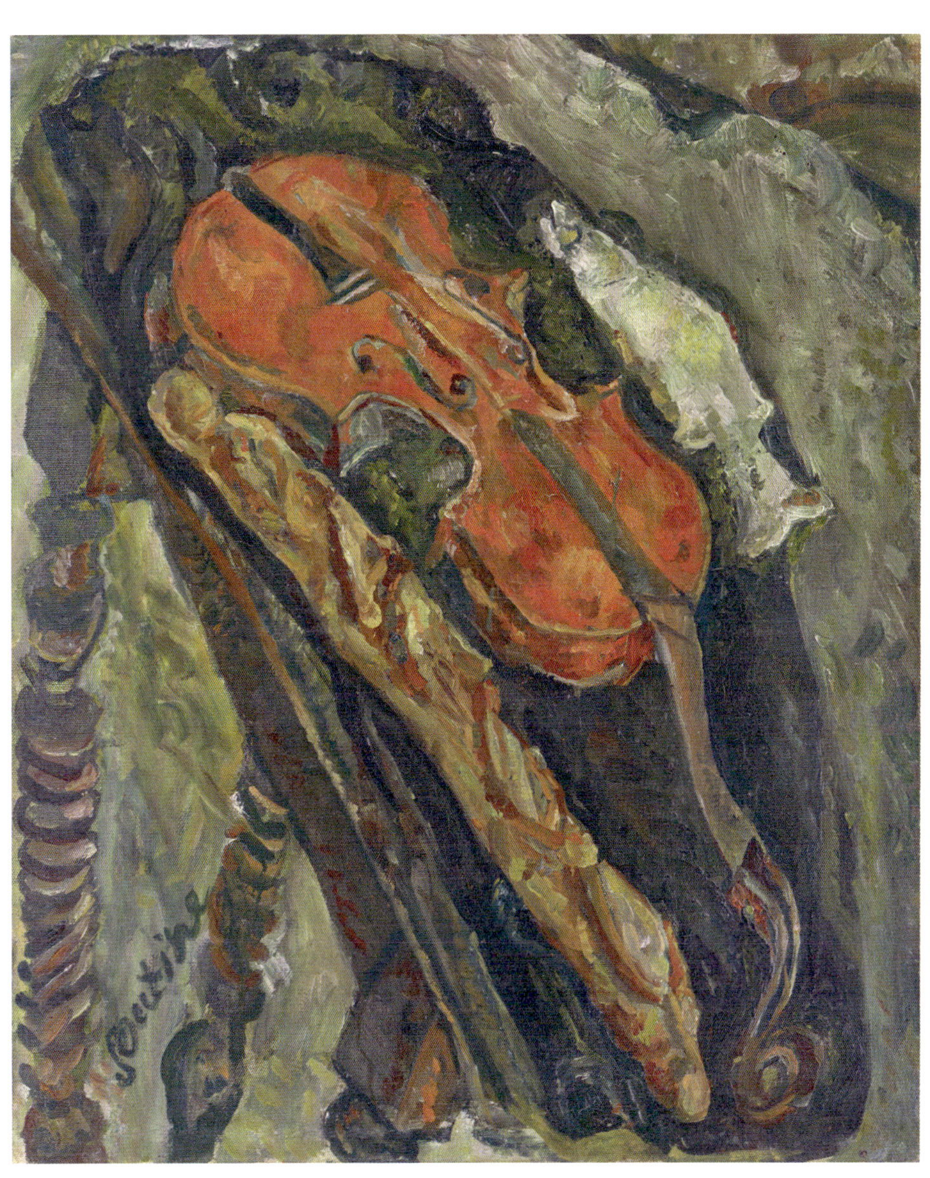

[21]
Landscape with Figures, ca. 1922
Oil on canvas
64.1 × 38.1 cm
Private Collection

[22]
Still Life with Violin, Bread, and Fish, ca. 1922
Oil on canvas
65 × 54 cm
Stiftung Im Obersteg
Depositum im Kunstmuseum Basel 2004

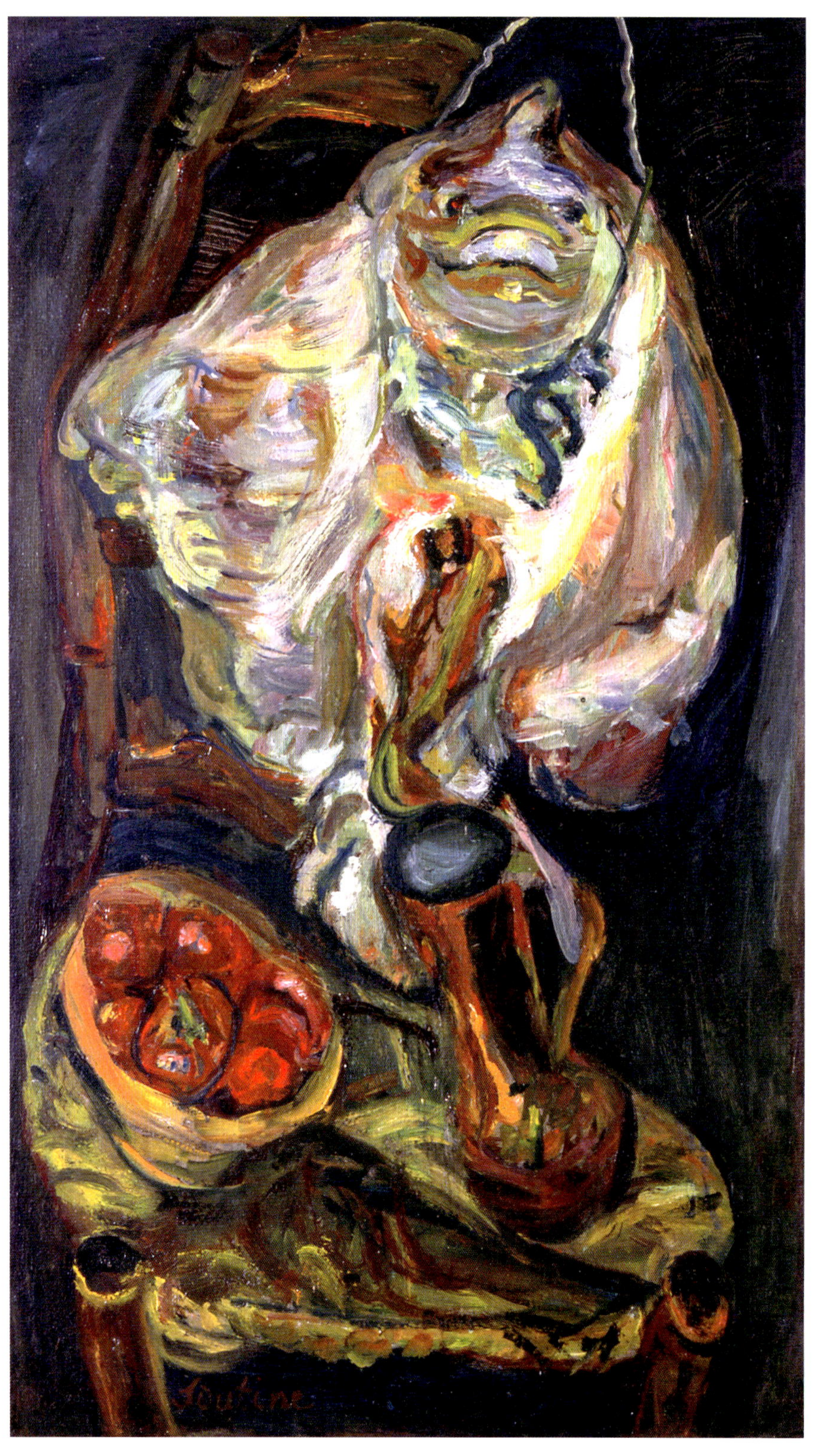

[23]
The Rayfish, 1922
Oil on canvas
81 × 47.5 cm
Musée Calvet, Avignon

[24]
Still Life with Rayfish, 1923
Oil on canvas
80.5 × 64.5 cm
The Cleveland Museum of Art

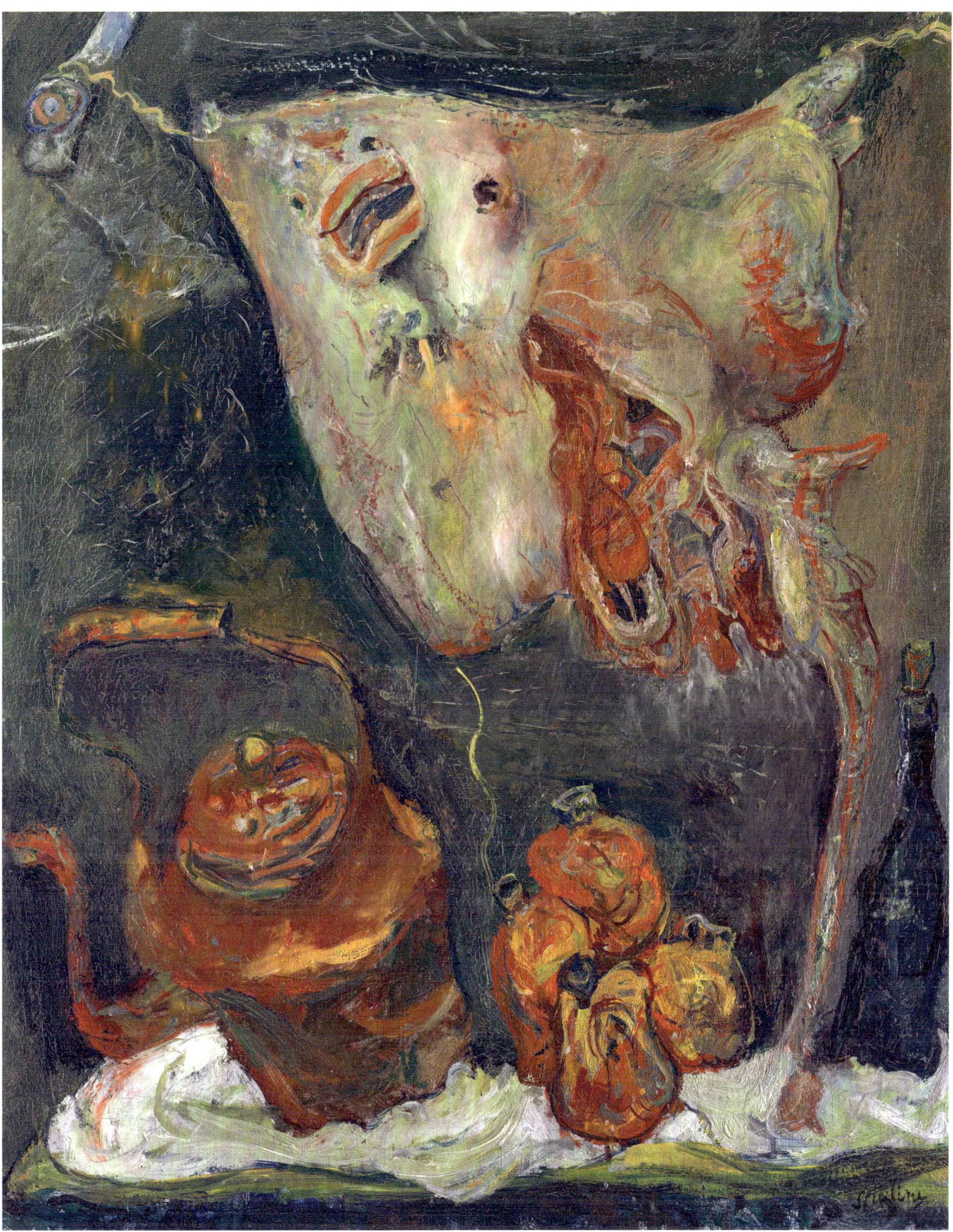

[25]
The Village, ca. 1923
Oil on canvas
73.5 × 92 cm
Musée de l'Orangerie, Paris

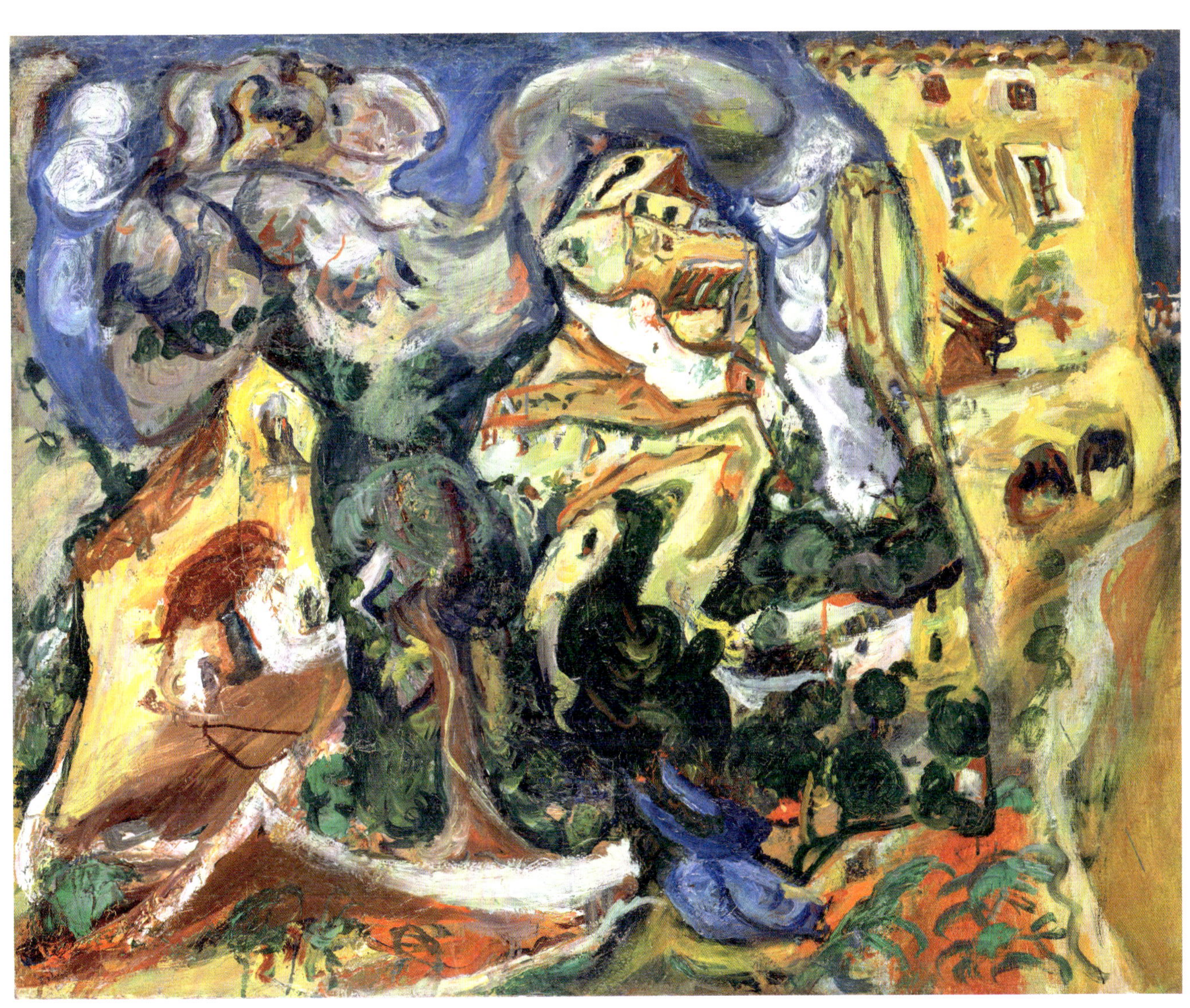

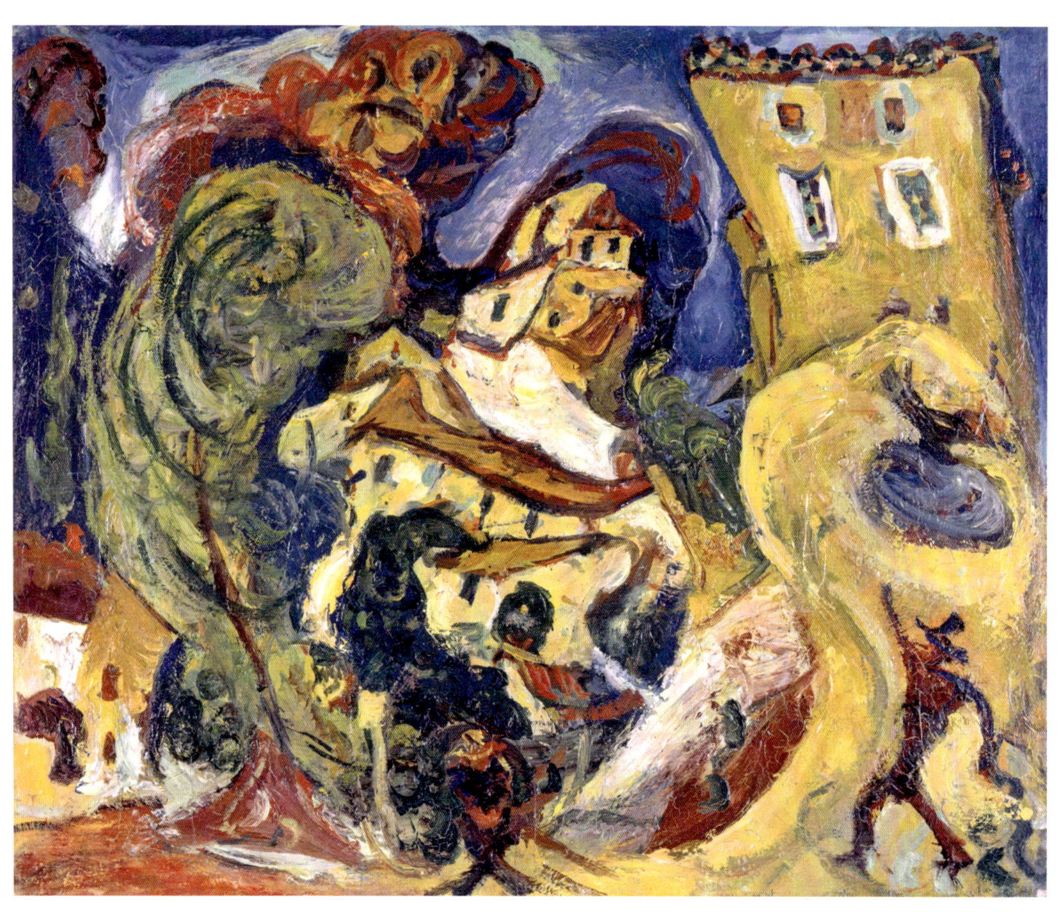

[26]
Landscape at Cagnes, ca. 1923
Oil on canvas
60 × 73 cm
Kunstmuseum Bern

[27]
Landscape at Cagnes (La Gaude), 1923
Oil on canvas
81 × 100 cm
Centre Pompidou, Paris

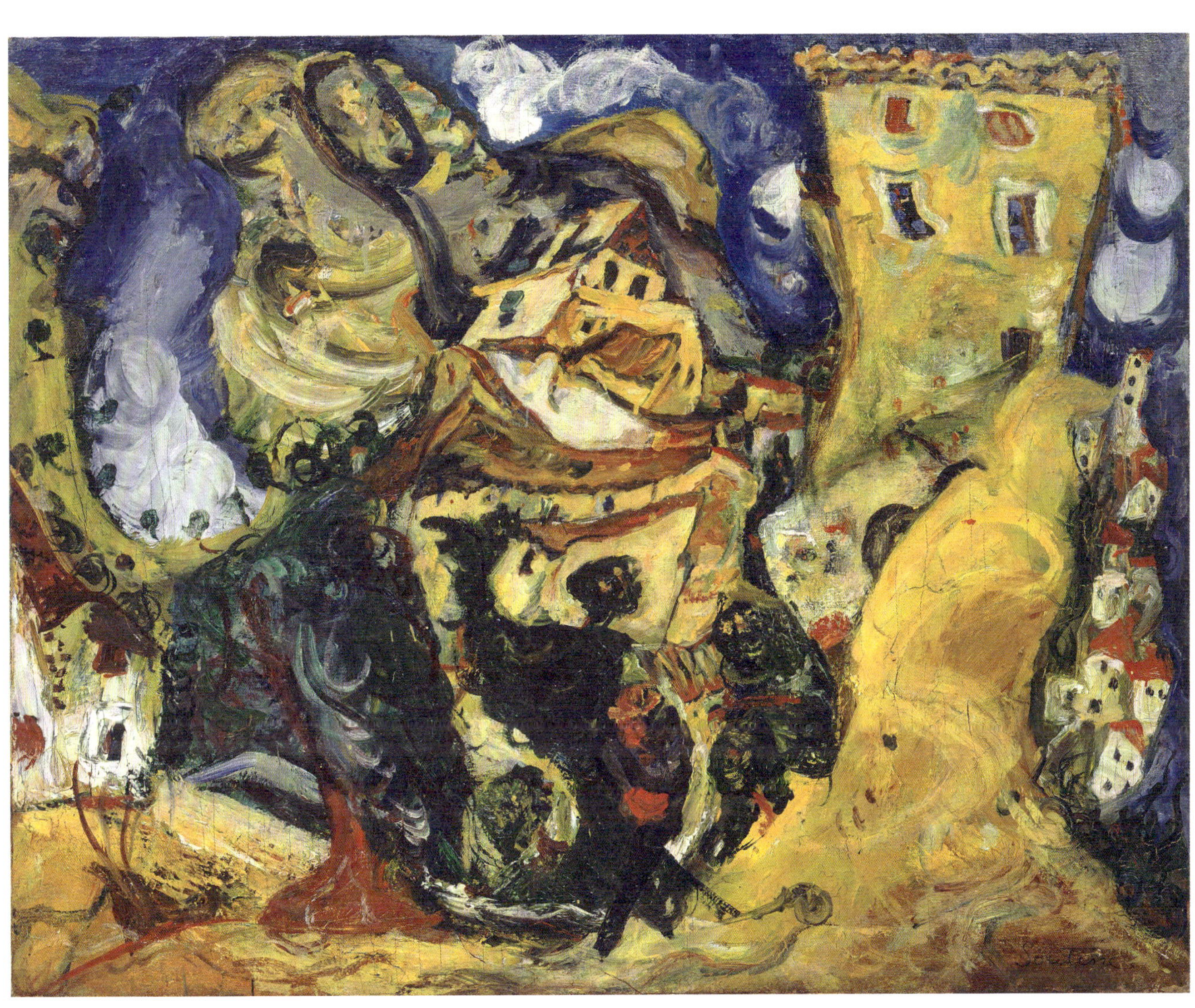

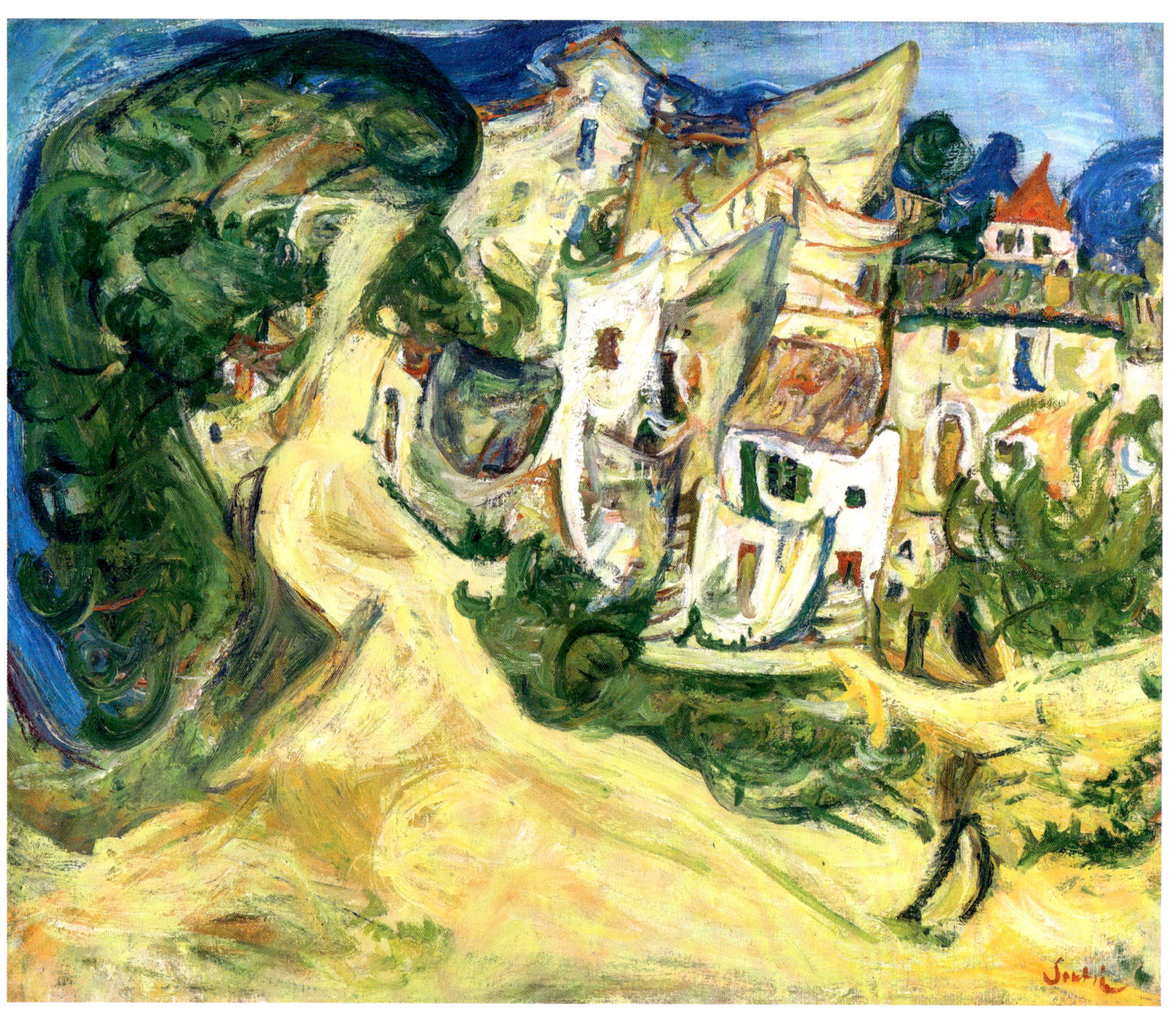

[28]
Landscape at Cagnes, 1923/24
Oil on canvas
60 × 73 cm
Courtesy Galerie Thomas, Munich

[29]
View of Cagnes (La Gaude and the Baous), 1922/23
Oil on canvas
60.5 × 72.5 cm
Musée des Beaux-Arts, La Chaux-de-Fonds

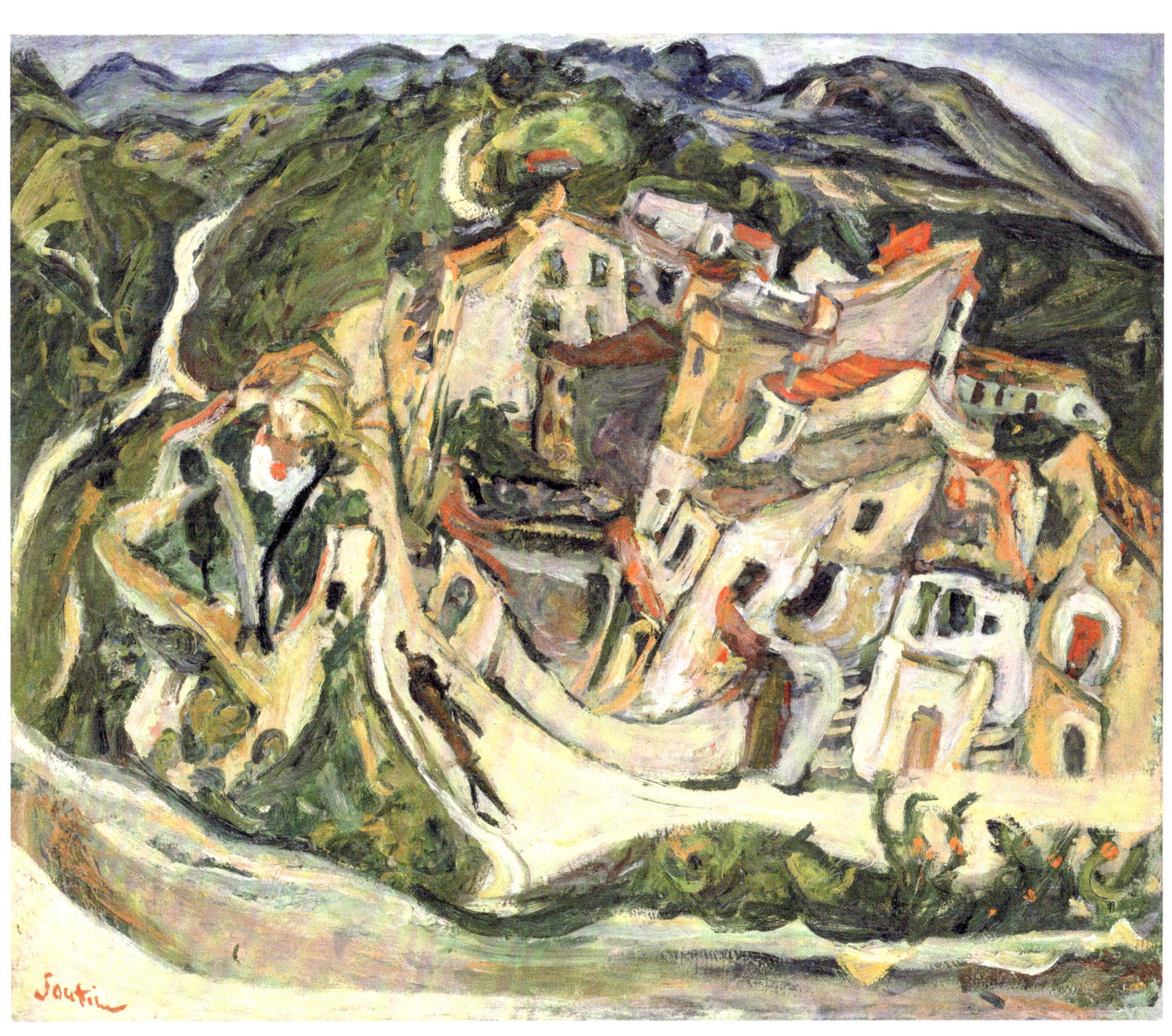

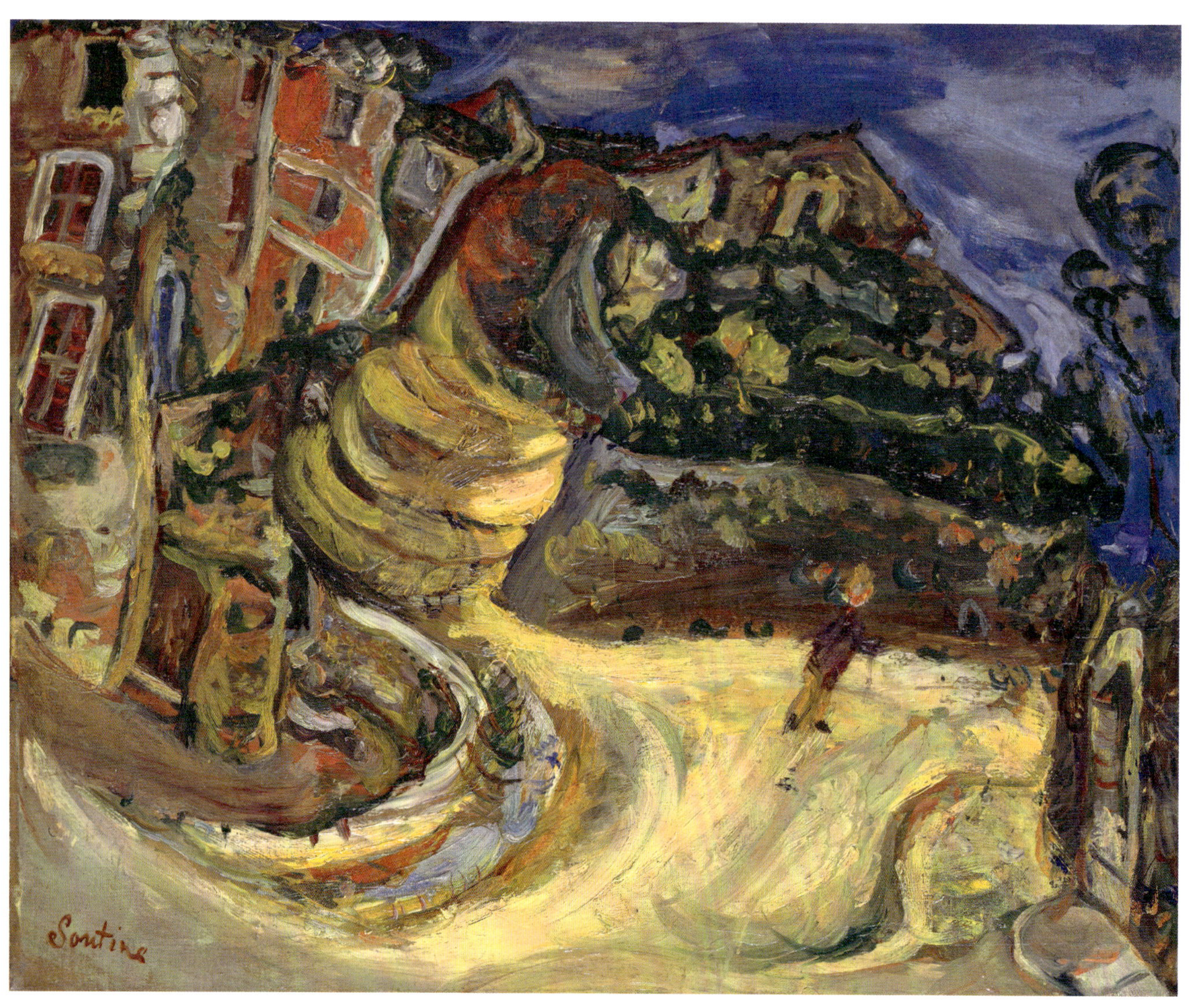

[30]
The Road, ca. 1923/24
Oil on canvas
65.1 × 81 cm
SMB Staatliche Museen zu Berlin,
Nationalgalerie

[31]
The Road up the Hill, ca. 1924
Oil on canvas
72.4 × 60 cm
Tate

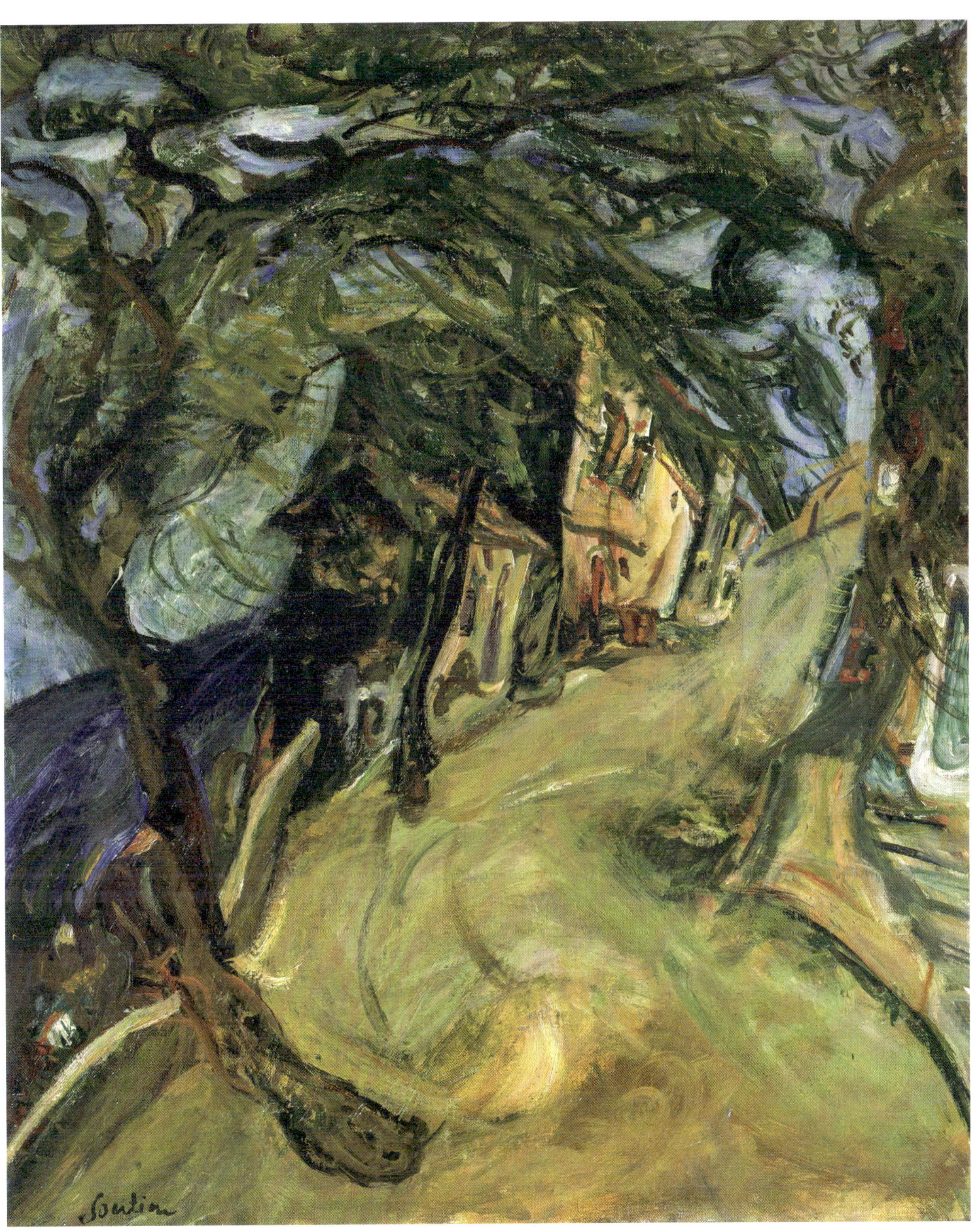

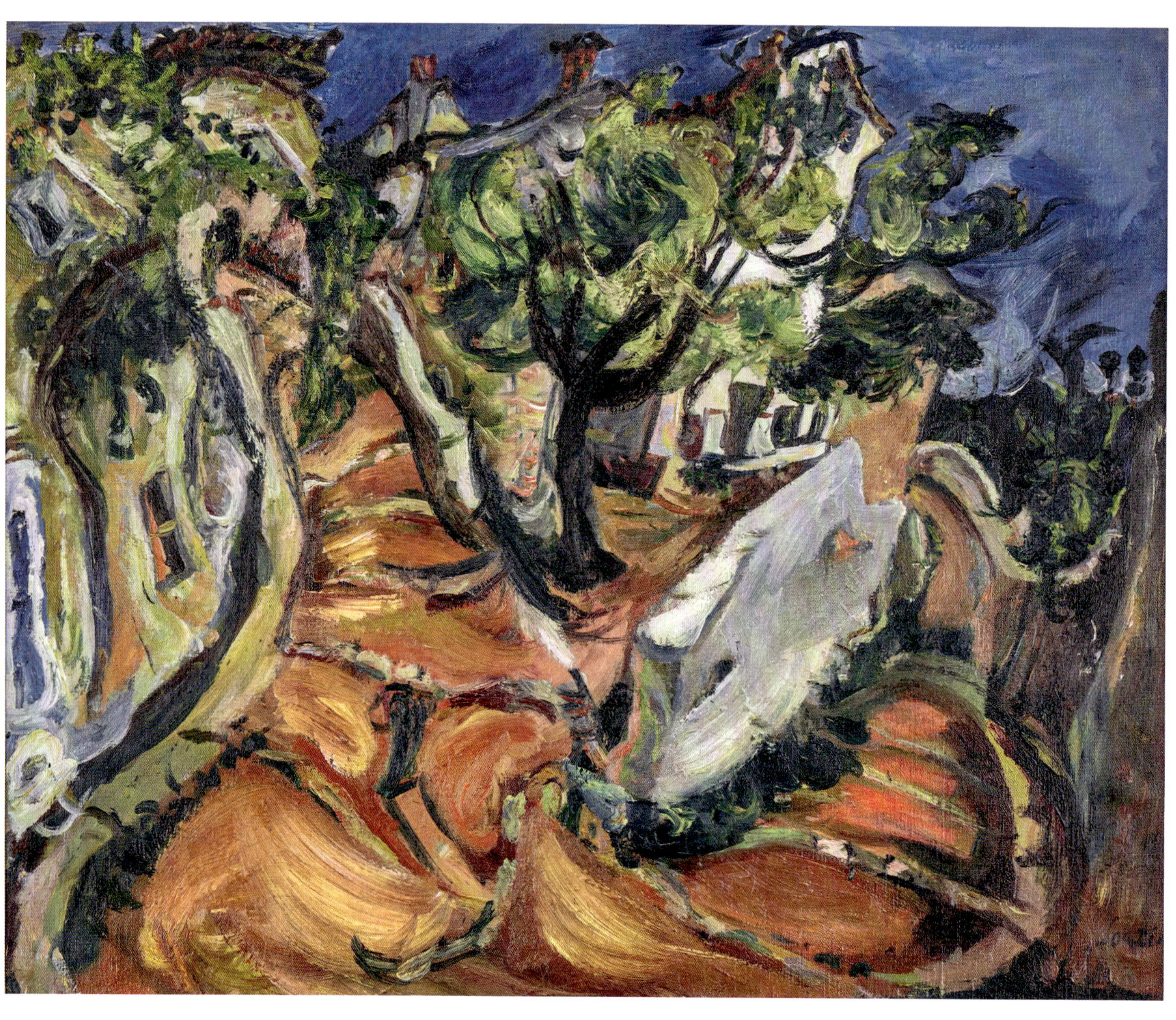

[32]
Stairway at Cagnes, ca. 1923/24
Oil on canvas
60 × 73 cm
Courtesy David Lévy et associés, Brussels

[33]
The Uphill Road in Cagnes
(Landscape at Cagnes), ca. 1923/24
Oil on canvas
55.2 × 38.1 cm
Courtesy David Lévy et associés, Brussels

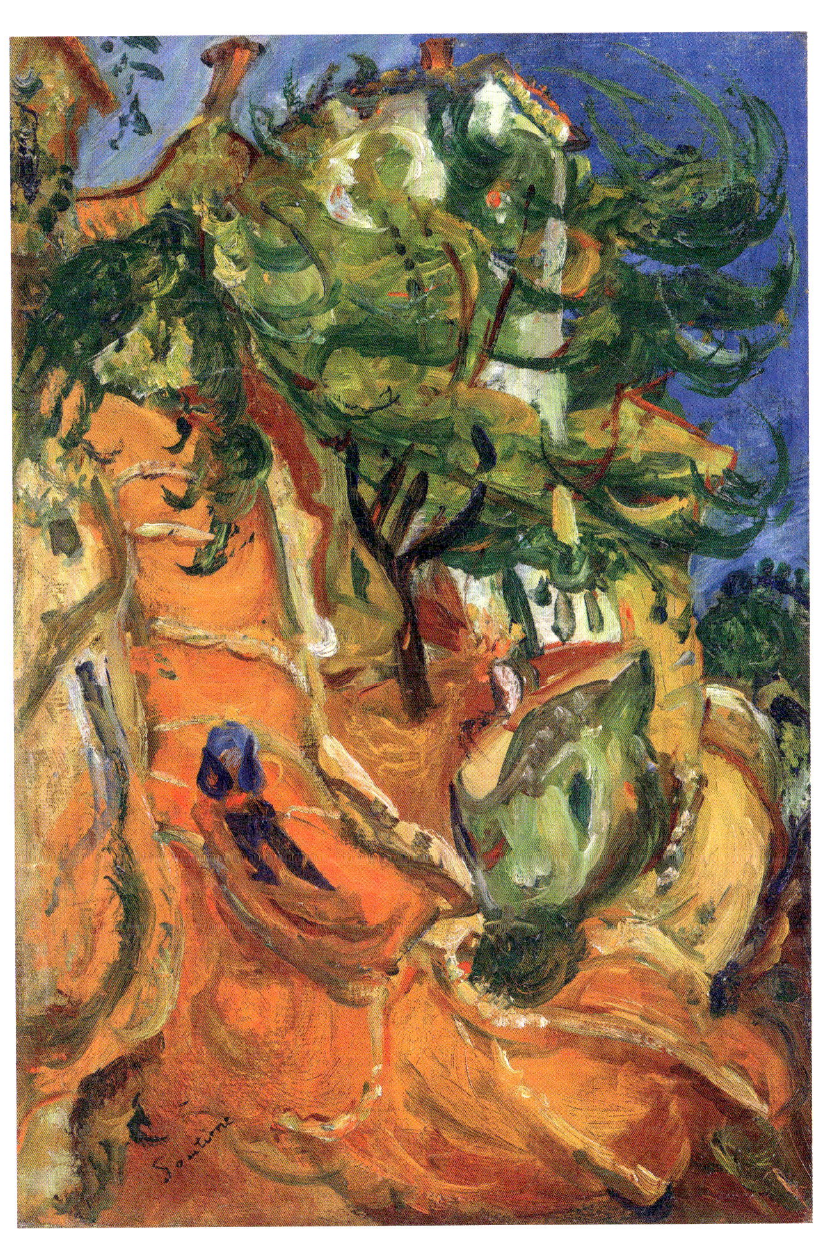

[34]
The Old Actress, 1922
Oil on canvas
92.1 × 65.1 cm
Private Collection
Courtesy McClain Gallery, Houston

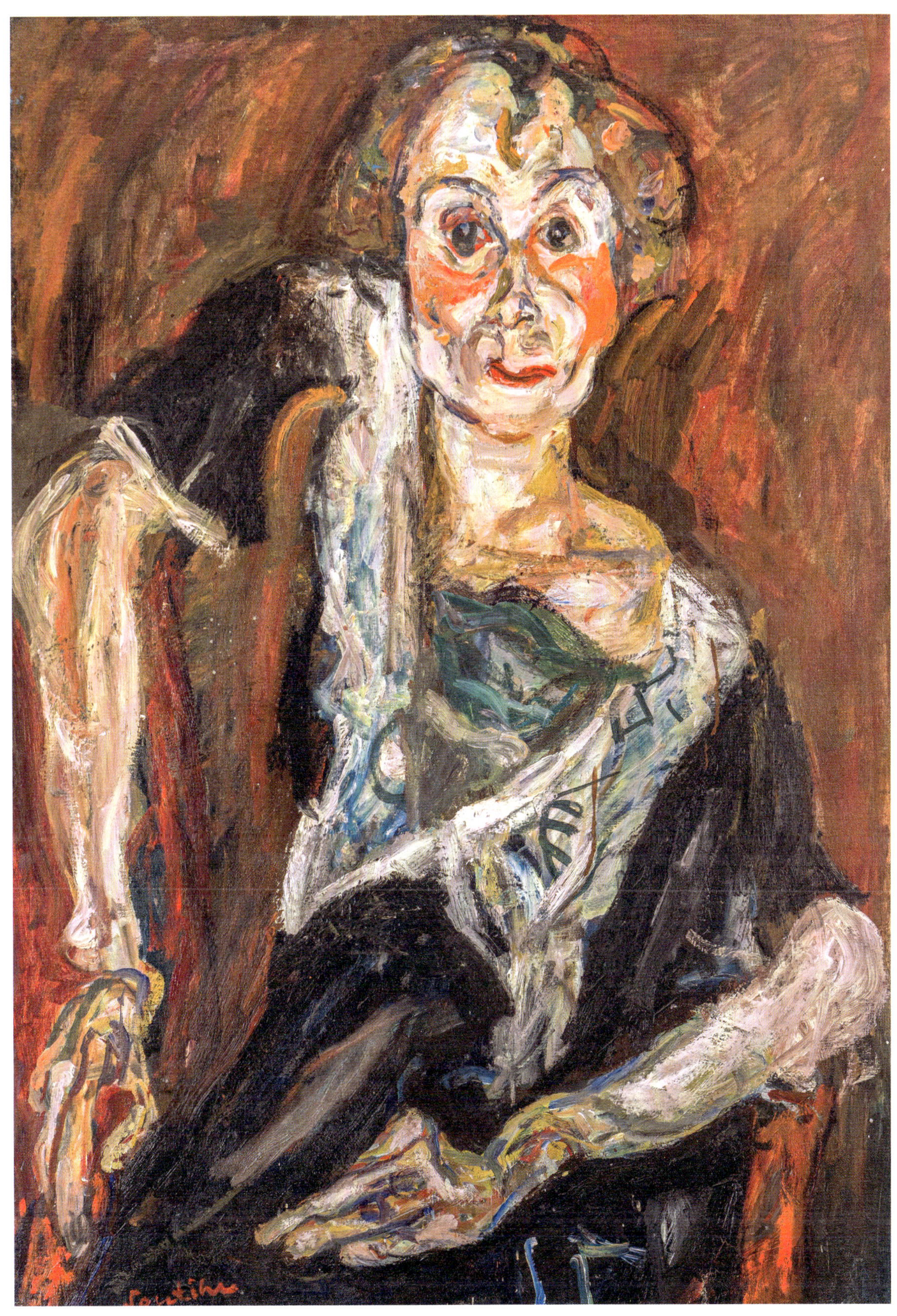

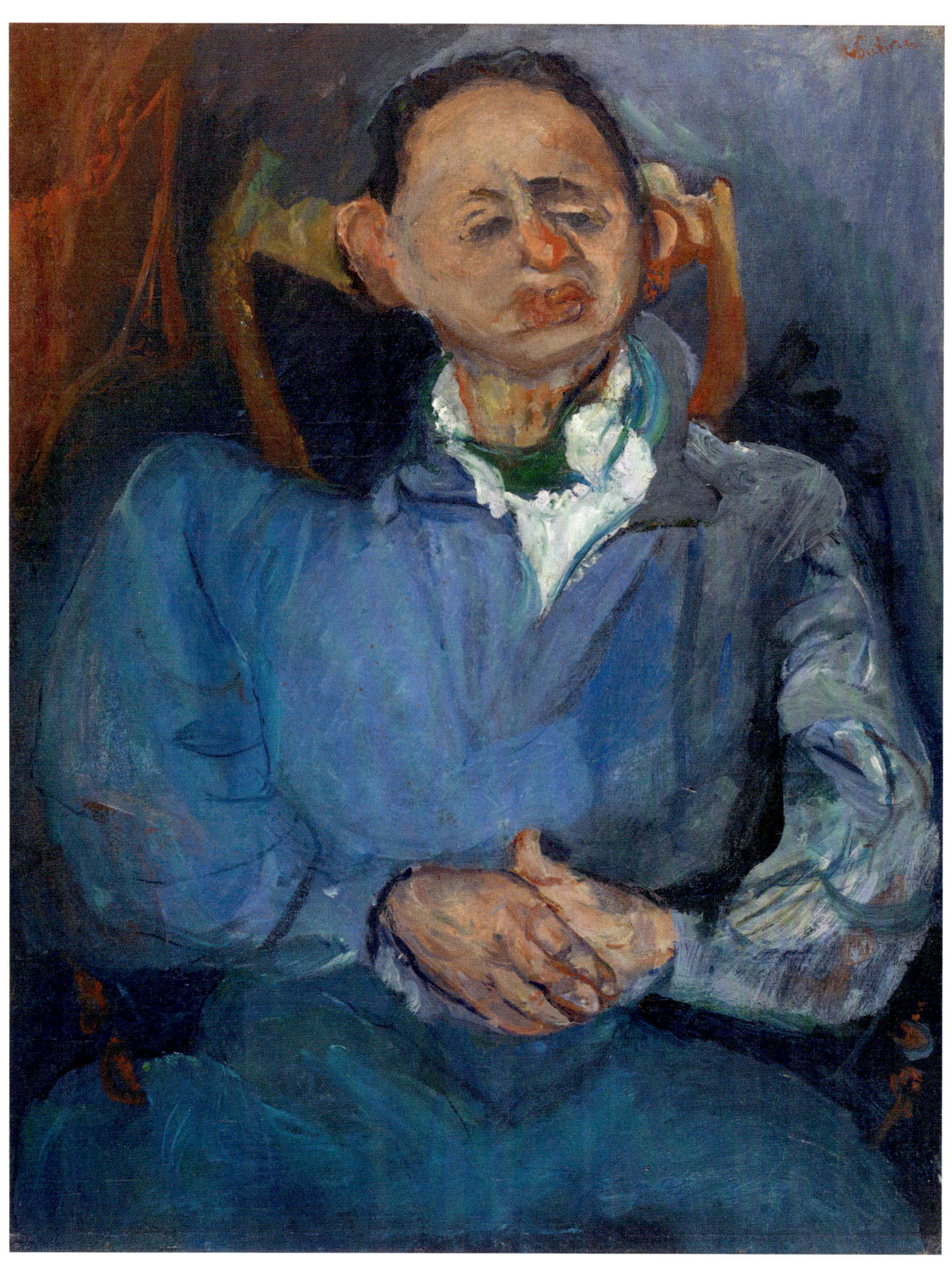

[35]
Portrait of the Sculptor Oscar Miestchaninoff, 1923/24
Oil on canvas
83 × 65 cm
Centre Pompidou, Paris

[36]
Woman in Red, 1923/24
Oil on canvas
92 × 65 cm
Musée d'Art moderne de Paris

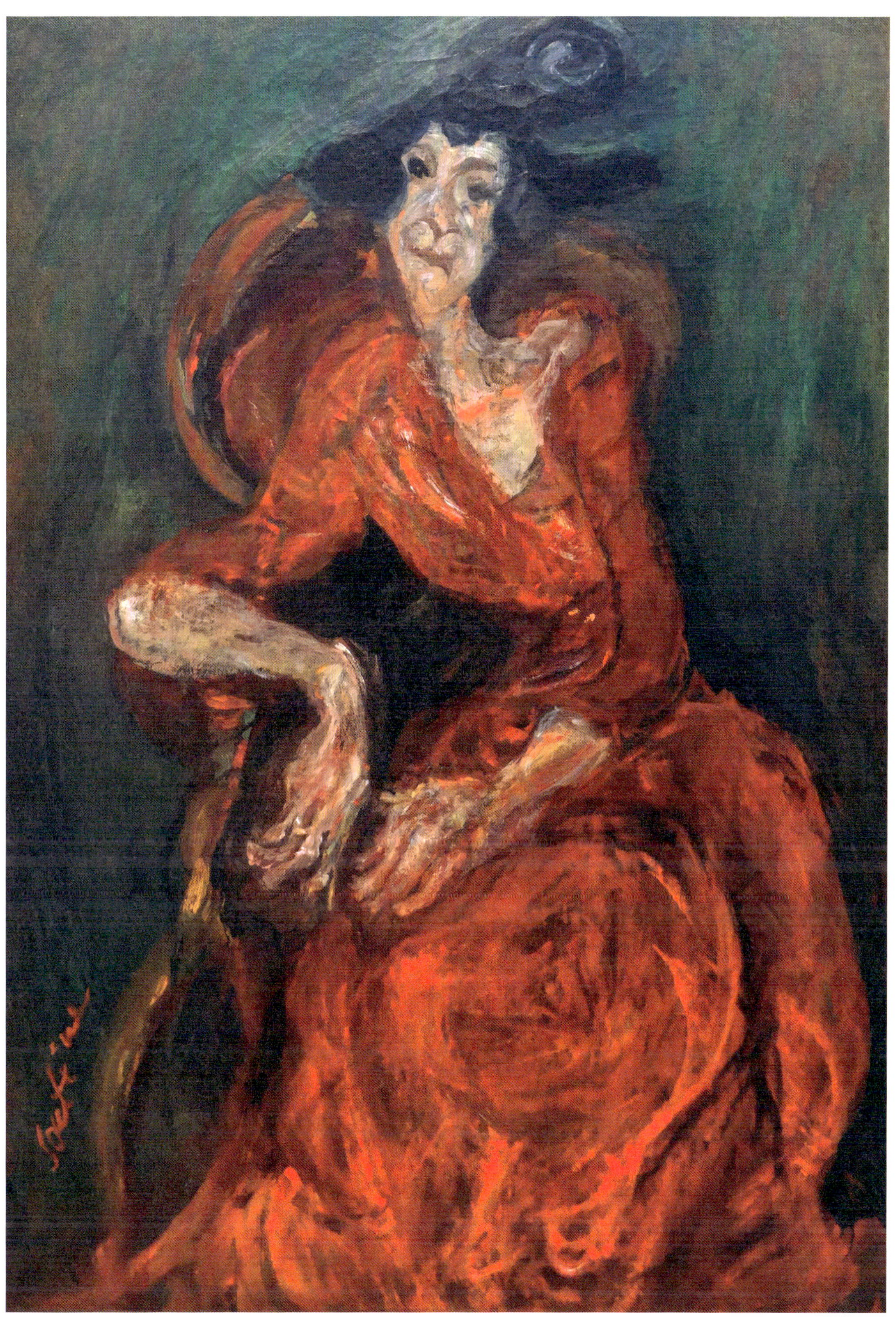

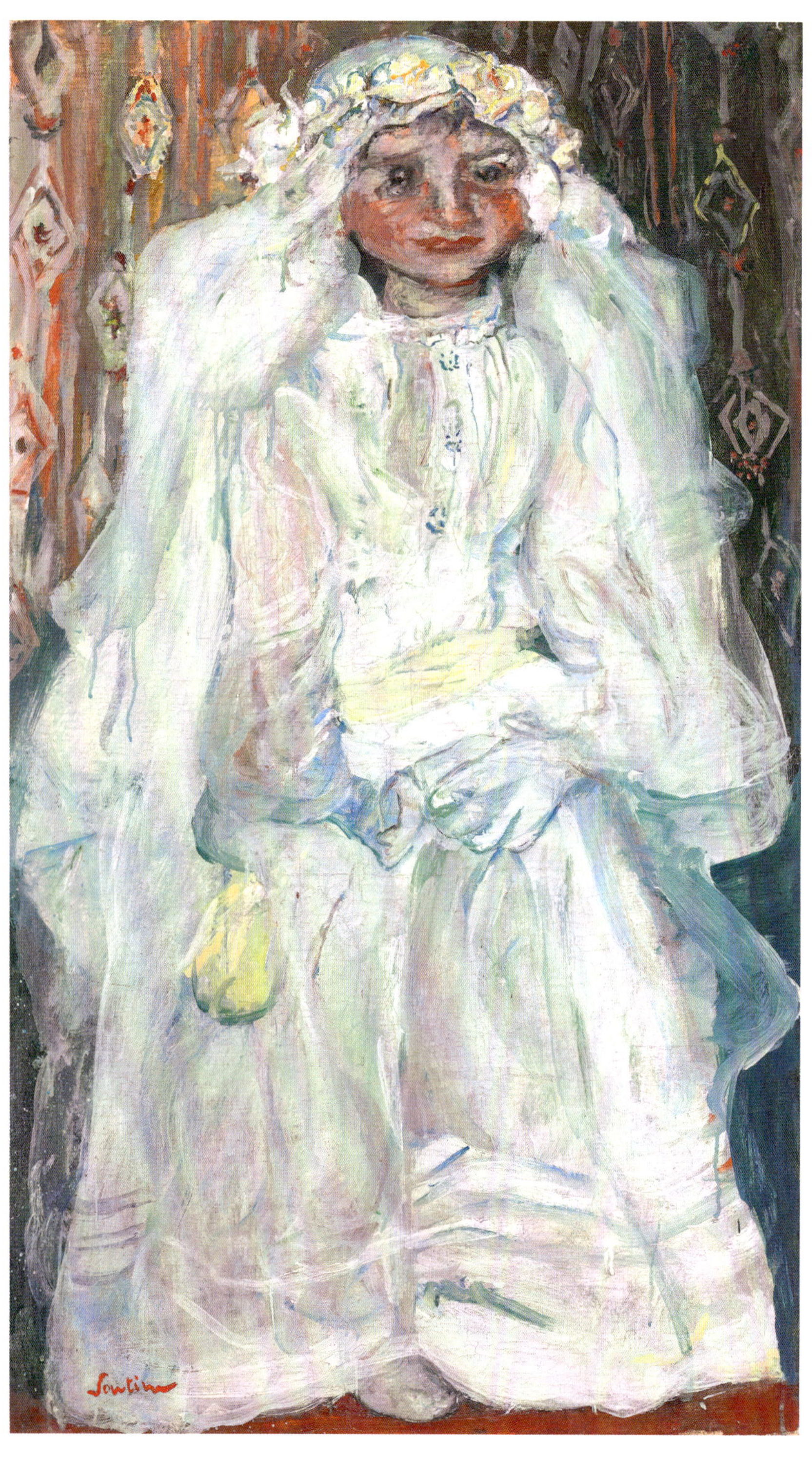

[37]
The Communicant (The Bride), ca. 1924
Oil on canvas
81.6 × 47.5 cm
The Lewis Collection, London

[38]
Woman in a Blue Dress, ca. 1924
Oil on canvas
81 × 60 cm
Musée d'Art moderne de Paris

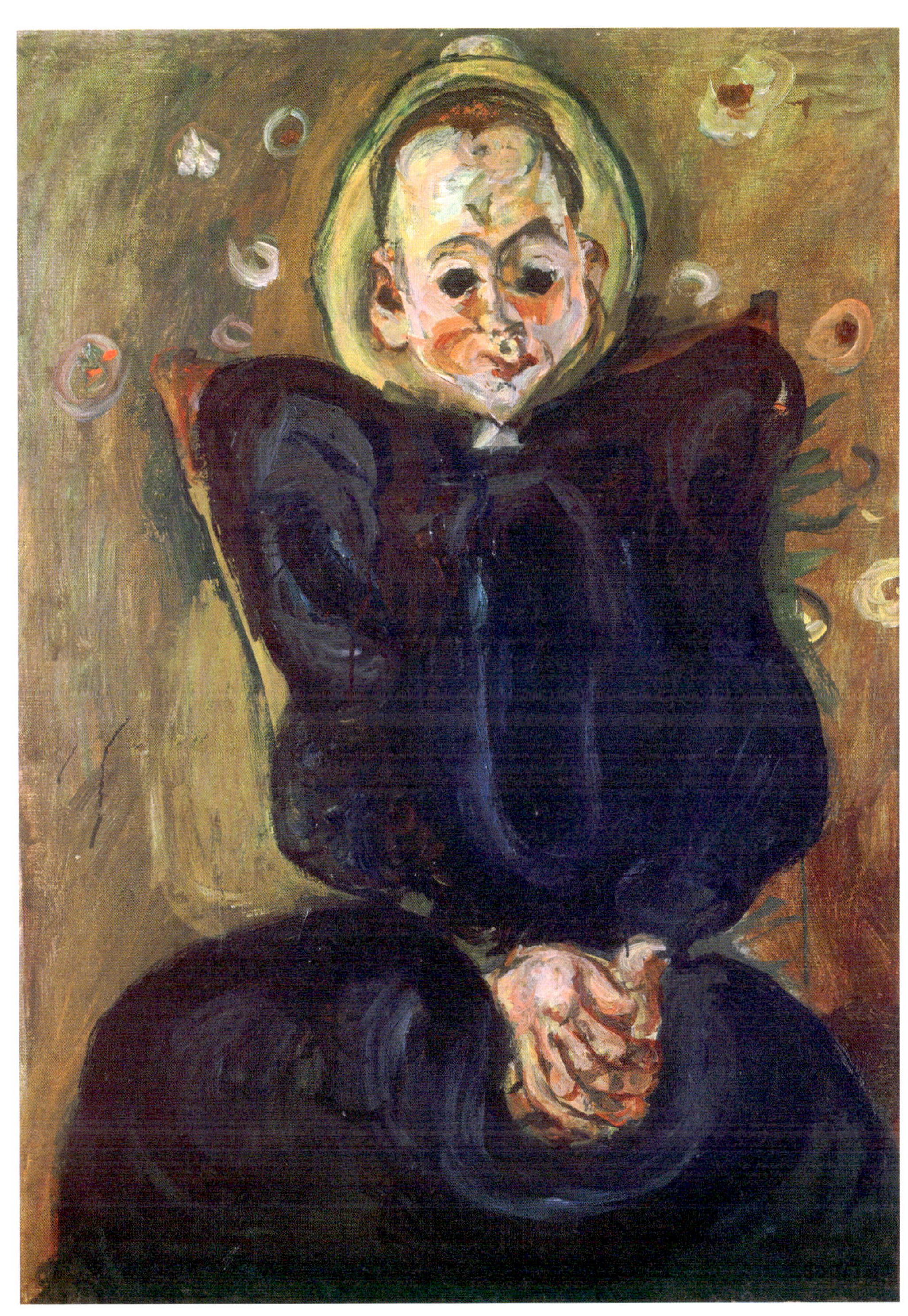

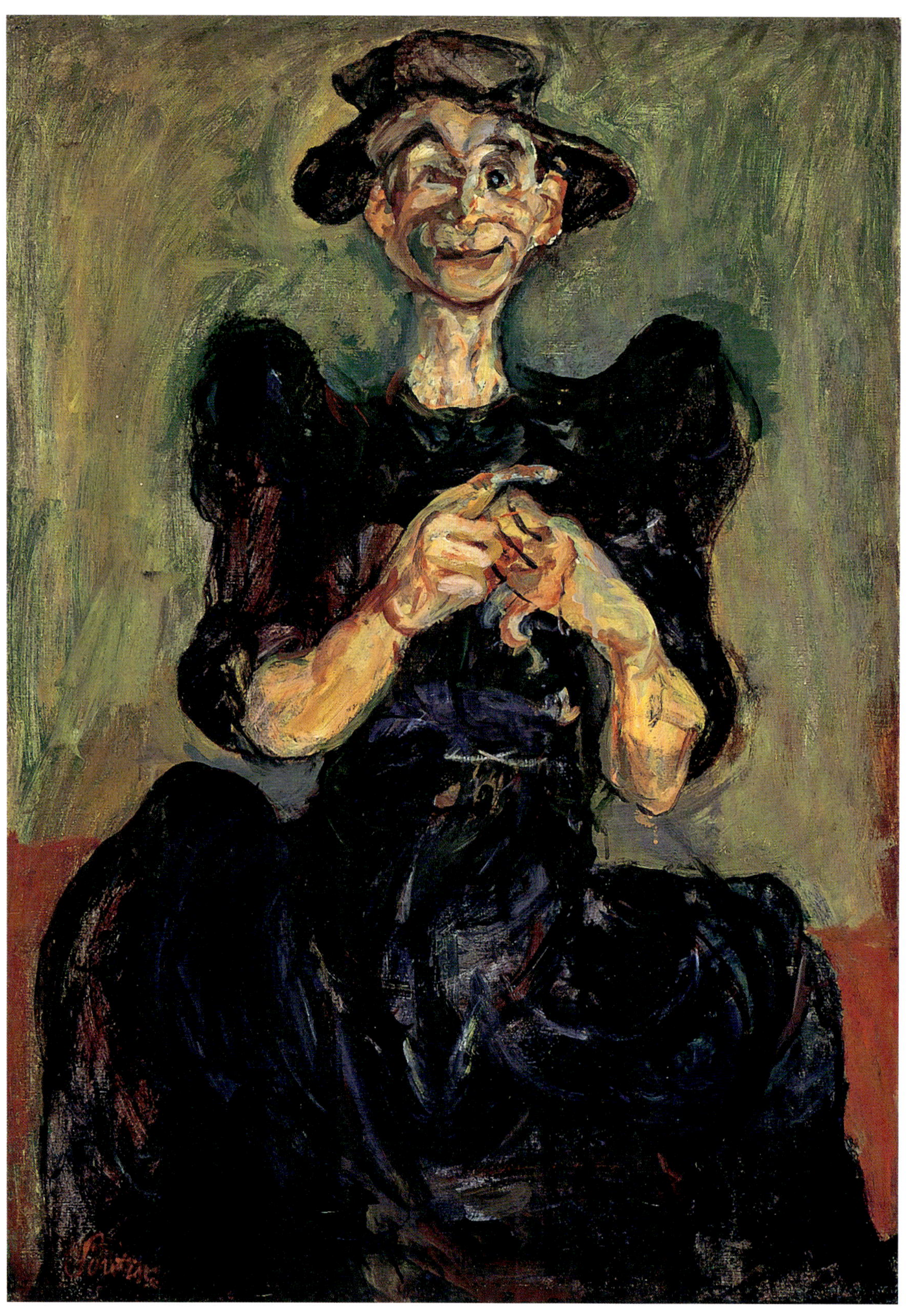

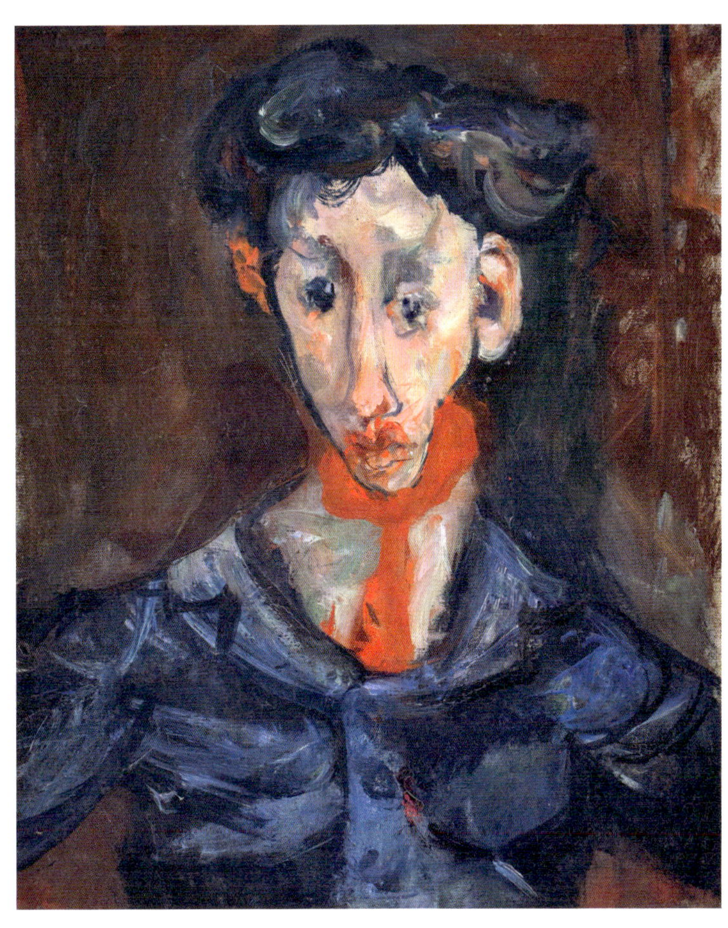

[39]
Woman Knitting, ca. 1924/25
Oil on canvas
82.55 × 59.69 cm
The Norton Simon Foundation, Pasadena

[40]
The Gypsy, 1926
Oil on canvas
46 × 38 cm
SMK Statens Museum for Kunst, Copenhagen

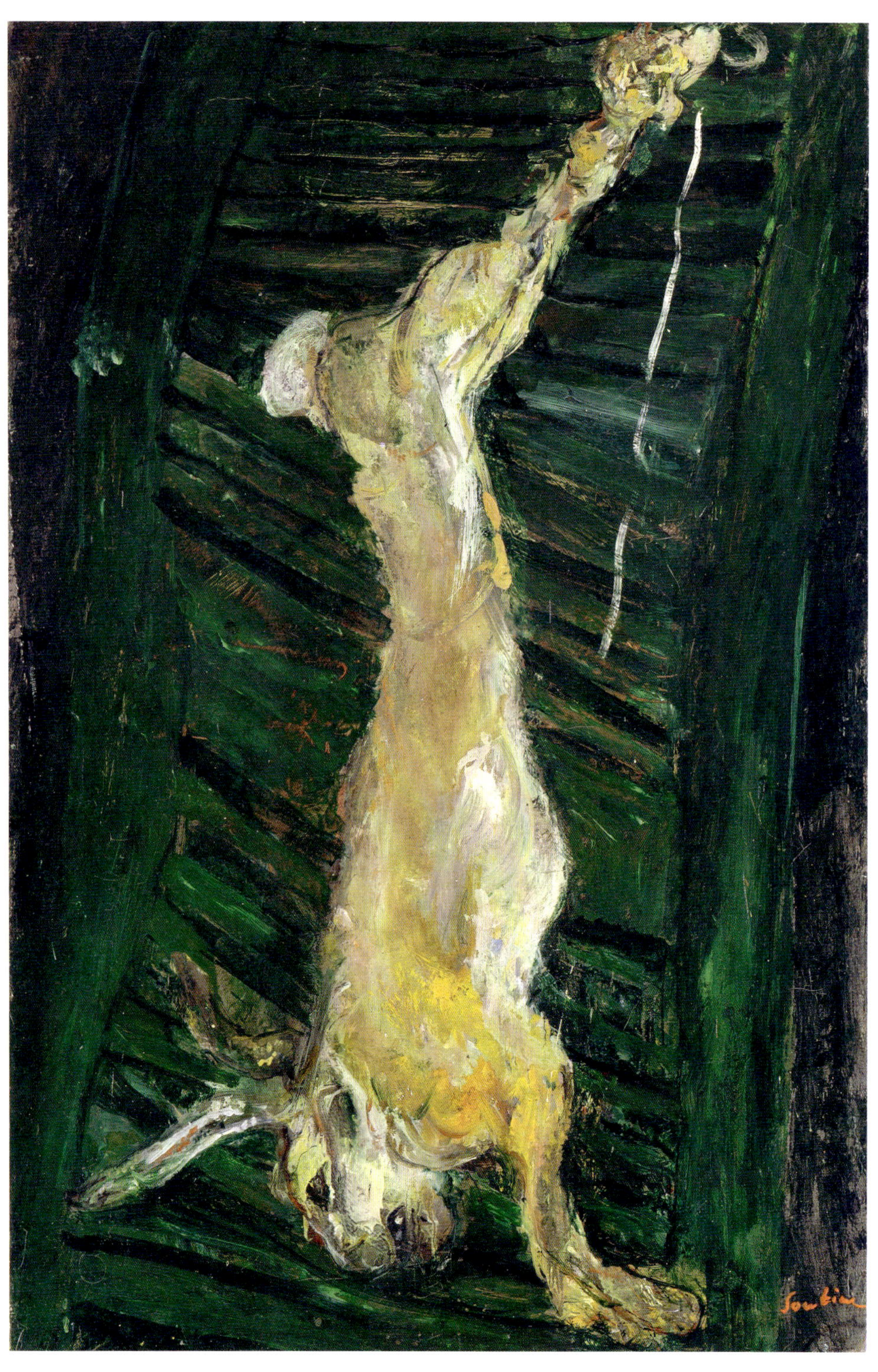

[41]
Hare against Green Shutter, ca. 1924/25
Oil on canvas
81.5 × 54.5 cm
Centre Pompidou, Paris /
Musée d'Art moderne de Troyes

[42]
Chicken Hanging against Brick Wall, 1925
Oil on canvas
65 × 46.5 cm
Kunstmuseum Bern

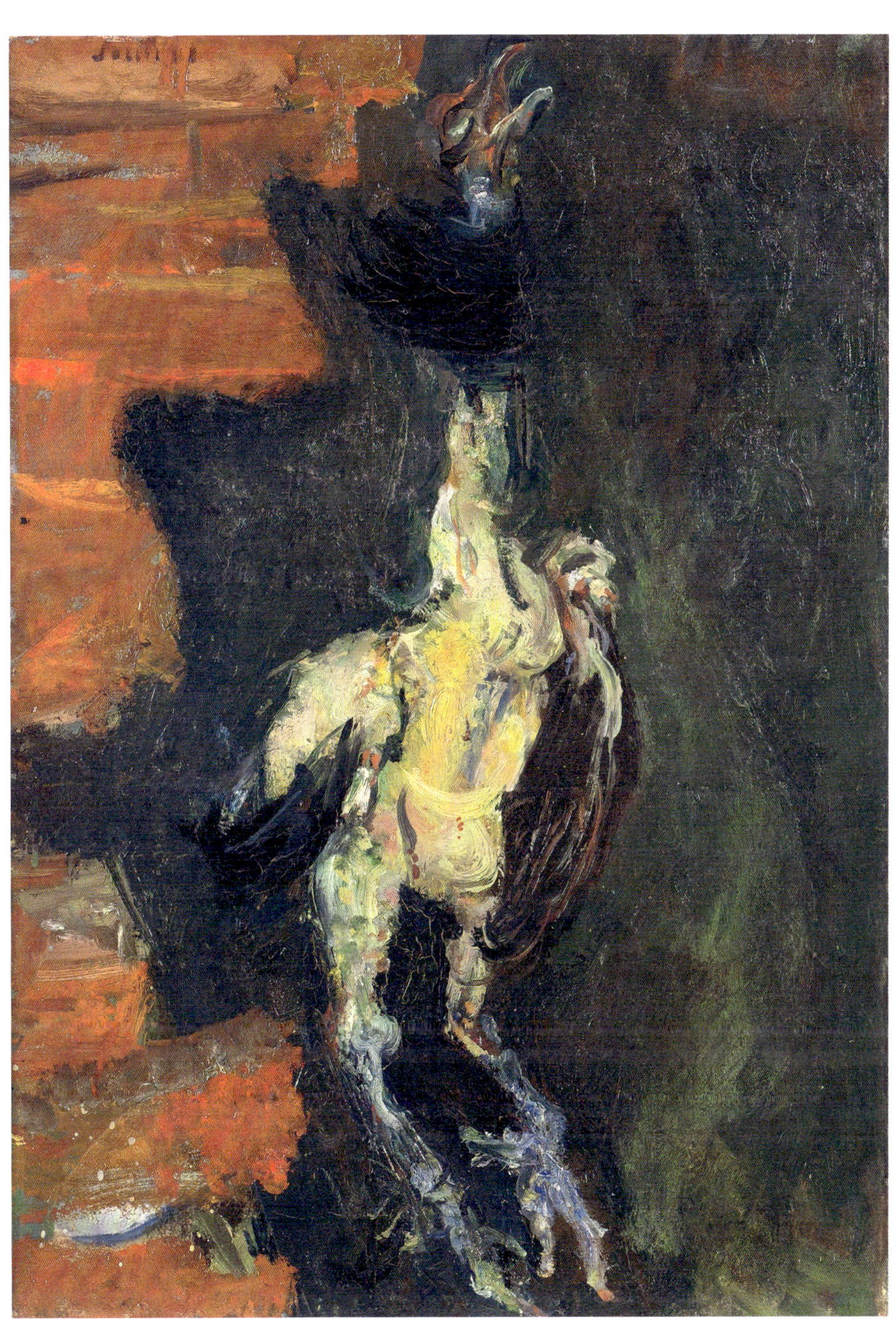

[43]
Chicken and Tomatoes, ca. 1924
Oil on canvas
92.5 x 45 cm
Staatsgalerie Stuttgart

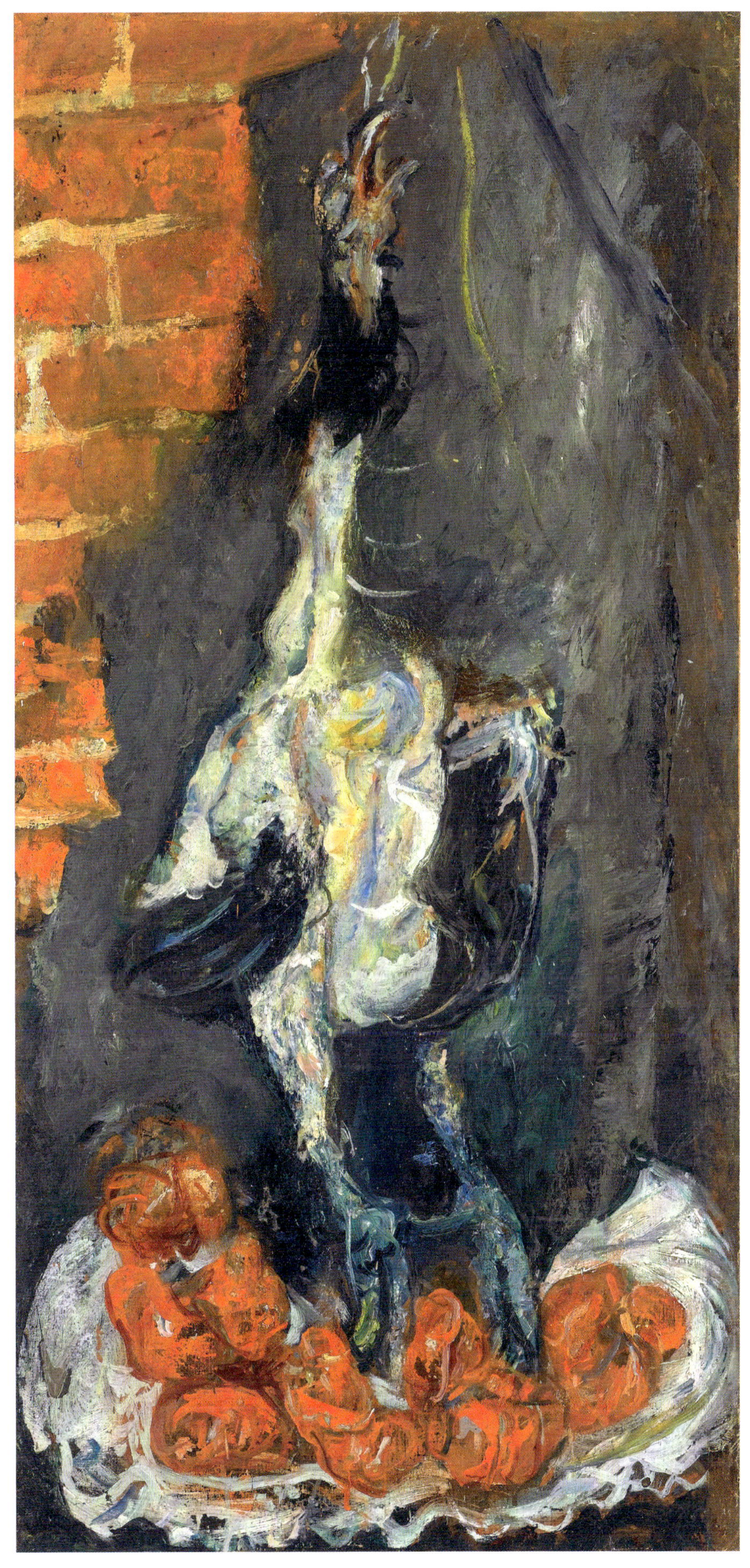

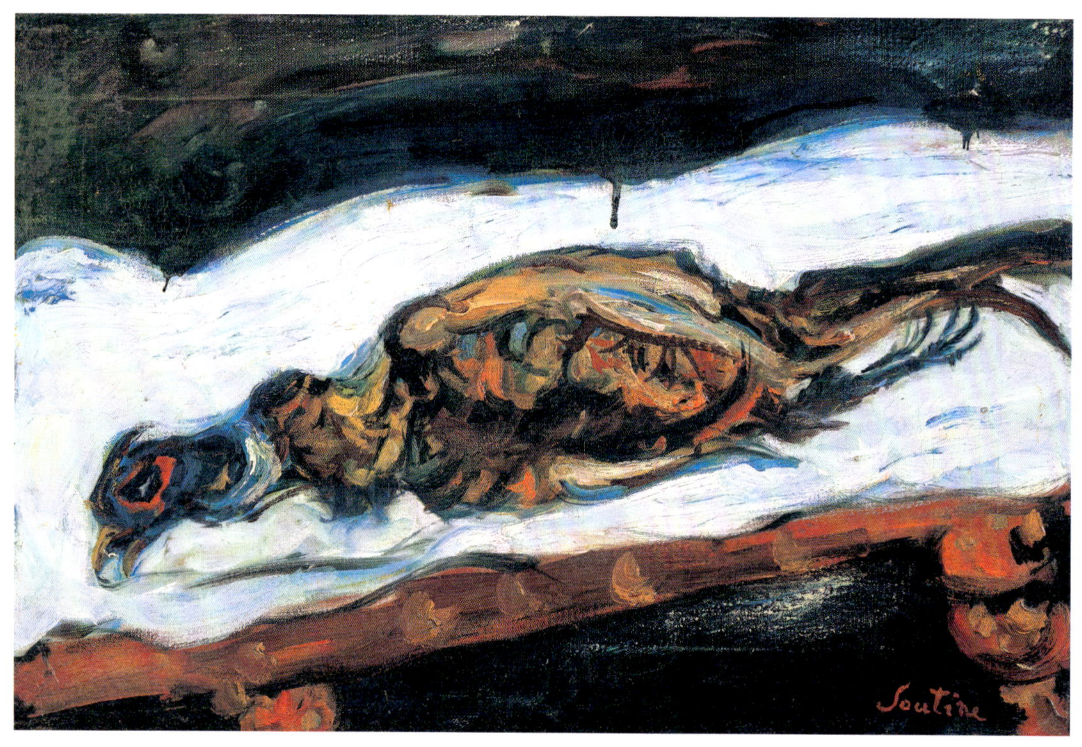

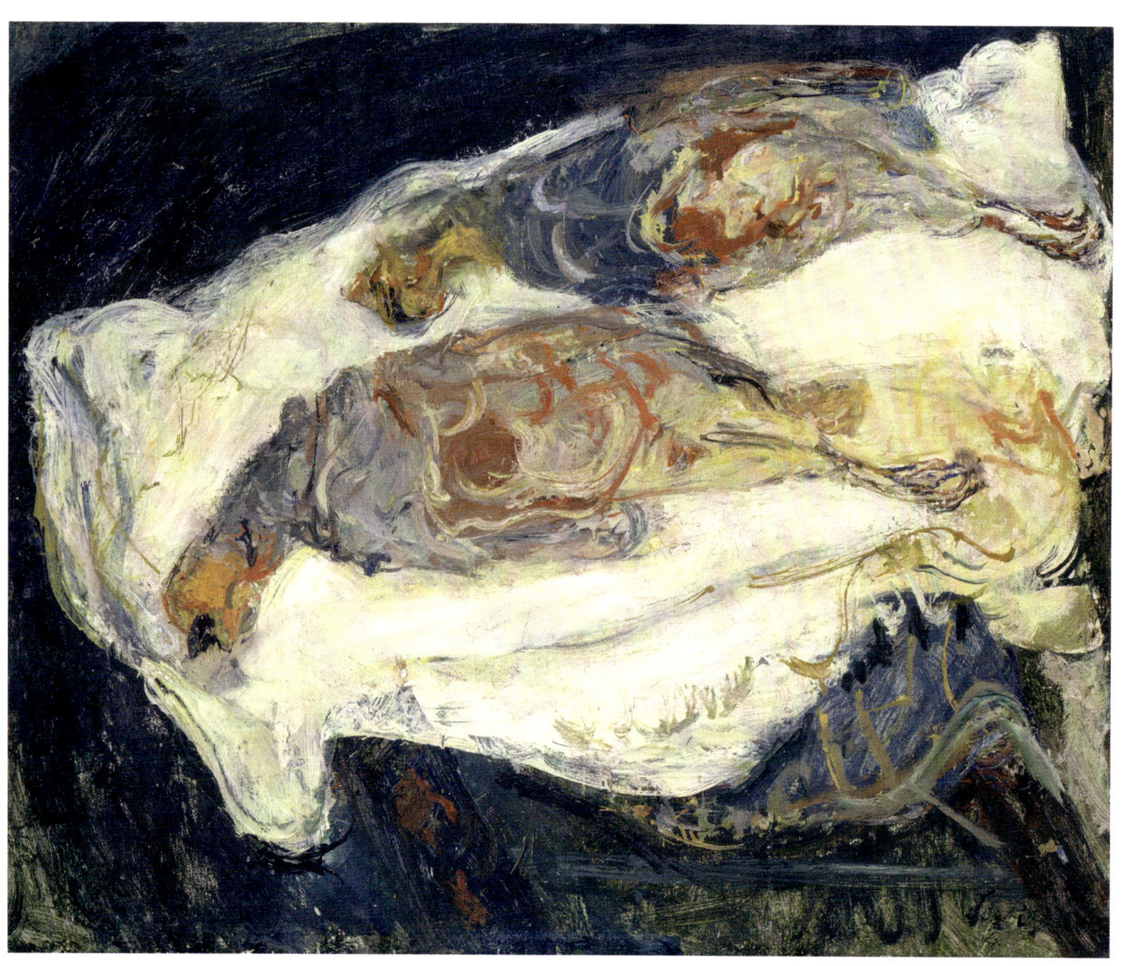

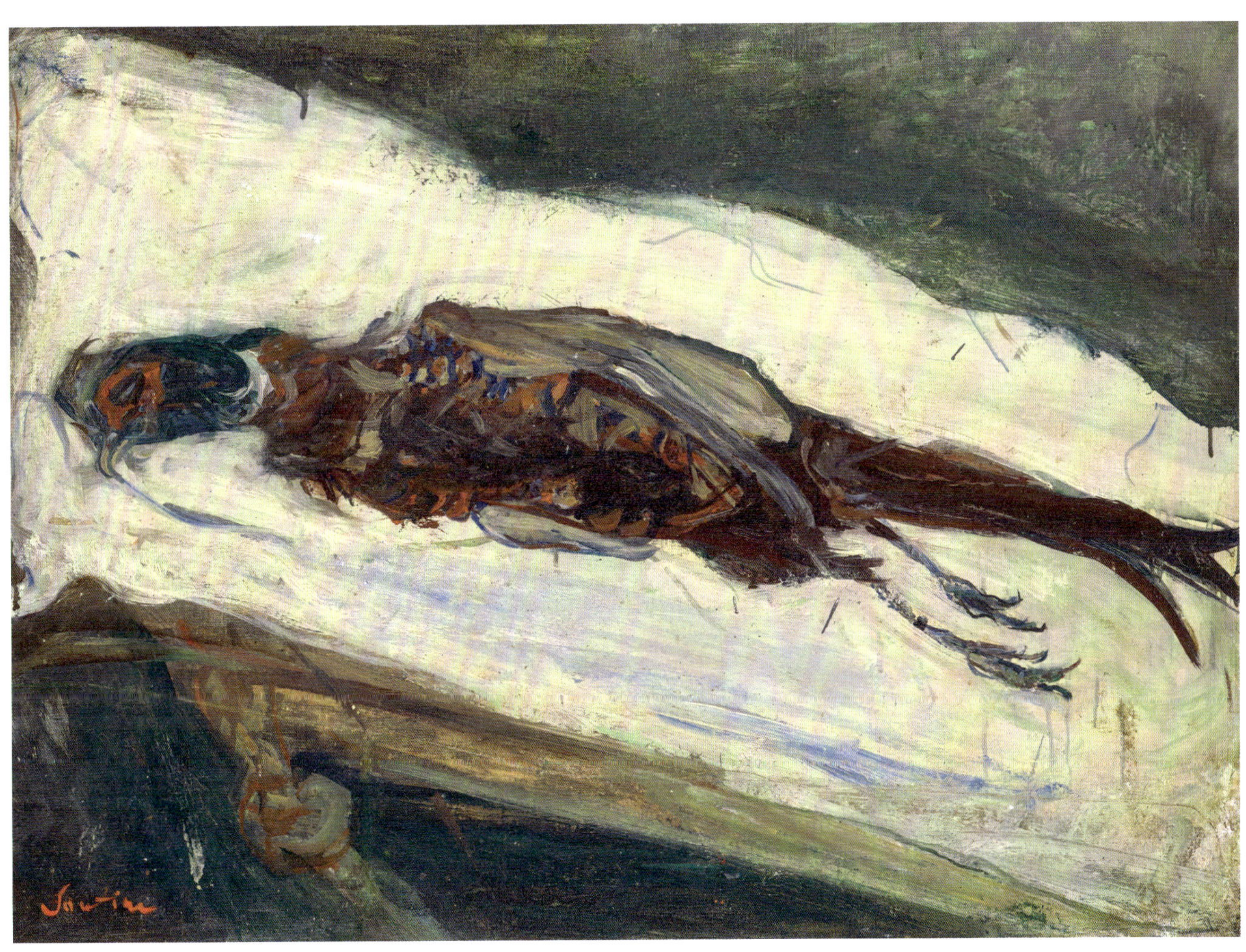

[44]
Two Pheasants, ca. 1924/25
Oil on canvas
50 × 61 cm
Collection Emil Bührle
On long-term loan to Kunsthaus Zürich

[45]
Pheasant, ca. 1924
Oil on canvas
38.5 × 58.5 cm
ALBERTINA, Vienna

[46]
Dead Pheasant, ca. 1926/27
Oil on canvas
52 × 72 cm
Stiftung Im Obersteg
Depositum im Kunstmuseum Basel 2004

[47]
Turkey and Tomatoes, 1923/24
Oil on canvas
81 × 49 cm
Musée de l'Orangerie, Paris

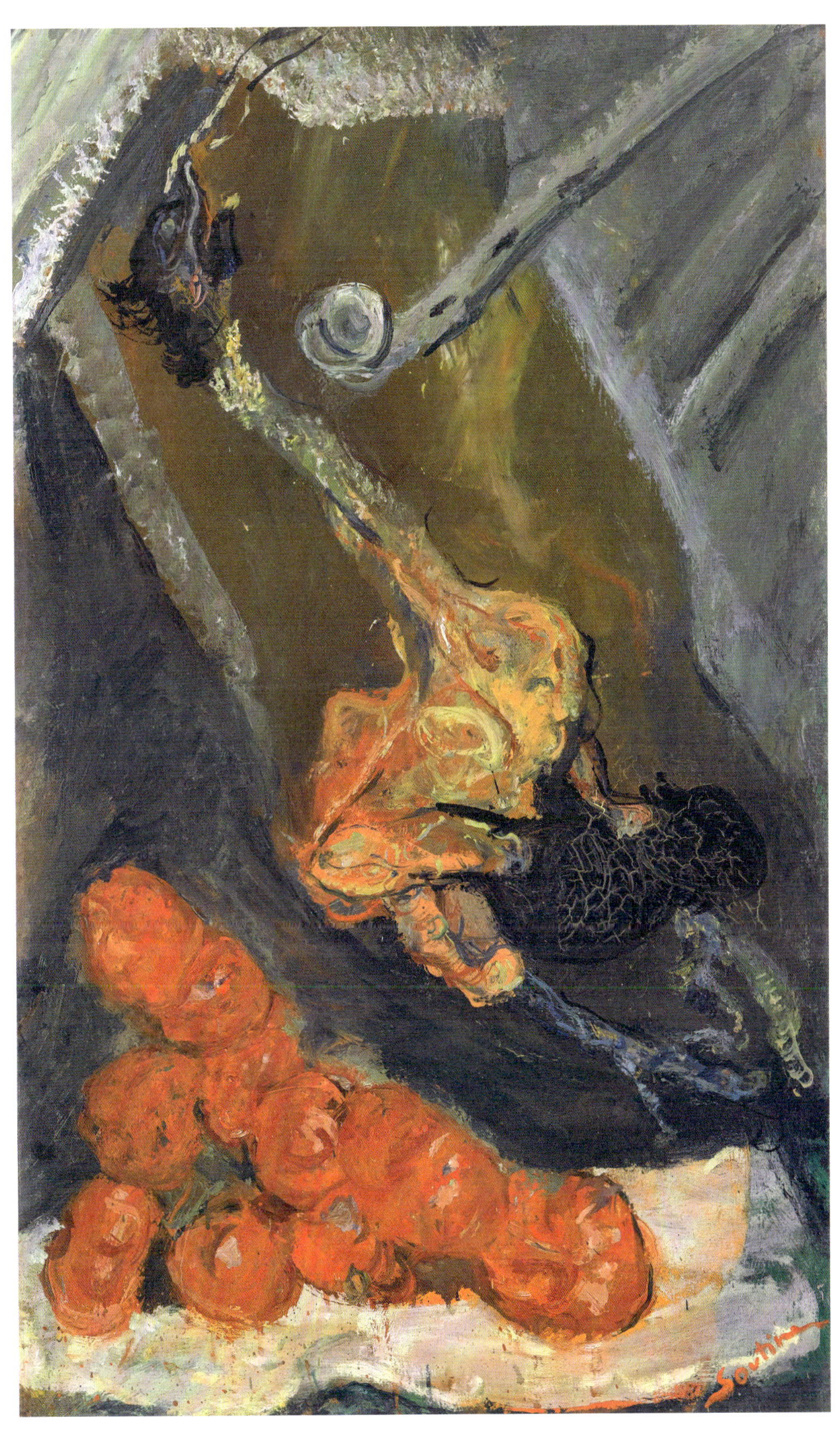

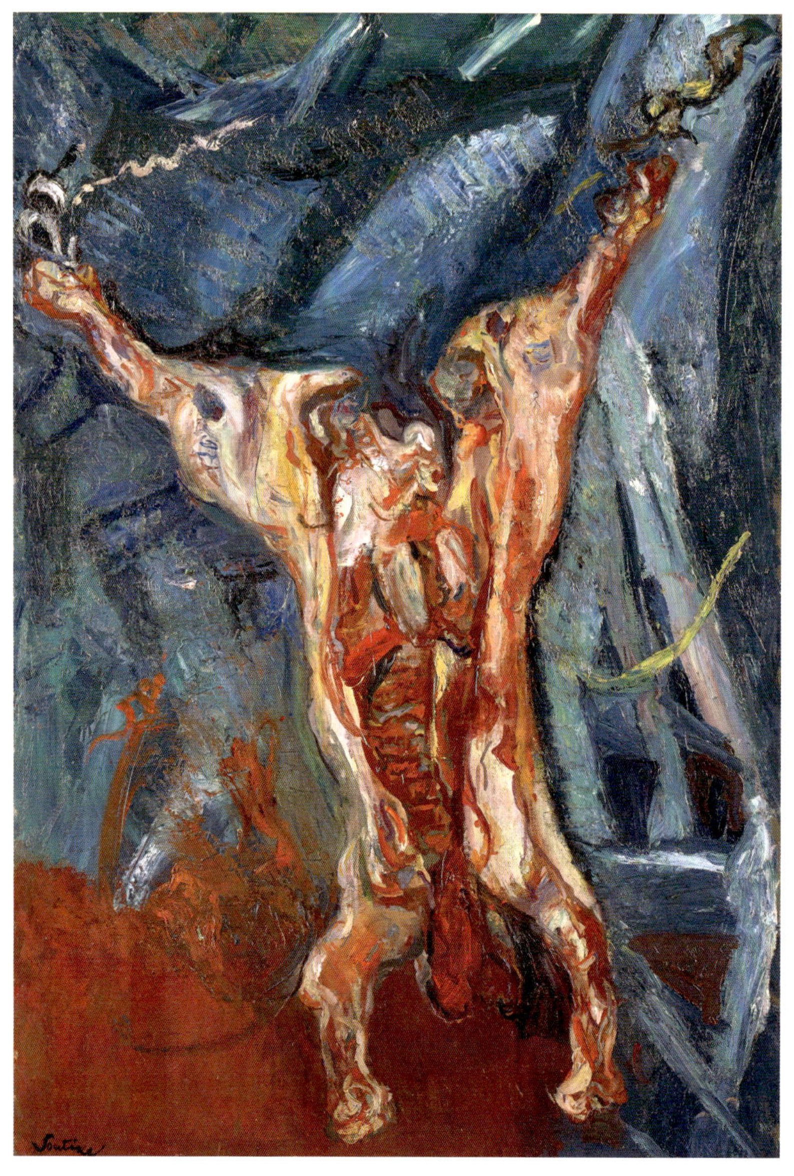

[48]
Carcass of Beef, 1925
Oil on canvas
116.21 × 80.65 cm
Minneapolis Institute of Art

[49]
Flayed Beef, 1925
Oil on canvas
202 × 114 cm
Musée de Grenoble

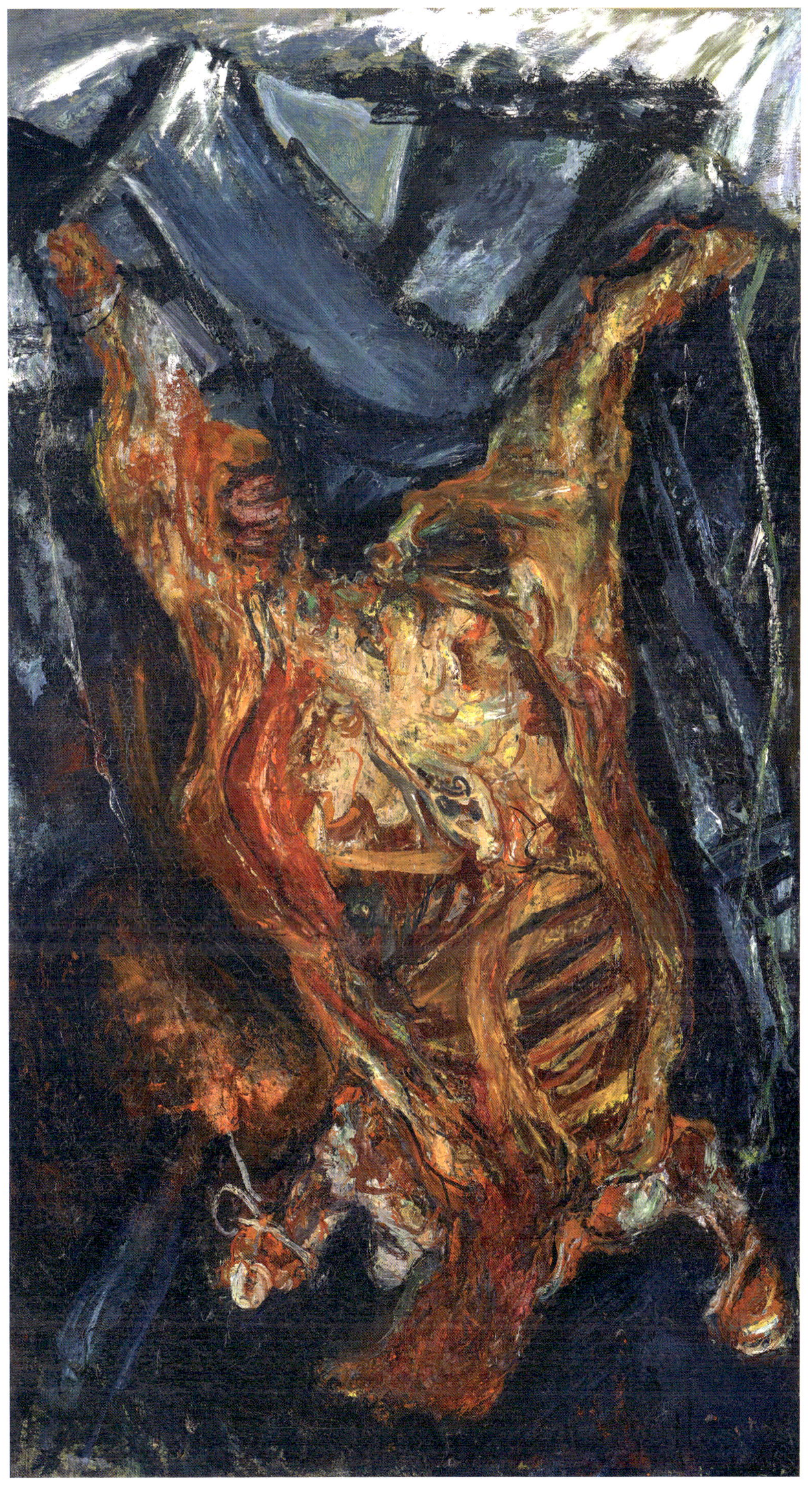

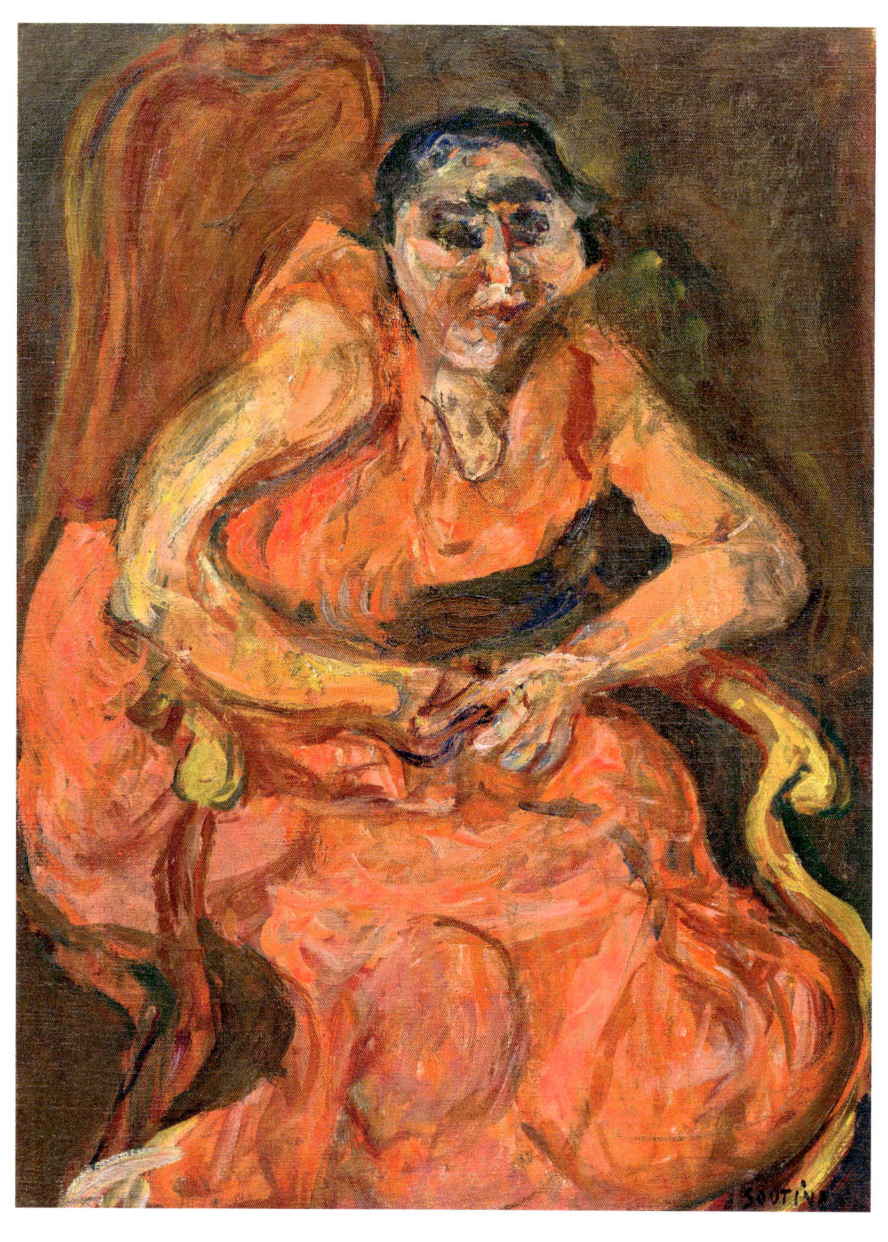

[50]
Woman in Pink, ca. 1924
Oil on canvas
73 × 54.3 cm
Saint Louis Art Museum

[51]
Grotesque, 1922–1925
Oil on canvas
81 × 45 cm
Musée d'Art moderne de Paris

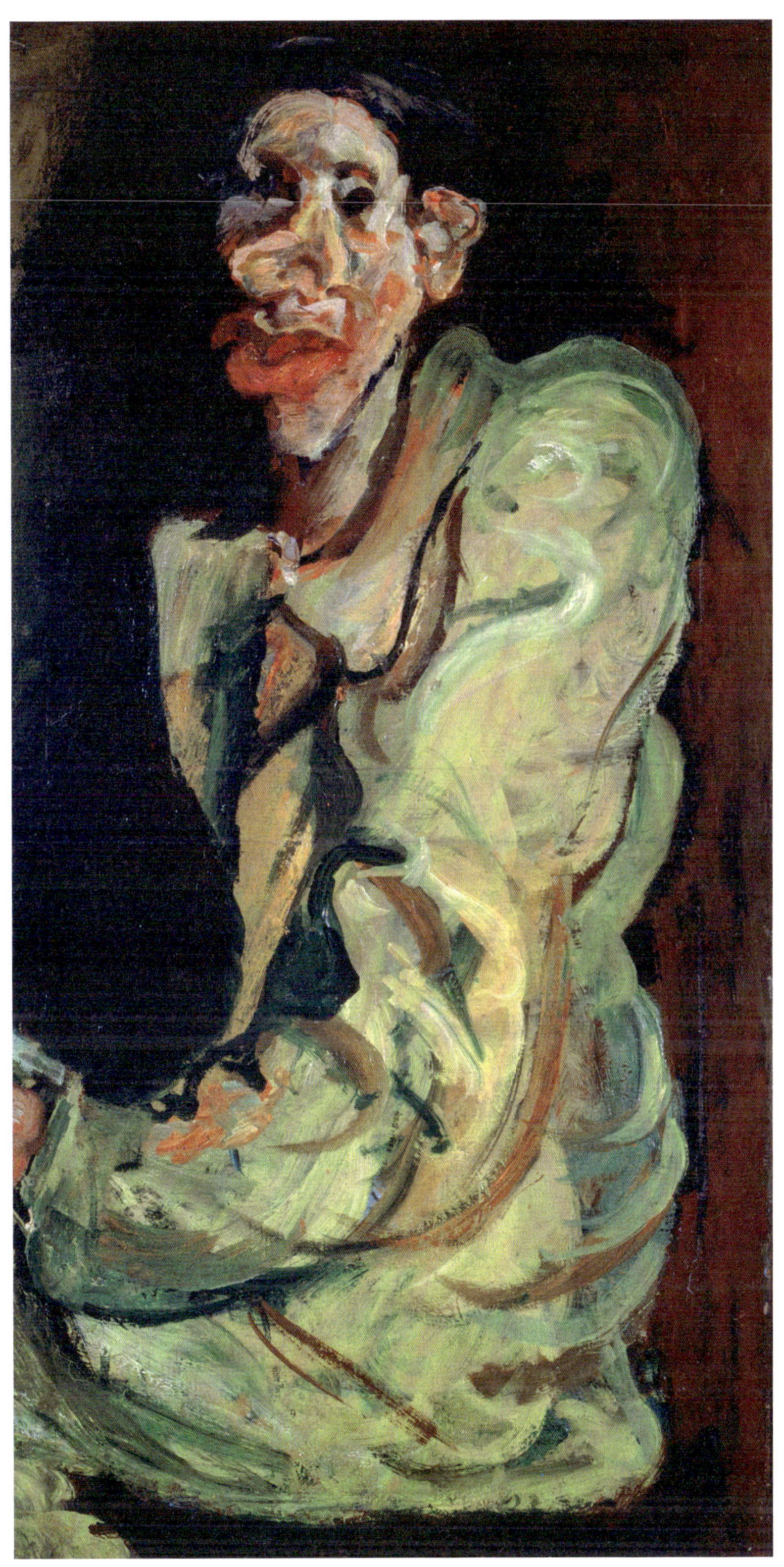

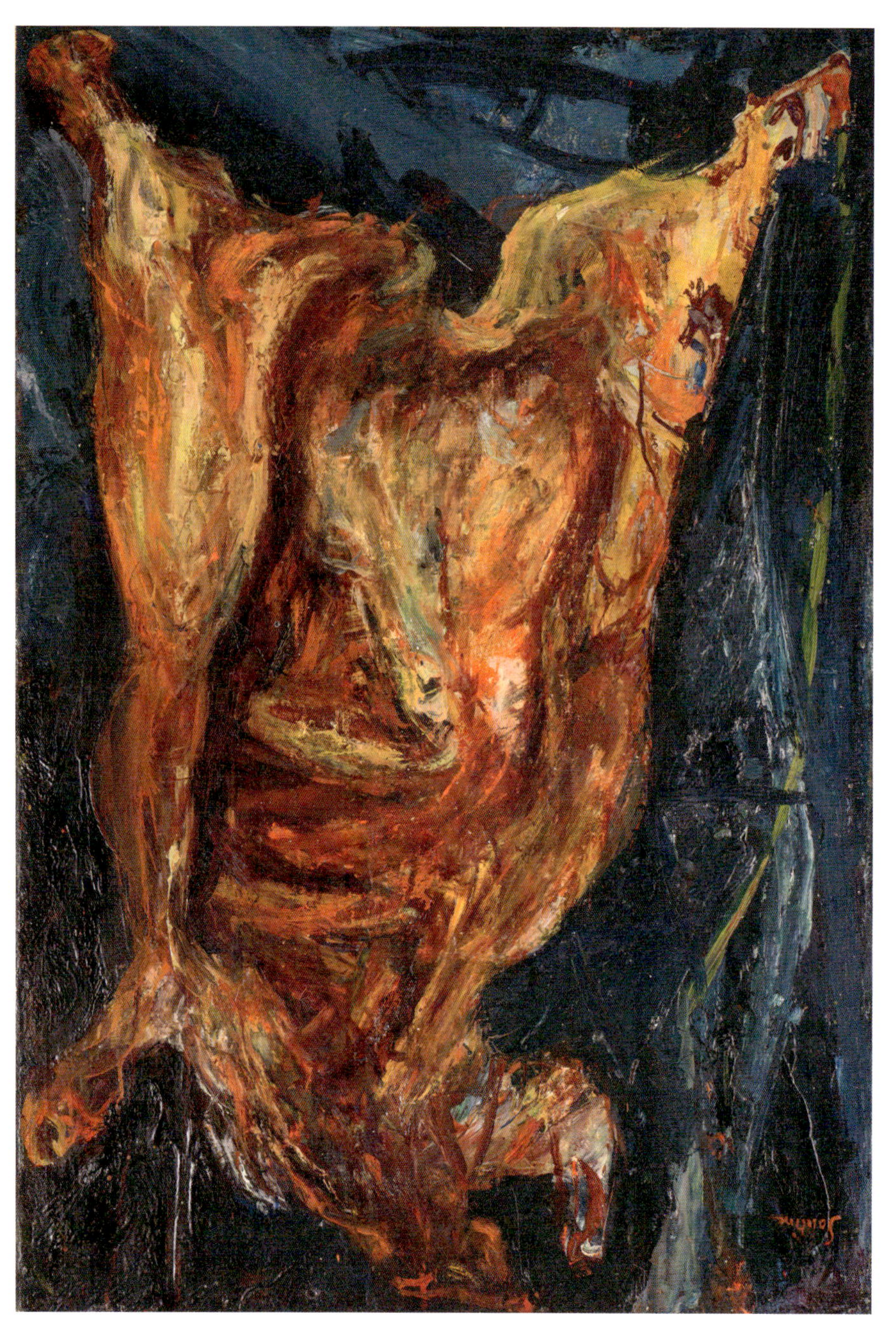

[52]
Flayed Beef, ca. 1925
Oil on canvas
72.5 × 49.9 cm
Kunstmuseum Bern

[53]
Side of Beef and Calf's Head, ca. 1925
Oil on canvas
92 × 73 cm
Musée de l'Orangerie, Paris

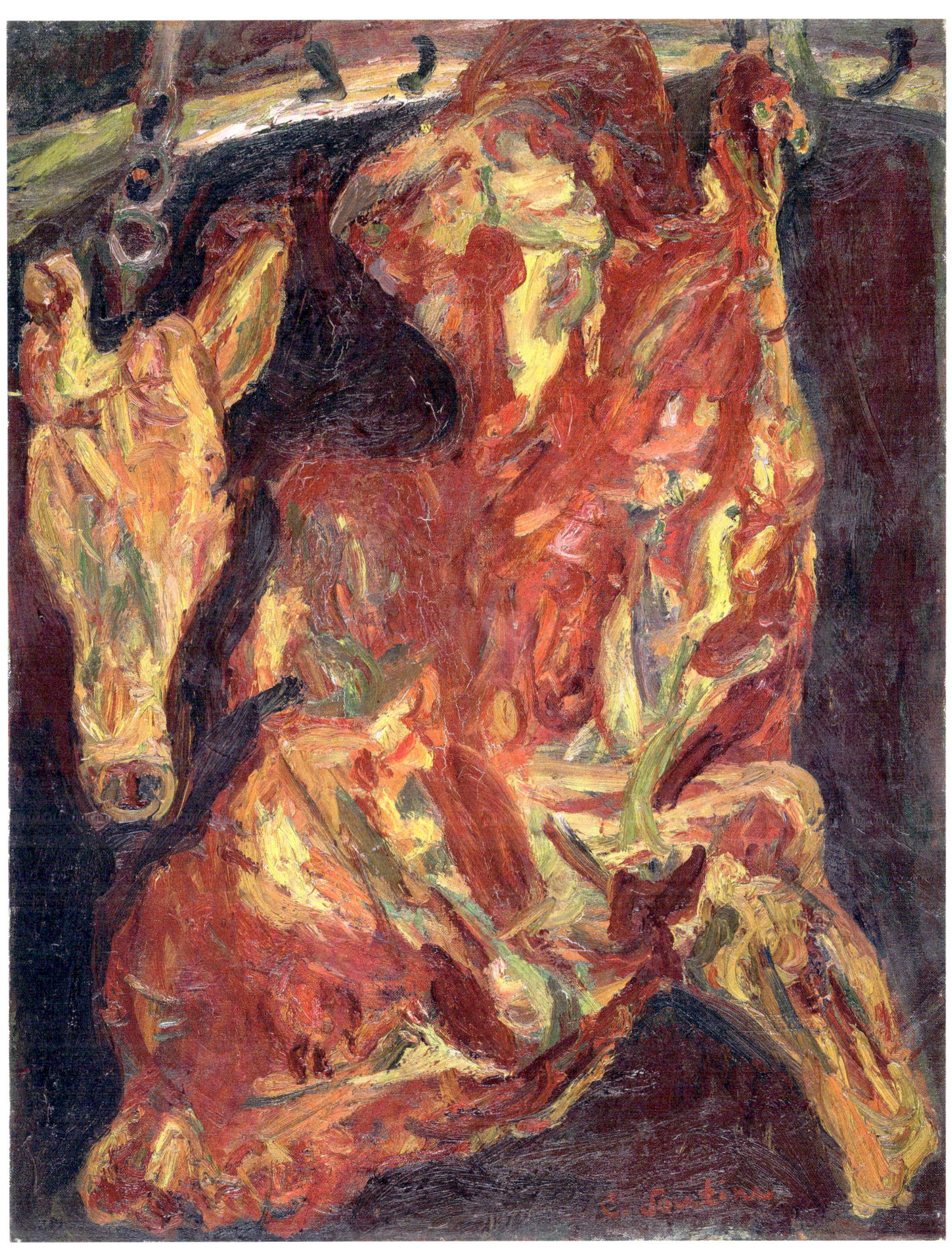

[54]
Hanging Fowl, 1925
Oil on wood
125 × 80 cm
Centre Pompidou, Paris

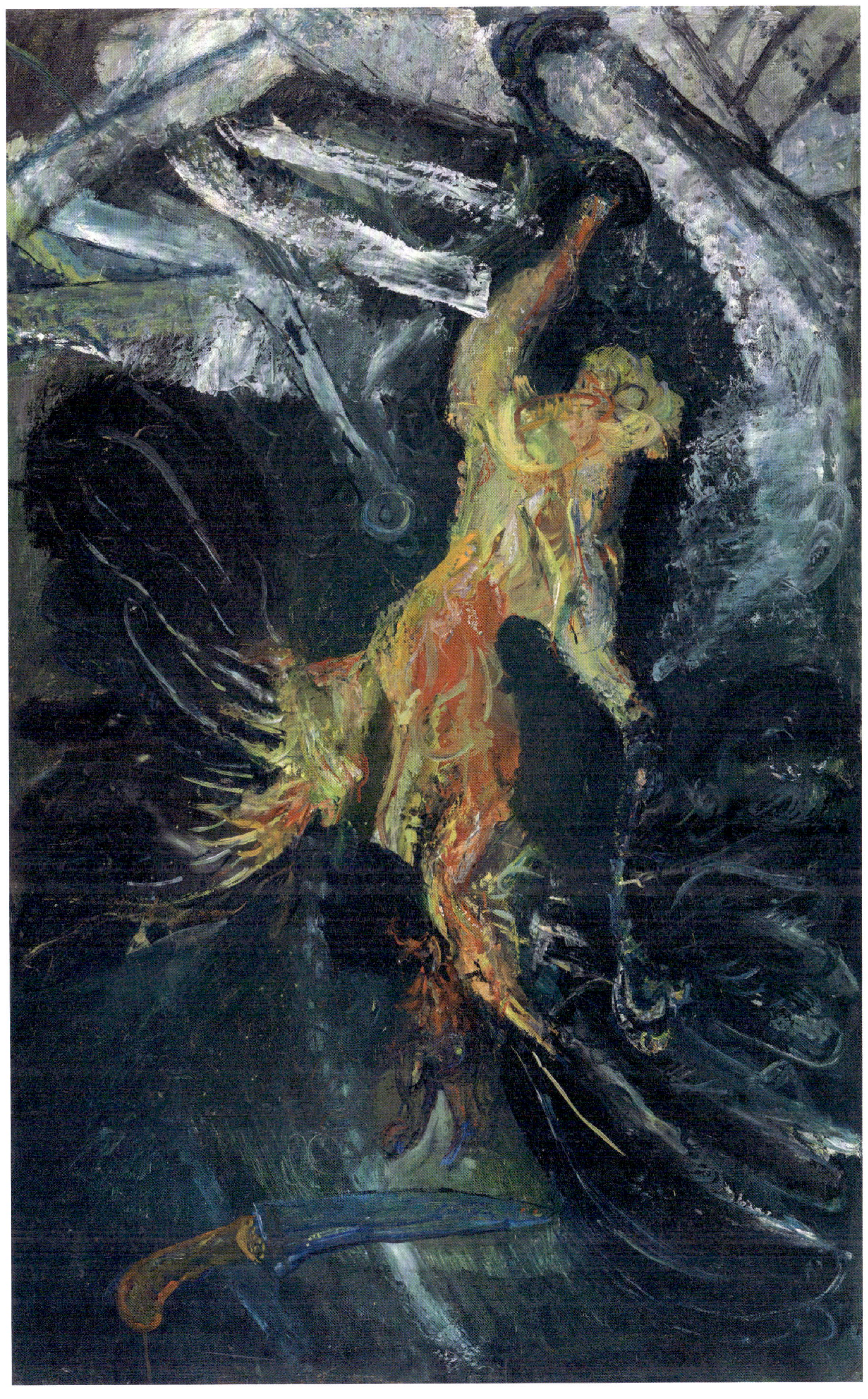

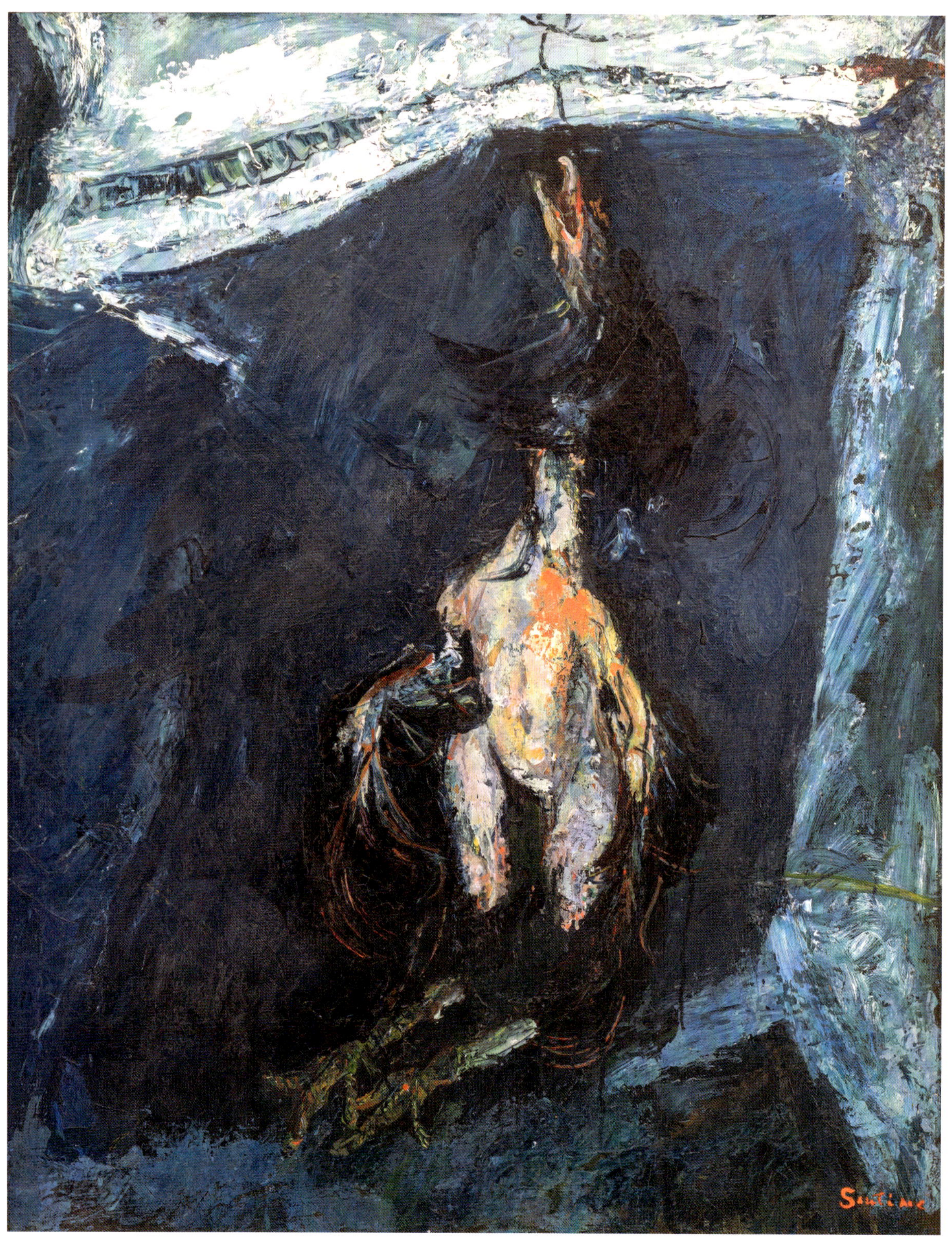

[55]
Hanging Turkey, 1925
Oil on canvas
91.4 × 72.4 cm
Private Collection
Courtesy McClain Gallery, Houston

[56]
Dead Fowl, ca. 1924
Oil on canvas
110.4 × 81.1 cm
The Museum of Modern Art, New York

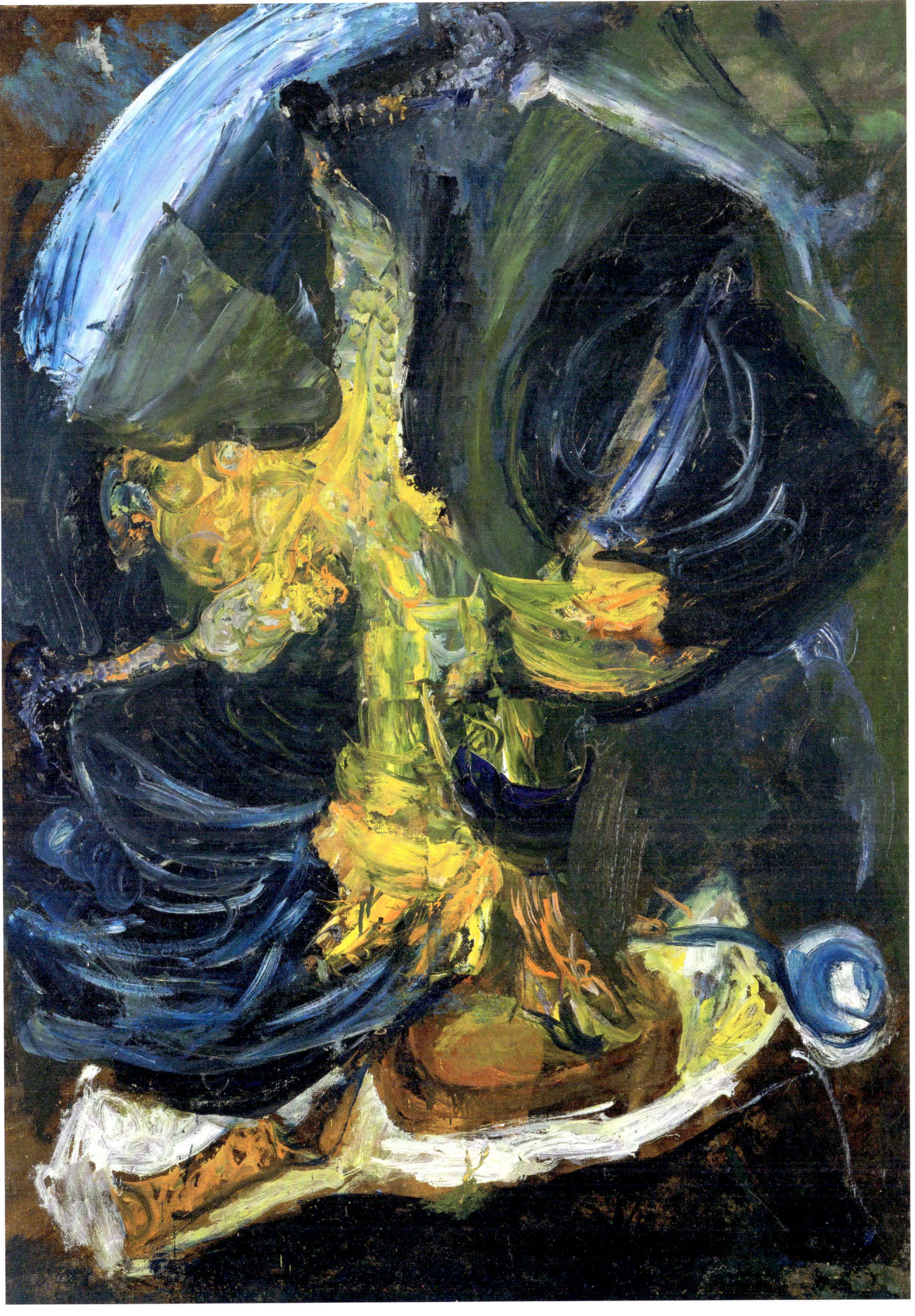

[57]
Bellboy (also known as *The Groom*), 1925
Oil on canvas
98 × 80.5 cm
Centre Pompidou, Paris

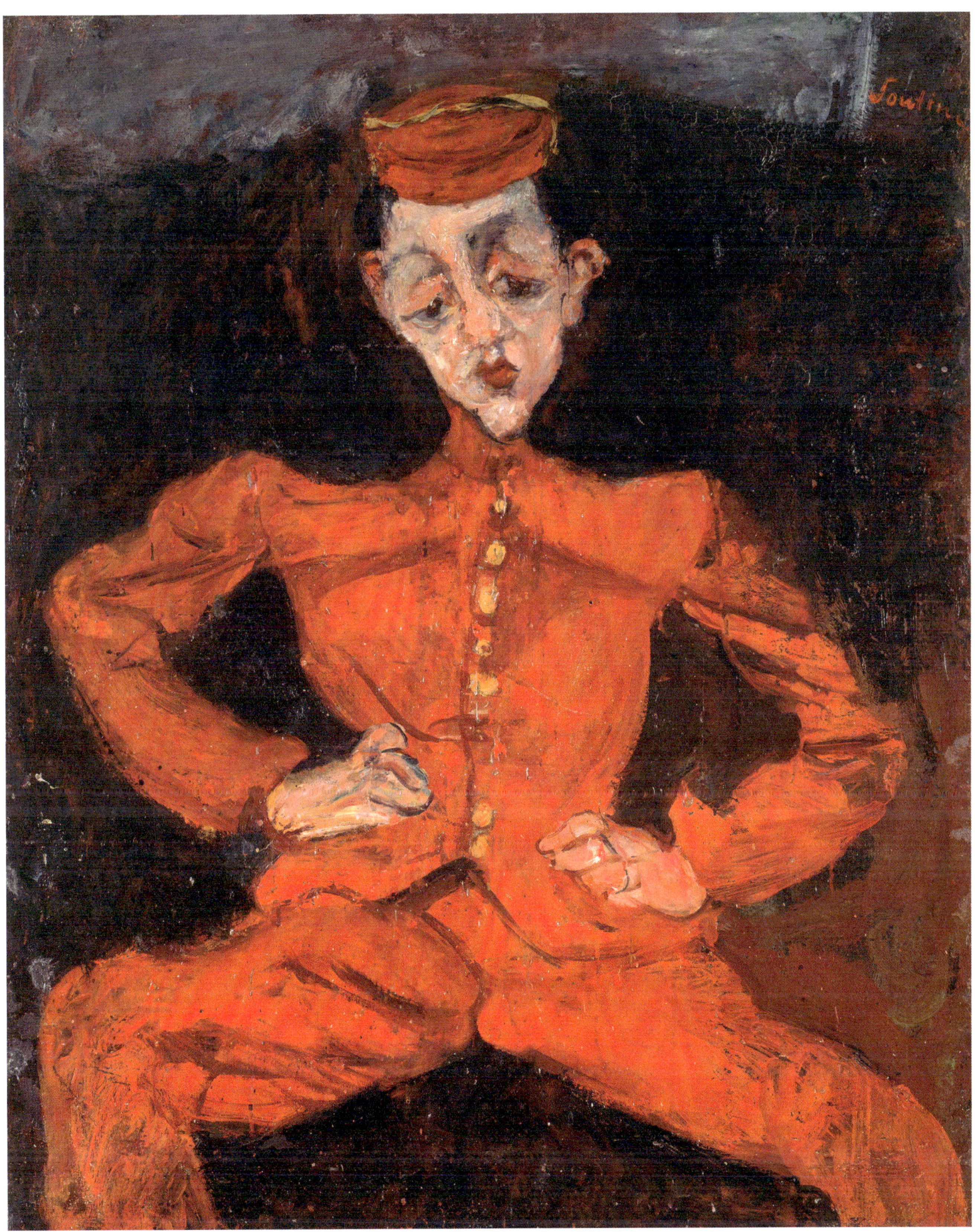
Soutine

[58]
Page Boy at Maxim's, ca. 1927
Oil on canvas
129.5 × 66 cm
Buffalo AKG Art Museum

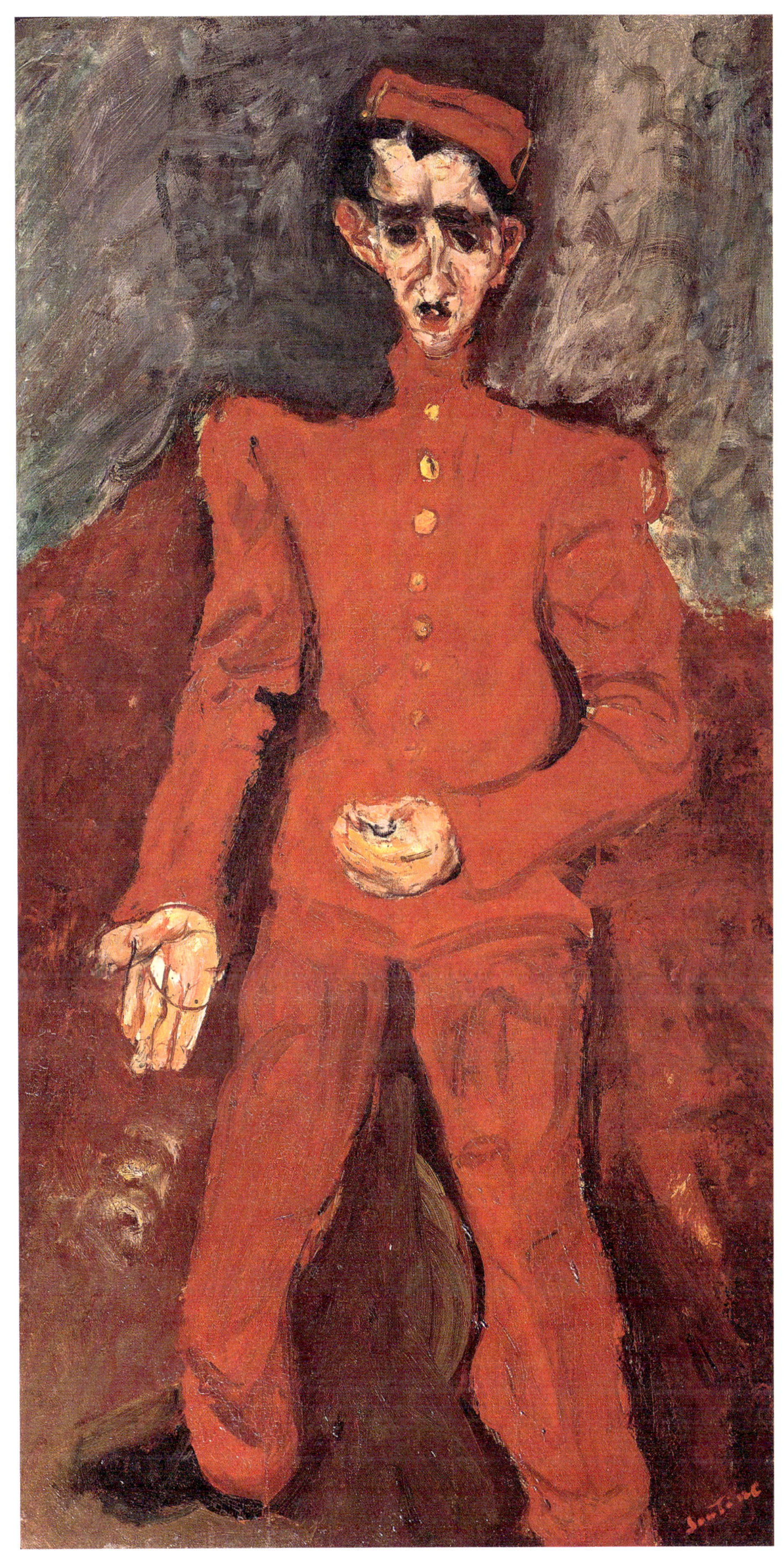

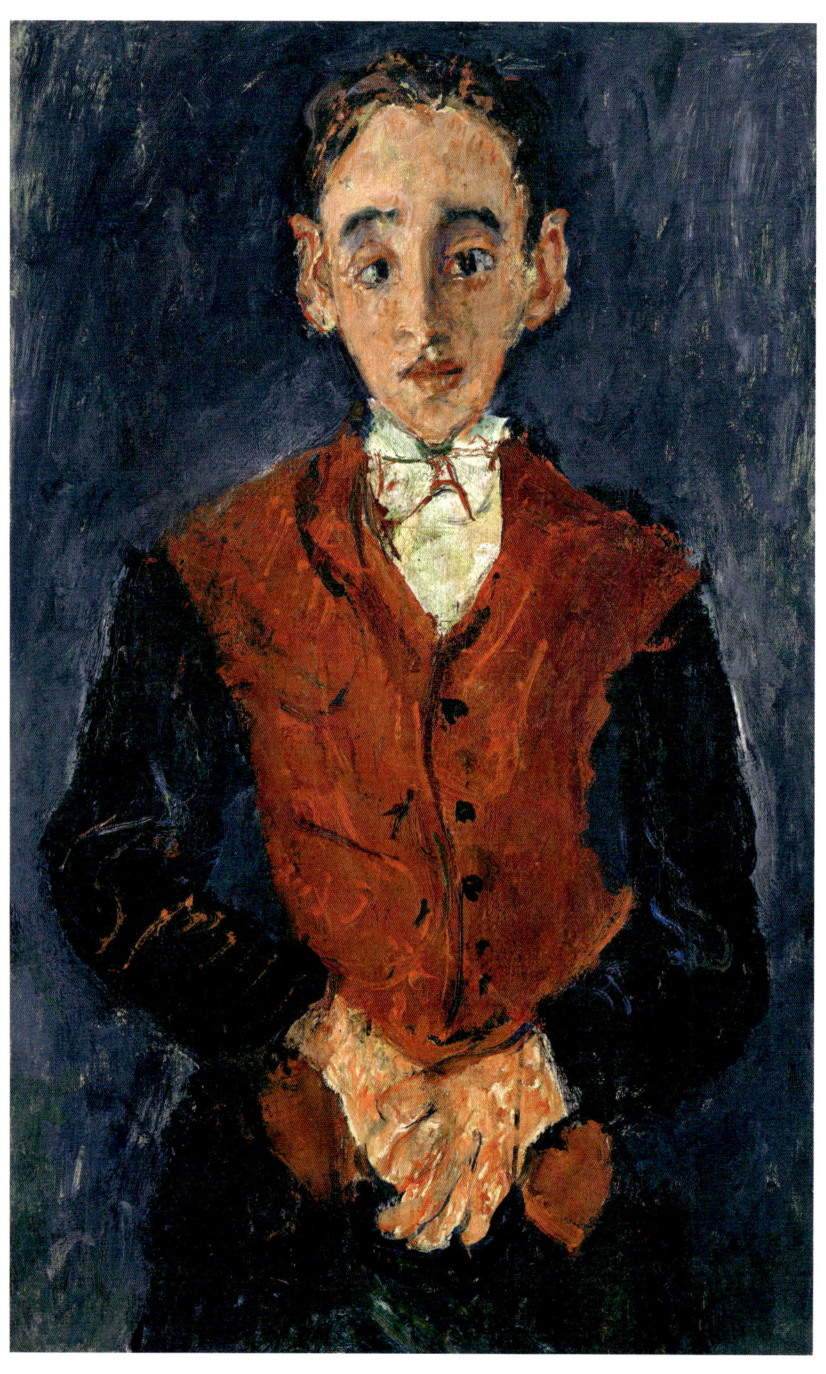

[59]
The Valet, ca. 1927
Oil on canvas
68.9 × 46 cm
The Lewis Collection, London

[60]
Head Waiter, ca. 1927
Oil on canvas
60 × 49.5 cm
Private Collection, Berlin
On long-term loan to the Museum Folkwang, Essen

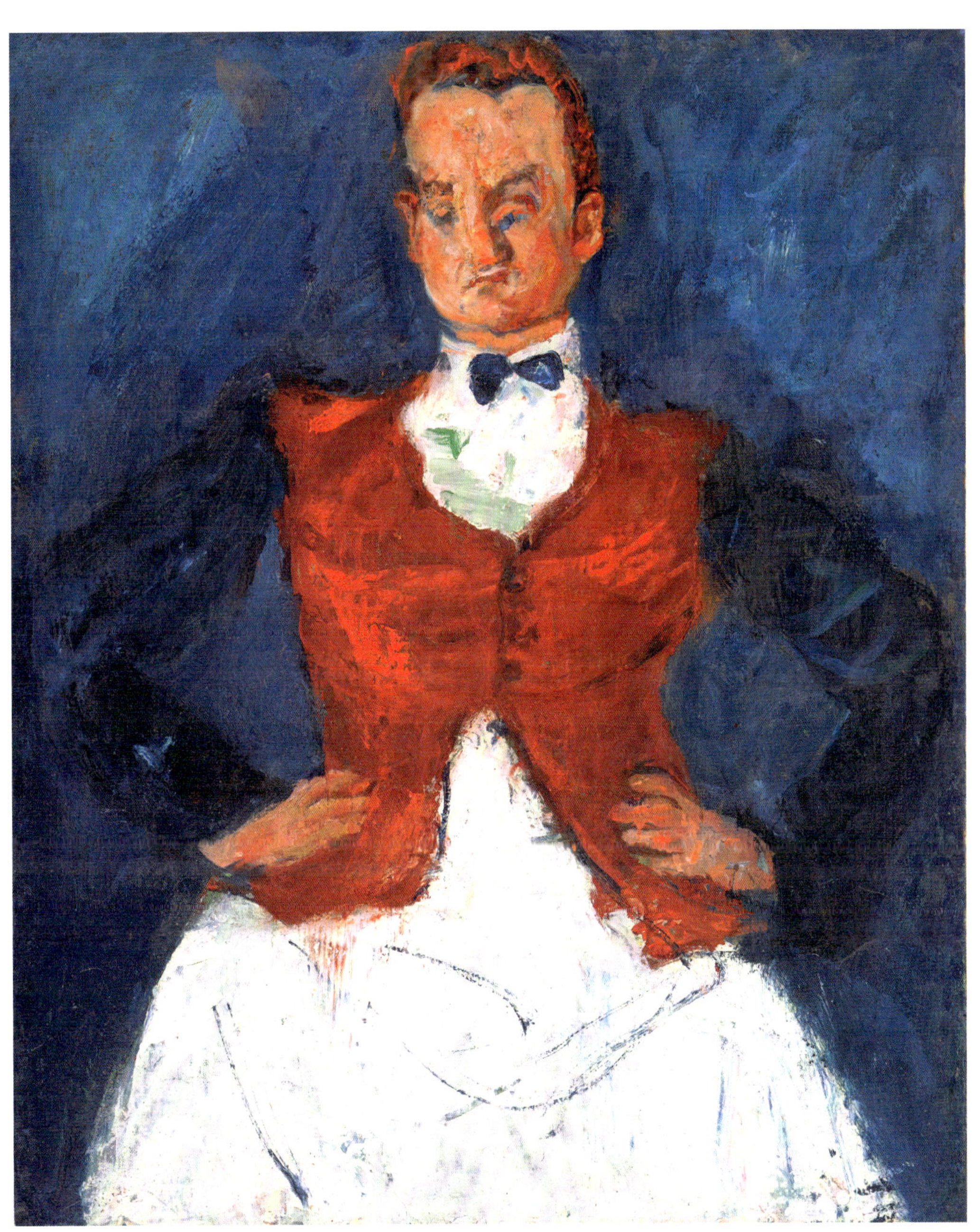

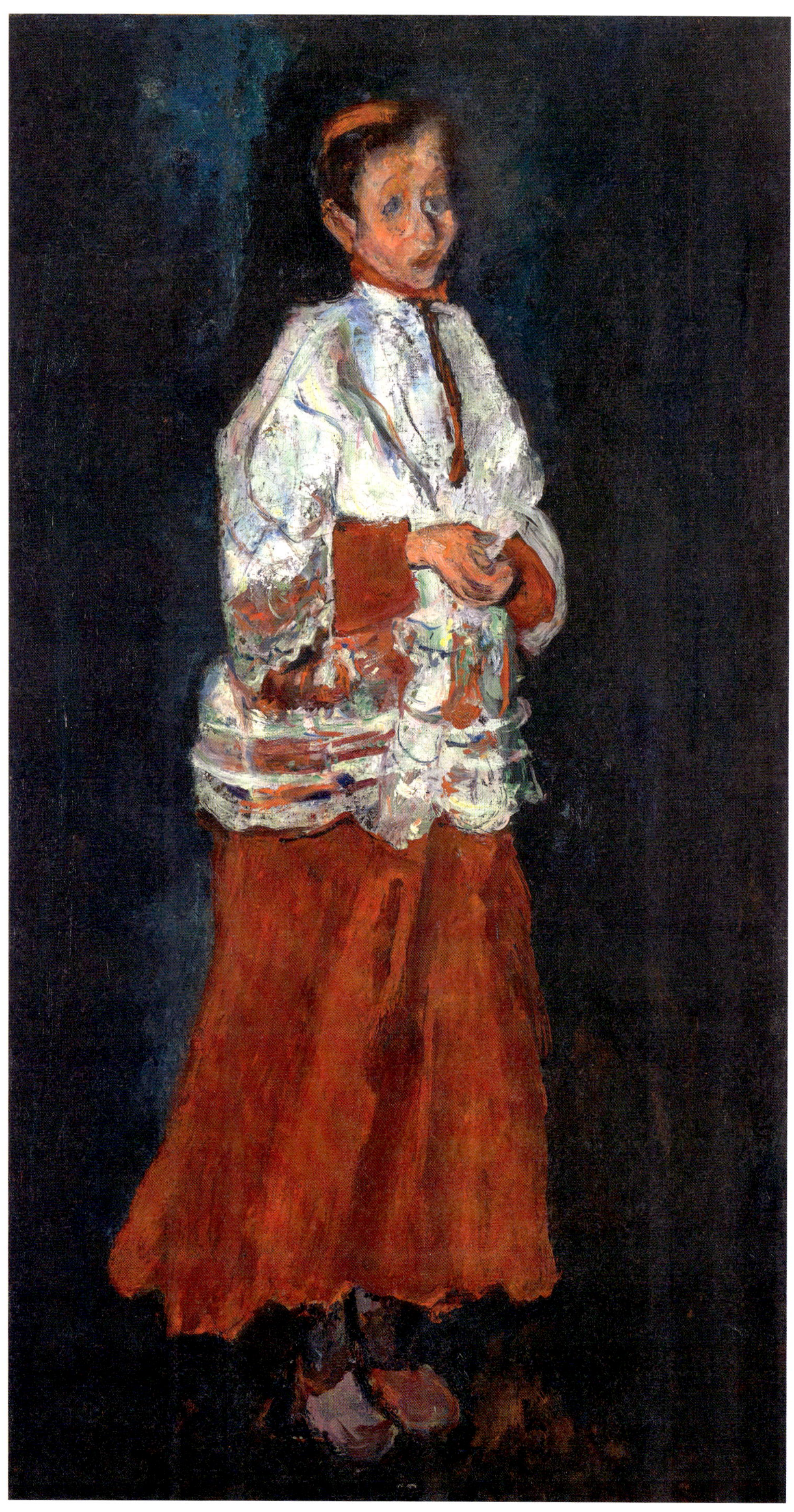

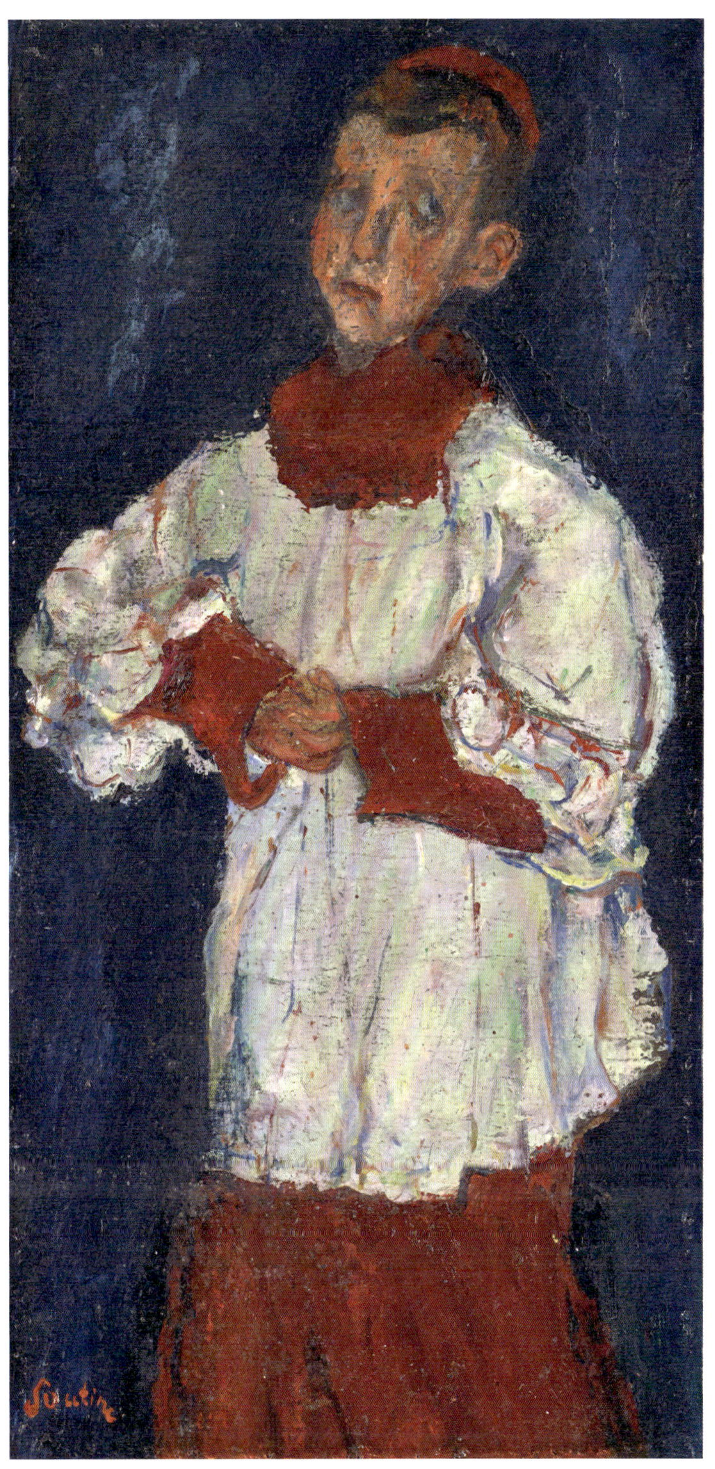

[61]
Large Choirboy, 1925
Oil on canvas
100 × 55.9 cm
Centre Pompidou, Paris /
Musée des Beaux-Arts de Chartres

[62]
The Choirboy, ca. 1927
Oil on canvas
77.5 × 39 cm
Stiftung Im Obersteg
Depositum im Kunstmuseum Basel 2004

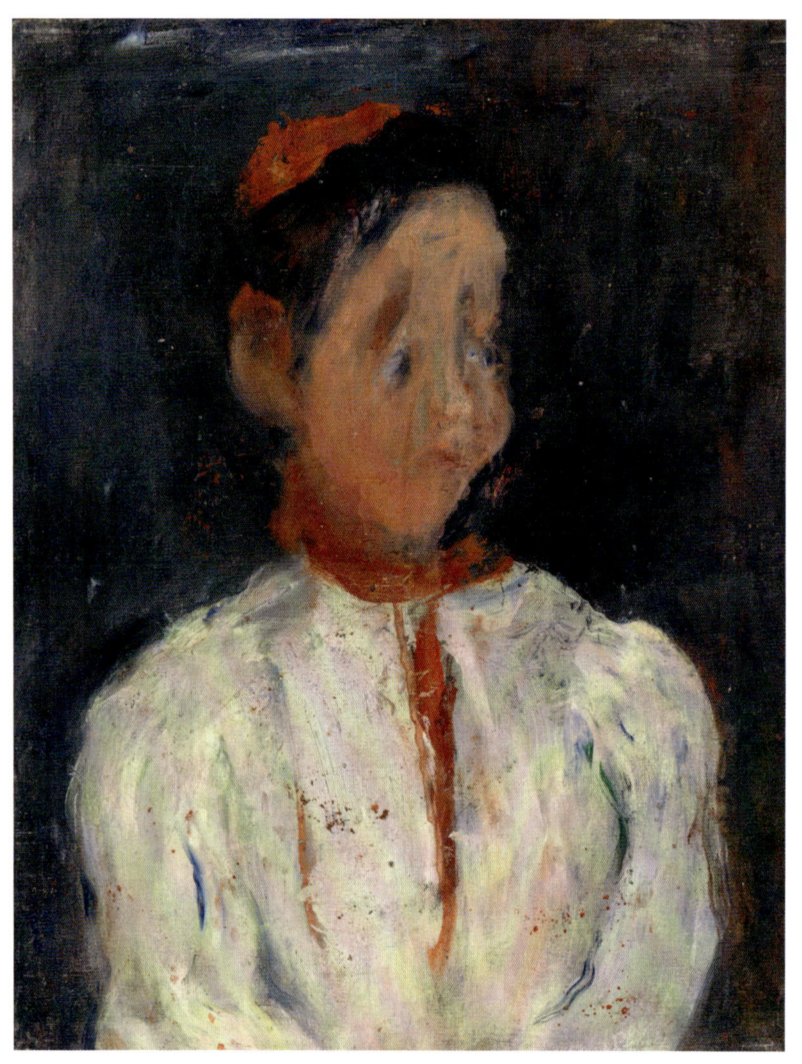

[63]
The Choirboy, 1925
Oil on canvas
35.6 × 27.9 cm
Princeton University Art Museum

[64]
The Choirboy, 1927/28
Oil on canvas
63.5 × 50 cm
Musée de l'Orangerie, Paris

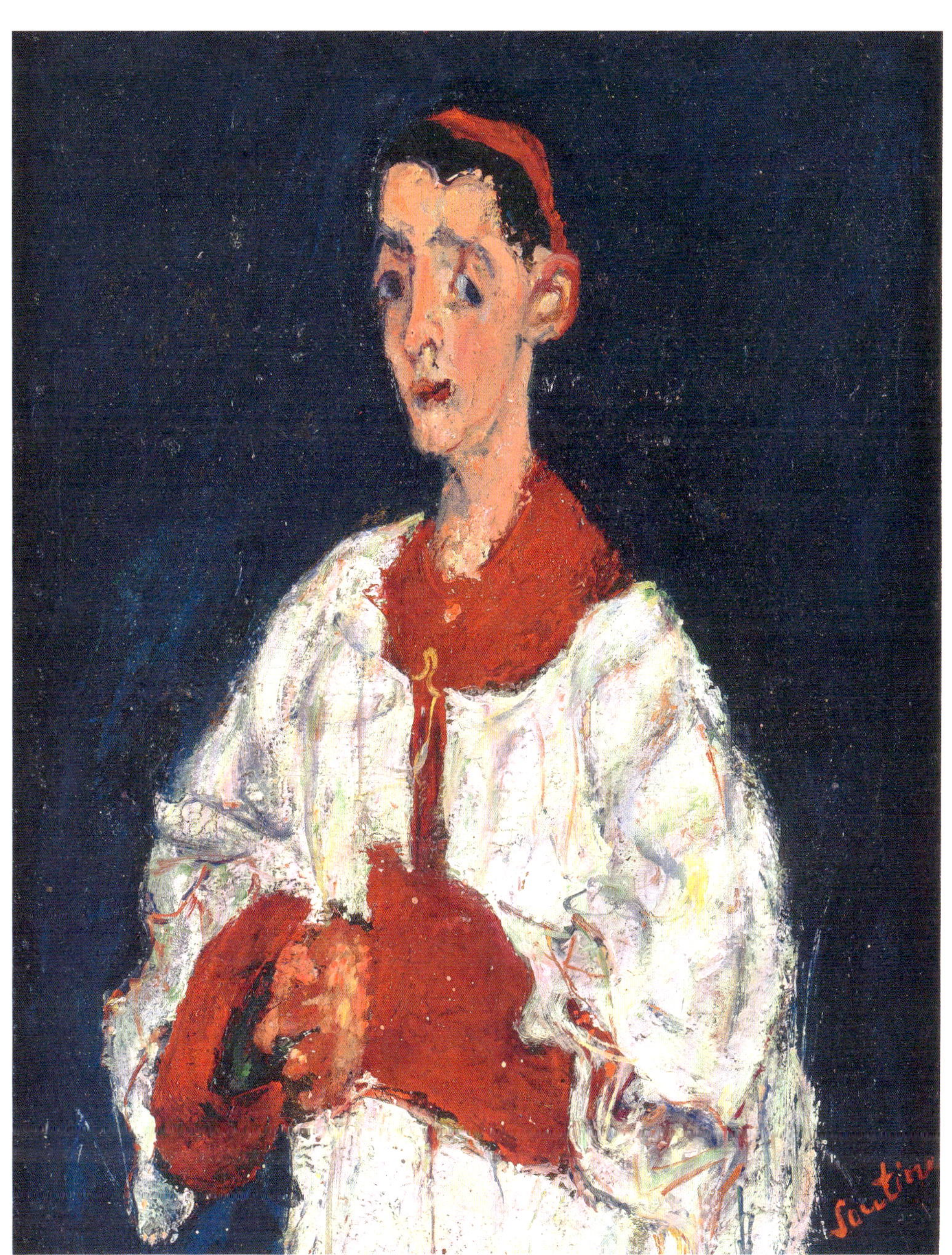

Soutine

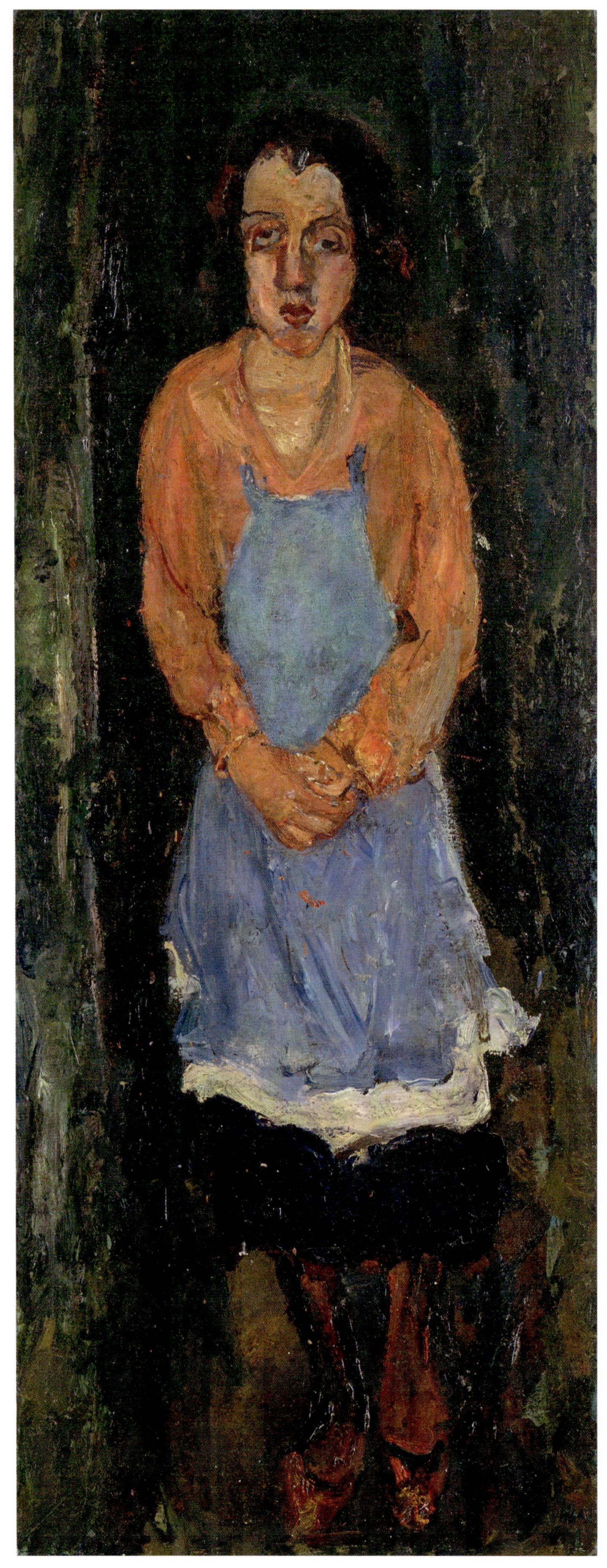

[65]
Cook with Blue Apron, ca. 1930
Oil on canvas
128 × 50.5 cm
Stiftung Im Obersteg
Depositum im Kunstmuseum Basel 2004

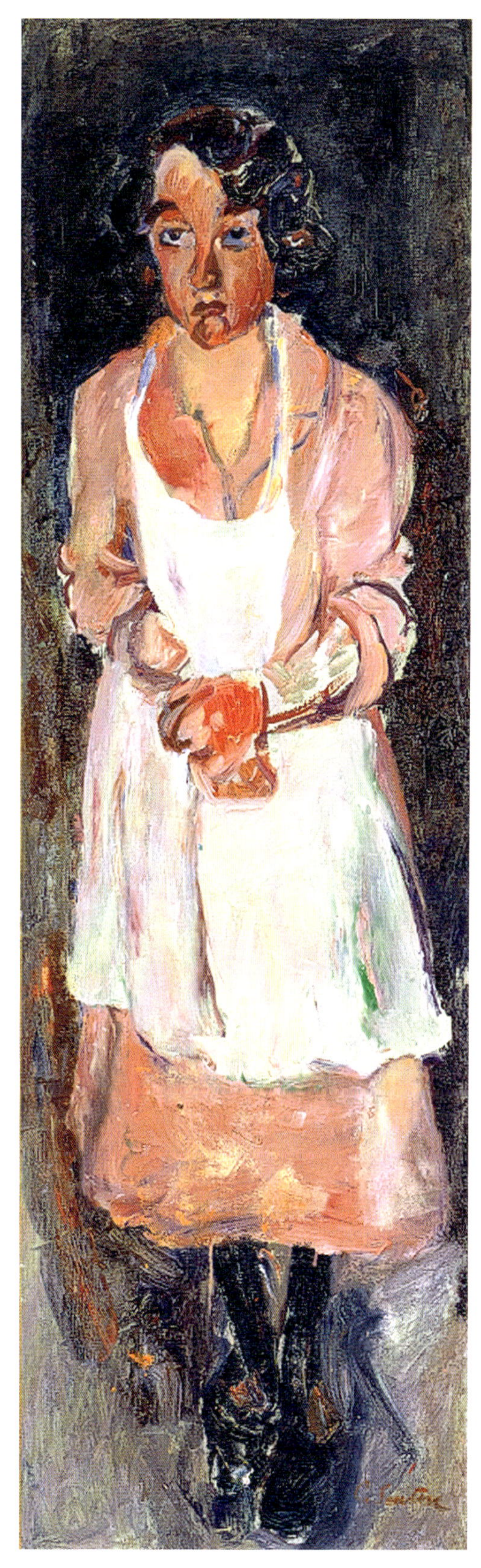

[66]
The Chambermaid, ca. 1930
Oil on canvas
110.3 × 34 cm
Kunstmuseum Luzern, Lucerne

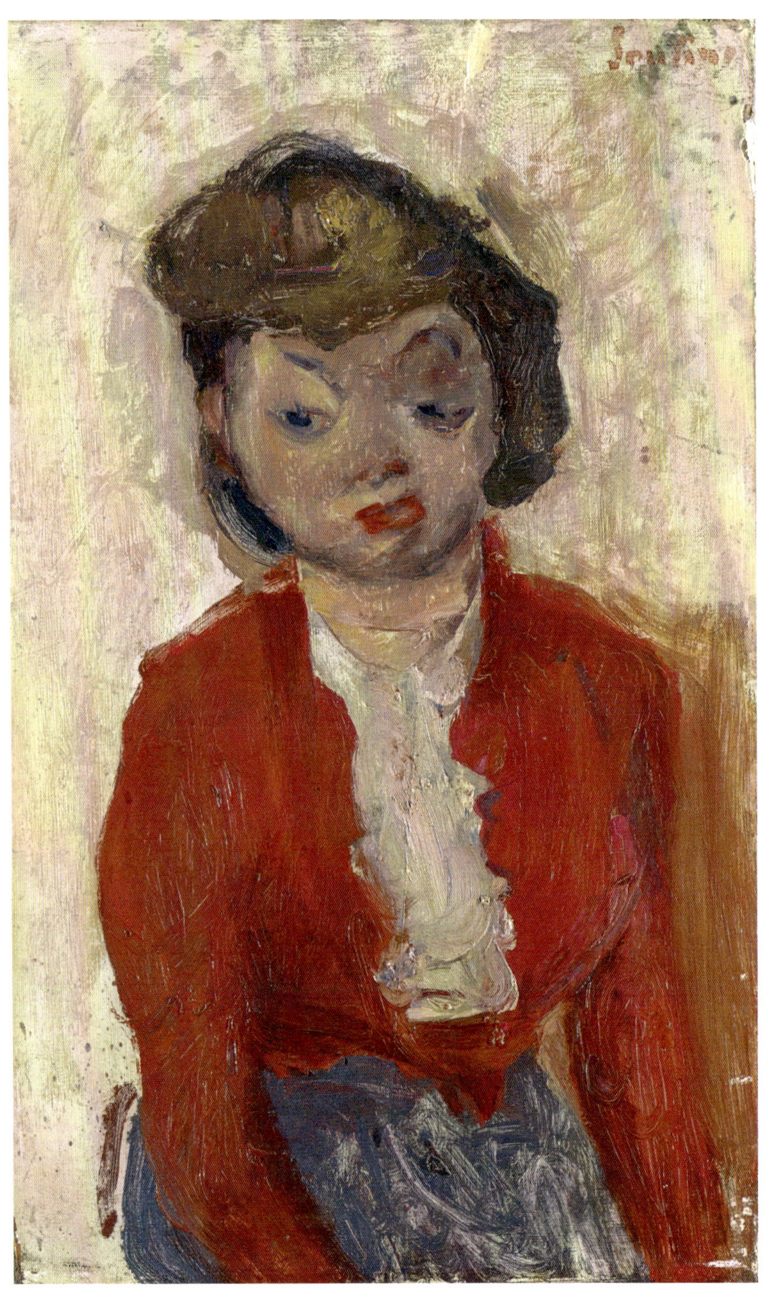

[67]
Young Englishwoman, ca. 1934
Oil on wood
56 × 34 cm
Stiftung Im Obersteg
Depositum im Kunstmuseum Basel 2004

[68]
Little Girl in Blue, ca. 1934/35
Oil on wood
73 × 31.5 cm
Kunstmuseum Bern

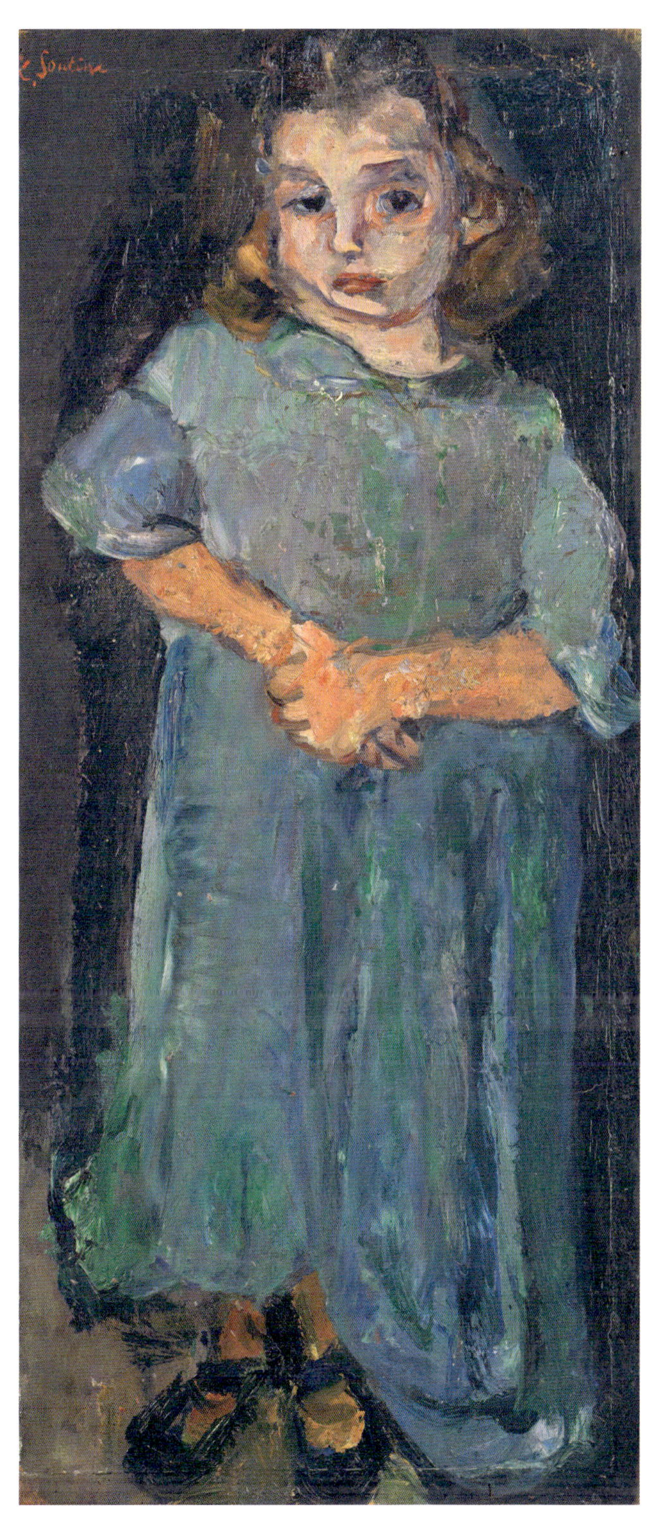

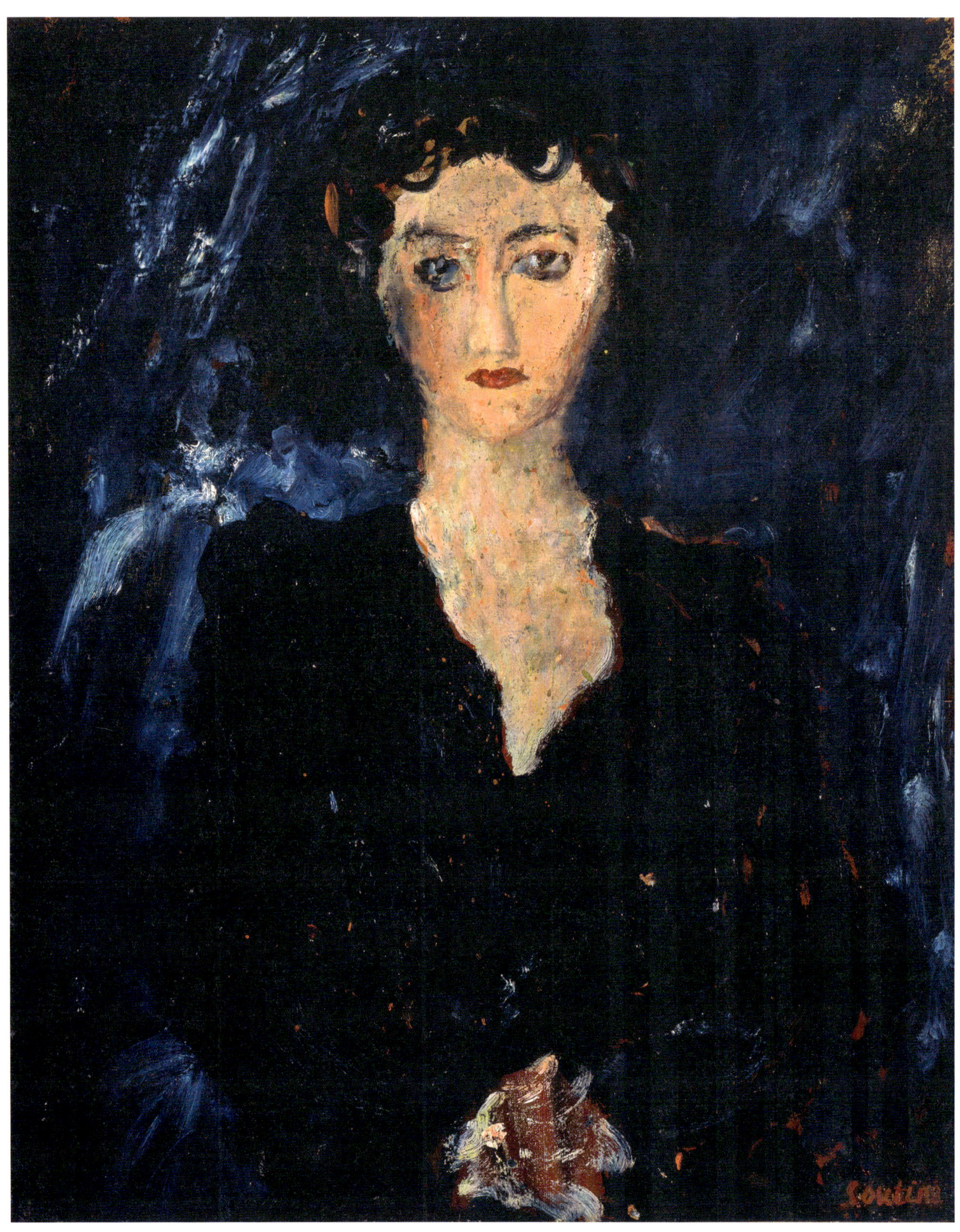

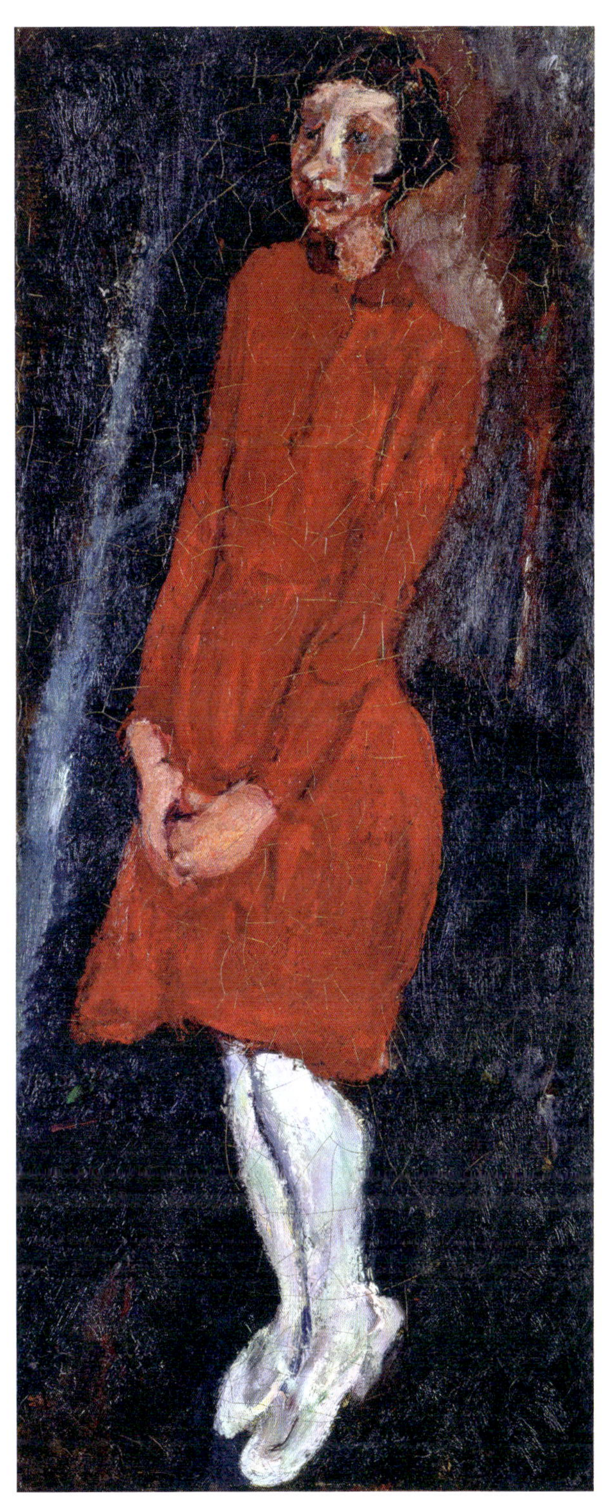

[69]
Portrait of a Lady, ca. 1928
Oil on canvas
73 × 60 cm
Collection Emil Bührle
On long-term loan to Kunstmuseum Basel

[70]
Young Girl in Red, 1928
Oil on canvas
81.3 ×34.3 cm
The Israel Museum, Jerusalem

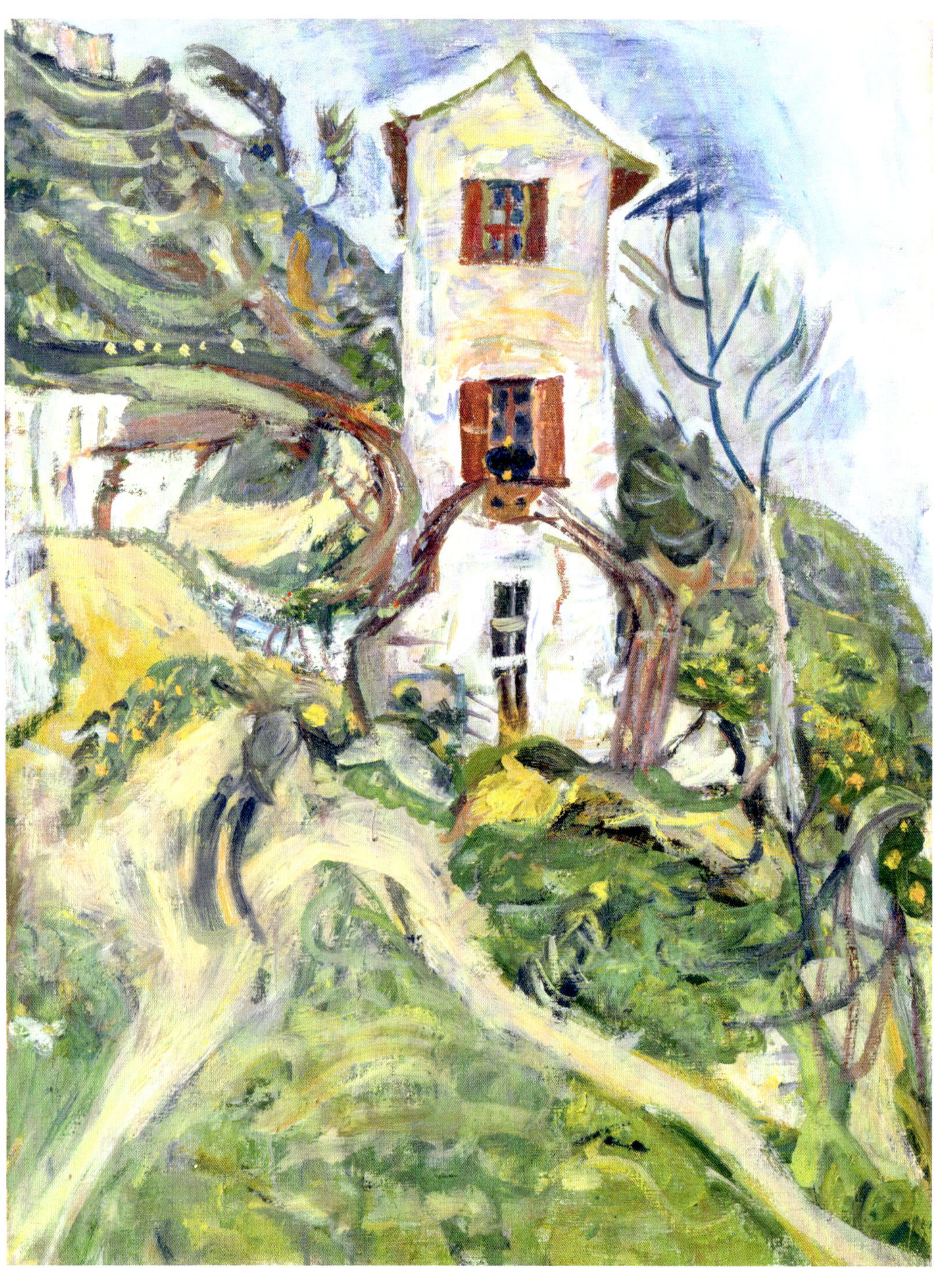

[71]
White House, ca. 1933
Oil on canvas
65 × 50 cm
Musée de l'Orangerie, Paris

[72]
Great Tree of Vence, ca. 1929
Oil on cardboard on plywood
61 × 44.5 cm
Kunstmuseum Bern

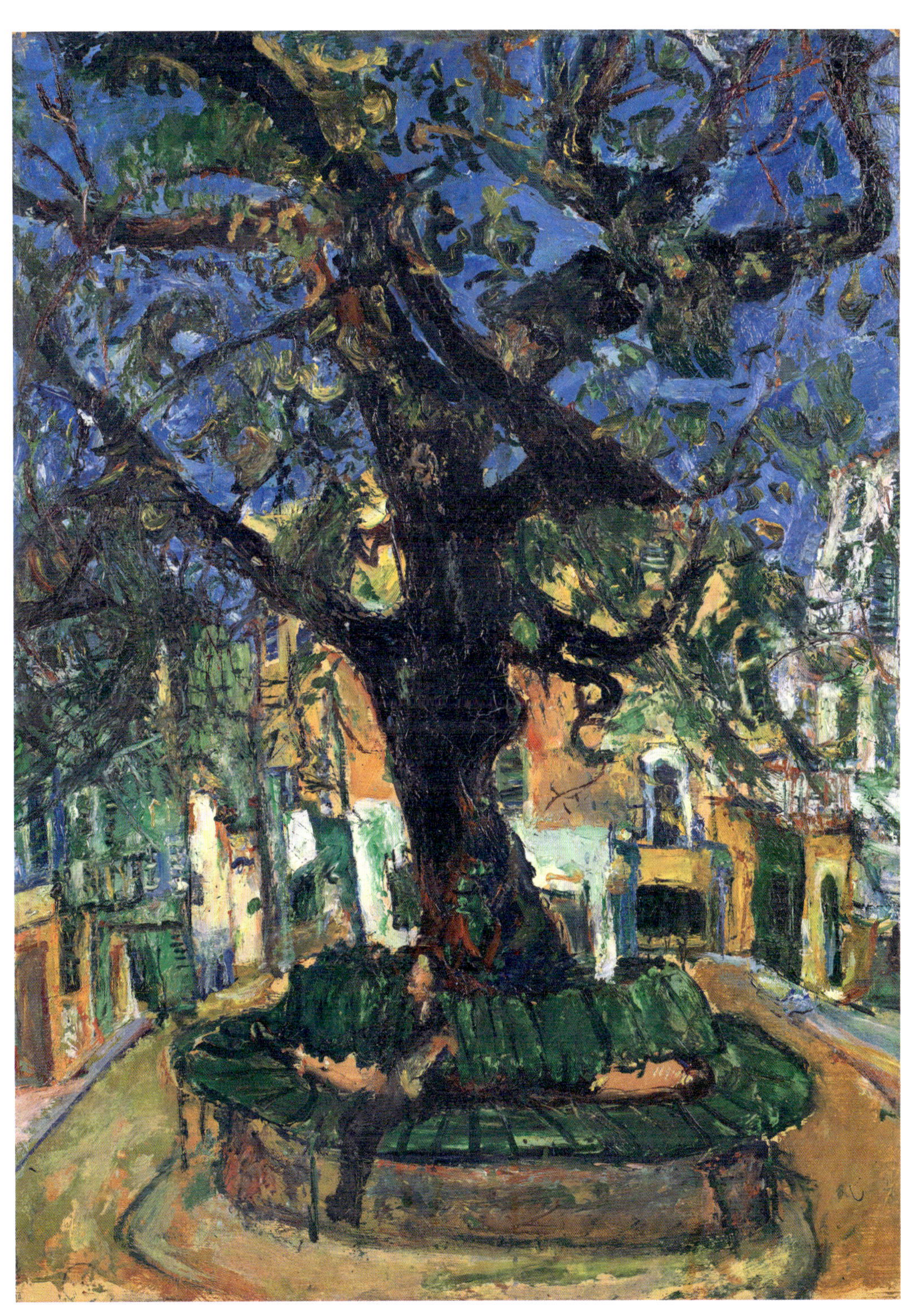

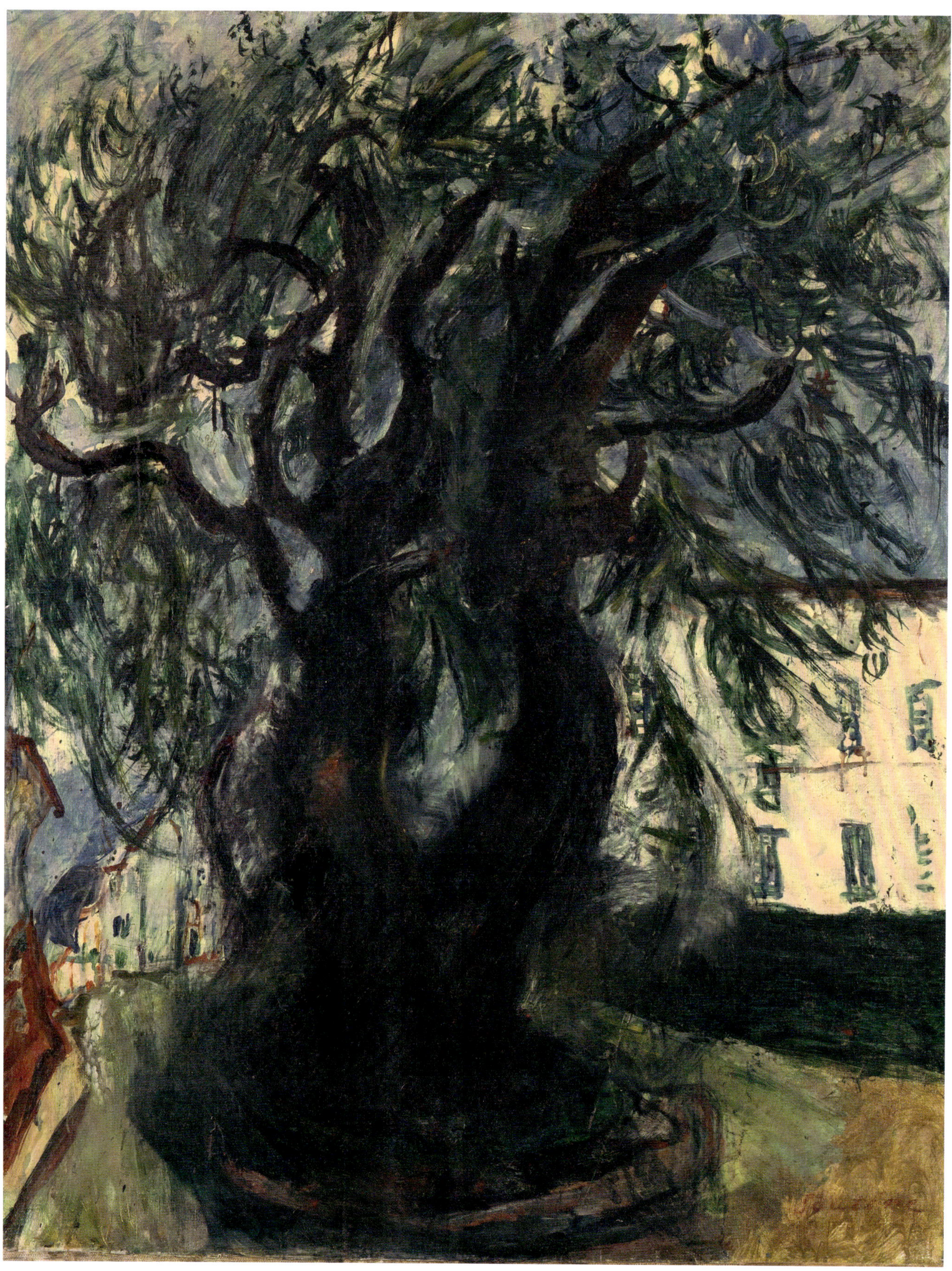

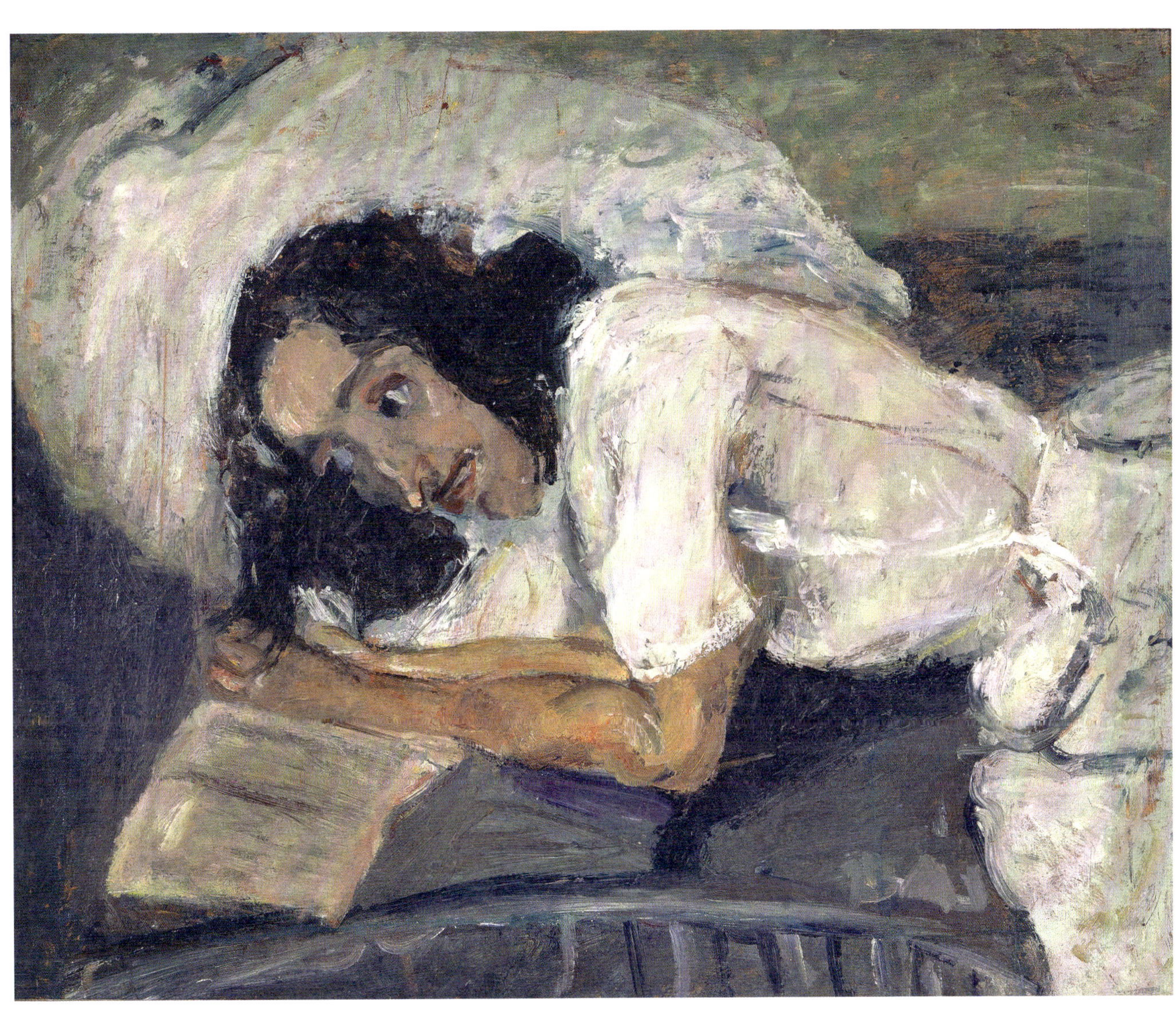

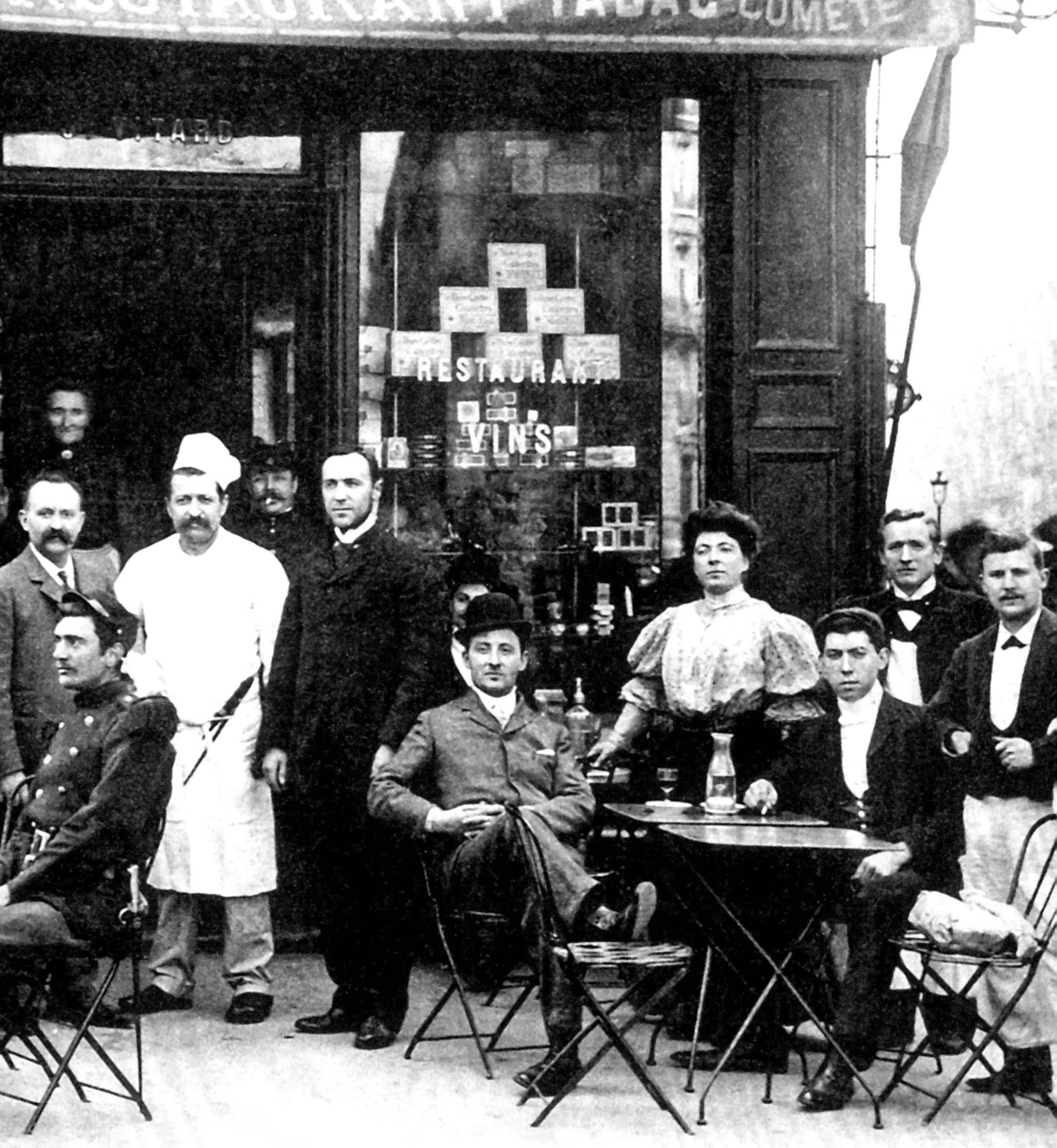

RESTAURANT TABAC
BIÈRE DE LA COMÈTE
TABA
RESTAURANT
VINS

Soutine

and the
École de Paris

Sophie Krebs

During the 1981/82 Soutine exhibition in Germany, museum director Peter Berghaus complained about the absence of works by Soutine in German private and public collections and the lack of publications on the artist. This was undoubtedly true, but it seems that this lack was largely due to the course of German history after 1914. Soutine could be considered the ideal "degenerate artist," even though none of his works were blacklisted: he was Jewish, Russian, and an expressionist. No foreign intermediaries, neither French nor German,[1] showed his work in Germany before the Nazis seized power. It is necessary to look back over the artist's career, with its many rough patches, even in France where he lived beginning in 1913. It can be argued, however, that Soutine's success was due to a handful of people who were brave enough to discover his "genius," closely associated with the figure of the troubled artist.[2] These are the same people who supported other foreign artists gathered under the label of the École de Paris (School of Paris)—which was not a movement, but a trick to include painters on the Parisian art scene while at the same time excluding them. This is a paradox of the crisis then ruffling that milieu, which at once mingled anarchist and cosmopolitan currents and nationalist ideologies.

Soutine and the École de Paris

From its outset, Soutine was attached to the École of Paris, being one of its few tutelary figures, along with such artists as Marc Chagall, Amedeo Modigliani, Jules Pascin, Tsuguharu Foujita, Moïse Kisling, and Ossip Zadkine. The ties between Modigliani and Soutine are the subject of a legendary account in which Modigliani, on his deathbed, is said to have predicted his friend's genius and hence his future glory.[3] This legend became a *posteriori* a kind of accreditation of Soutine's legitimacy as a painter (fig. 1).

However, a definition is first necessary. The term, "École de Paris," was born from the pen of critic Roger Allard in 1923, during a polemic that shook the entire art world. In order to cope with the influx of new artists from across the globe (a reason given by its president, Paul Signac), the Salon des Indépendants decided to change its classification system—alphabetical in 1922—along a basis of nationality the following year.[4] Despite the protests of French and foreign artists, and the dramatic resignation of Fernand Léger, nothing happened: Signac was inflexible. The polemic swelled in the press and lasted for more than a year.

The decision of the organizing committee of the Salon des Indépendants reveals all the ambiguities of this measure. Jules Pascin for example, so intrinsically linked to the Paris of the Roaring Twenties, was placed in the section for "American painting" because he had been naturalized in order to avoid the undesirable status of statelessness during the First World War. Roger Allard coined the term, "École de Paris," in order to place certain foreigners, who had been living in Paris for a long time and who were associated with the so-called "École française" (French School), in a sort of transit zone: "Let us also say that foreign artists, some of them at least, tend to forget what they owe to our modern French schools. Trained for the most part in our classrooms, they try to accredit outside of France the notion of a certain School of Paris where masters and instructors, on the one hand, pupils and copyists, on the other, would be confused for the benefit of the latter. The most mediocre being the most interested in the confusion, which, understandably, they push with all their might."[5] Or again: "Certainly, one would not know how to be too grateful to the foreign artists who bring us a particular sensitivity, a turn of singular imagination, but one must push back against any pretension of barbarism, real or simulated, to direct the evolution of contemporary art. A certain School of Montparnasse would like to pass itself off abroad as the School of Paris (the term French School being suspiciously jingoistic)."[6] This sets the tone and reveals all the nationalist undercurrents of this immediate postwar period, in which anxiety about "Otherness" overshadowed contemporary creation.

André Warnod,[7] to whom the coining of the term, "École de Paris," has often been attributed, entered a plea for the foreign artists who vitalized Montmartre and Montparnasse alongside the French, though without singling out an artistic group with even the vaguest of manifestos. These foreigners practiced a restrained form of modern art from the beginning of the twentieth century until the start of the Second World War.

As for Soutine, he never exhibited at the Salon des Indépendants or in any other salon exhibition for that matter. But he was one of those foreigners who are themselves unsettling because they were, *de facto*, associated with French art. The well-known affair of the millionaire industrialist Albert C. Barnes and his interest in Modigliani and Soutine,[8] the latter then still completely unknown, made this artist one of the masters of French painting.[9] The event put the whole art scene in a state of excitement, and anecdotes are rife.[10] A true phenomenon was unleashed: "Everyone is running after Soutine."[11]

The dealers, quick off the mark, were ahead of the critics in establishing the success of the painter. In a 1923 article devoted to Soutine, Paul Guillaume himself (fig. 2),[12] Barnes's skillful agent,[13] "denounced" the role of these "profiteering" collectors, driven by the lure of capital gains and easy investments. In fact, Soutine was the object of commercial transactions of the highest order. The critic Camille Mauclair went to town over the attitude of dealers establishing the careers in their galleries of foreign artists newly arrived at Paris.[14] For him, it was this École de Paris that was "contaminating" French art.

Thus, Soutine was one of the sparks that ignited the "Querelle des étrangers," this feud over foreigners at the Salon des Indépendants.[15] Around him all the resentments and hatred crystallized. The perfect scapegoat, Soutine's career was launched, but under a cloud of suspicion that would follow him all his life; this success—as unlikely as it was unexpected—would awaken a reaction that was both xenophobic and anti-Semitic,[16] all because of the "arbitrary" choice of one collector, and an American to boot.

The first articles on Soutine were written by Barnes and Guillaume, his first collector and dealer, before those of Waldemar George,[17] the critic in thrall to Guillaume. The support that George gave to Soutine, however sincere, was contingent on these circumstances. Waldemar George preferred to deny him the status of a French painter, instead according him, along with Chagall, the new status of one of the great painters of the modern Jewish School.

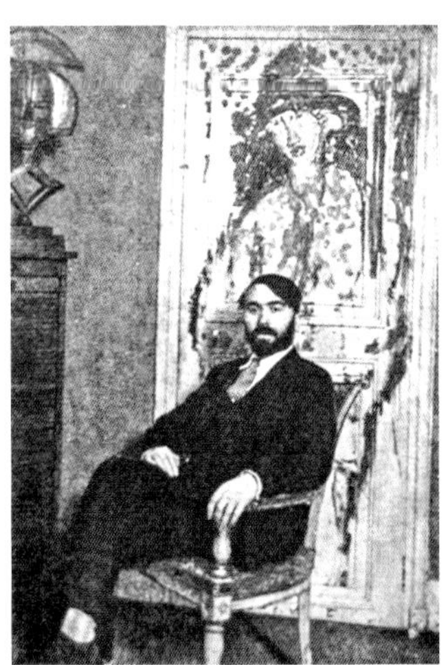

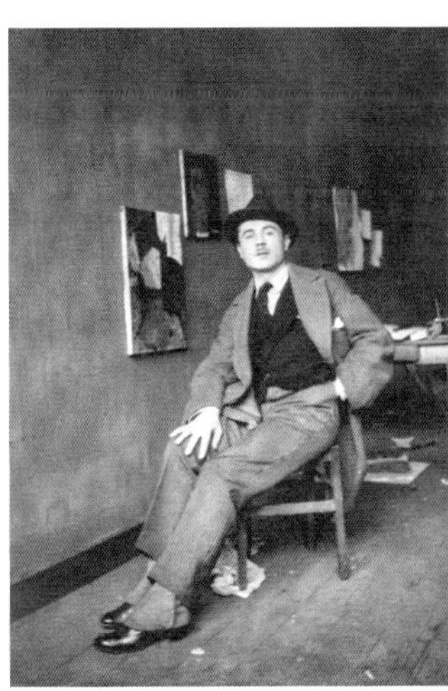

1
Léopold Zborowski, dealer of Amedeo Modigliani, in his apartment at 3, rue Joseph Bara in Paris, in front of the door with the portrait of Soutine painted by Modigliani (lower panel is lost, upper panel in Private Collection), 1918
Photographer unknown

2
Paul Guillaume in the studio he rented for Modigliani in rue Ravignan Paris, 1915
Photographer unknown

Soutine and Expressionism

It is not uncommon to find critics of the time applying such derogatory terms as "daub," "smear," "dirty rag," or "barbarian art" (which were also associated with Expressionism) to describe the painting of the artists in Montparnasse, those "Slavs disguised as representatives of French art."[18]

Expressionism had had a bad reputation in France since the First World War.[19] It was irremediably associated with Germany, to the point that people on the other side of the Rhine were convinced that it was a mark of German identity. Moreover, the few French painters who could be associated with expressionism,[20] such as Maurice de Vlaminck, Jean Fautrier, and Georges Rouault (fig. 3), were never referred to as such, but by terms like "Fauve" or realist painter.

To compare Soutine with Expressionist artists only served to marginalize him even more, associating him with the "Boche art" of the enemy of the moment. However, the impetus behind Soutine's work is not like that of the German painters of Die Brücke or of any other Expressionist. It contained no politics, no critique of urban life, no relationship between man and nature, no claimed anti-academism, no tendency toward abstraction, etc.

Waldemar George wrote in 1926 about Soutine's search for a pedigree: "Nevertheless, it seems to me necessary to lay out the civil status of a painter whose

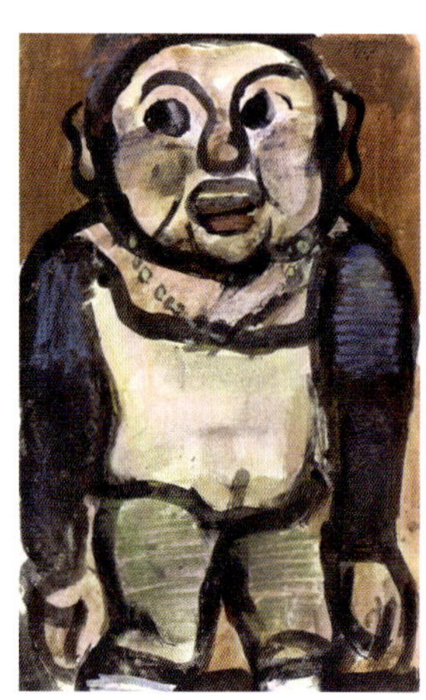

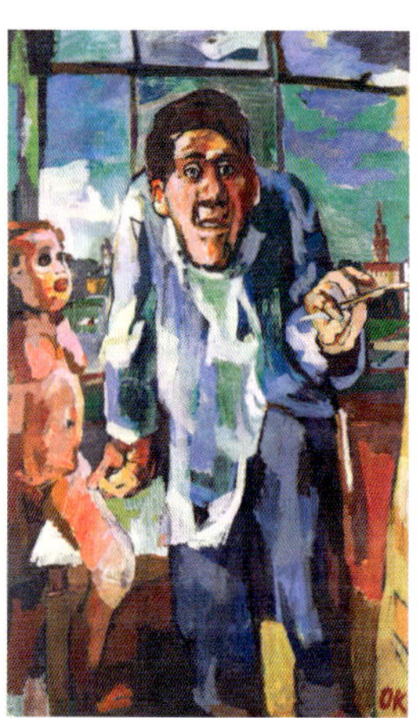

3
Georges Rouault
Grotesque, 1917
Musée d'Art moderne de Paris

4
Oskar Kokoschka
Selbstbildnis an der Staffelei, 1922
(*Self-Portrait at an Easel*)
Private Collection

work arouses the greatest interest, even if it goes against the French tradition . . . But, however broadly we define French painting, Soutine will never become a French painter. . . . Soutine owes nothing to the country in which he lives and has adopted. He does not even strive to equal the French, nor to acquire that sense of lofty and considered harmony which, to some, is the hallmark of their art. . . . Soutine's work seems to be, first of all, a symptom of the decline of intellectual art—a decline, not only of cerebral tendencies in painting, but of the intellectual himself. A Soutine painting, before being a homogeneous whole and a normally formed body, is the subjective expression of an individual, whose first concern is to externalize his latent state of mind." George continues: "And yet, despite certain apparent similarities, one cannot unfortunately establish a genuine relationship between Soutine and the German Expressionists. Expressionism is a composite phenomenon, not a style, not an artistic school, but a state of mind, codified a *posteriori*. . . . These figures, pastrycooks, first communicants, young boys and girls, are harrowing images, in which Soutine's pessimism and his penchant for dramatic distortion are much better conveyed than in the other paintings. It is here above all that he is gothic in spirit, if not in form—although he does tend to elongate the figures he paints."[21]

A trip to Berlin was even imagined to establish more convincingly this link between Soutine and Germany. That is something Soutine himself never mentioned, but one gets a clear sense that this critic, who was to veer toward fascism in the thirties, was using Soutine in support of his own discourse on decadence.

However, one comparison often made is that with the Austrian artist Oskar Kokoschka (fig. 4).[22] Waldemar George made it, of course, but so did the dealer, art connoisseur, and critic Wilhelm Uhde: "The Russian Jew Soutine also lives there, in whom I don't know what spirit, what lunacy akin to Van Gogh persists, and whose admirers detect a resemblance to Kokoschka, whom they consider inferior. But they err; Kokoschka's flamboyant baroque is one of the greatest positives in the art of today and is superior to the drunken disorder of Soutine, who, despite some pictorially beautiful results, remains purely negative."[23]

Soutine, abused by the critics who pulled no punches, never said a word. We know that—as with Jean Siméon Chardin, Gustave Courbet, Jean-Baptiste Camille Corot—Rembrandt van Rijn was his god (his only known trip was to Holland); that contemporary art did not interest him; and that he instead dreamed of the art of Classical Greece! He exhibited very little during his lifetime,[24] and one could see his work only in the collection of Paul Guillaume and at the Barnes Foundation, or else in his studio—though the man was so disconcerting that few ventured there. Nevertheless, he left no one indifferent, and he was well regarded by painters: Jean Fautrier (fig. 5), the young Jean Hélion (fig. 6), André Derain, and of course, the artists of the École de Paris.

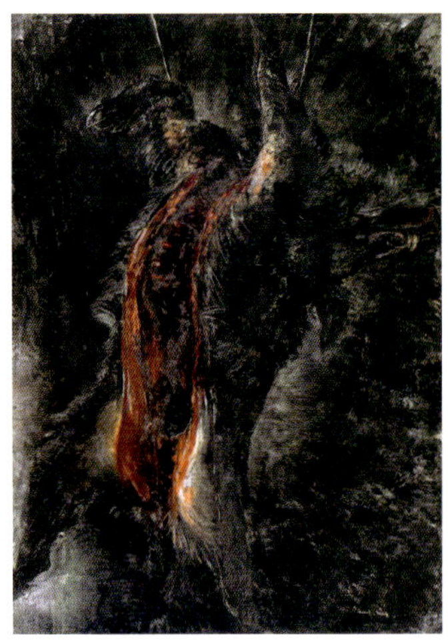

5
Jean Fautrier
Le Grand Sanglier noir, 1926
(*The Big Black Boar*)
Musée d'Art moderne de Paris

Soutine did not arouse curiosity on the German art scene, at least not during his lifetime, and this—it must be admitted—was heavily influenced by his need to survive in the interwar period. This artist was certainly unique, but he was not ambitious to renew modern art, but only to exist by means of perpetuating the masters of the past. Having been caught in the upheavals of history, he provoked a profound disgust among his contemporaries who were not used to seeing such violent visual expression. Today, in contrast, he is well on his way to becoming a benchmark artist, on a par with Francis Bacon, Willem de Kooning, and Jackson Pollock. And his life remains the stuff of novels![25]

6
Jean Hélion
L'Homme assis, 1928
(*The Seated Man*)
Galerie Alain Margaron, Paris

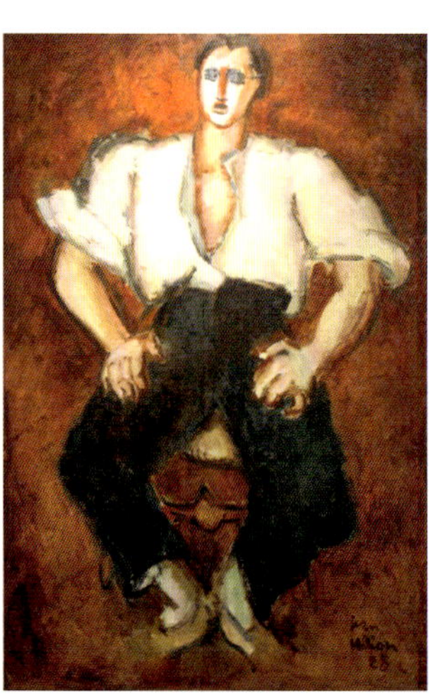

1 For example, the critics Emil Szittya, Adolphe Basler, and Waldemar George who wrote for German periodicals *Der Cicerone*, *Das Kunstblatt*, *Der Querschnitt*, etc., or German personalities connected with France, such as Ernst Cassirer, Alfred Flechtheim, and Paul Westheim, who did not support Soutine on the other side of the Rhine. He is mentioned in Karl Schwarz, *Die Juden in der Kunst* [The Jews in Art] (Vienna: Löwit, 1936), but it was not until the article by Ernst-Gerhard Güse in 1981 that Soutine was really noticed in Germany: see the English edition of Güse's essay, "Death and Destruction in the Work of Chaim Soutine," in C. *Soutine: 1893–1943*, ed. Ernst-Gerhard Güse, exh. cat. Westfälisches Landesmuseum, Münster 1981/82; Kunsthalle Tübingen 1982; Hayward Gallery, London (Arts Council of Great Britain) 1982; Kunstmuseum Luzern, Lucerne 1982 (London: Arts Council of Great Britain, 1982).

2 Soutine lived destitute for nine years before enjoying twenty years of success and patronage. However, his death in 1943 from an untreated gastric ulcer, after more than two years in hiding during the German occupation of France, placed him squarely among the Jewish painters who fell victim to the Holocaust and have attained a status as martyrs.

3 Modigliani, on his deathbed, is said to have told their art dealer, Léopold Zborowski, that he had nothing to fear as Soutine was a "great artist."

4 Many French painters, veterans of the salons, were jealous of the success of foreign artists and the place they occupied on the Parisian art scene.

5 Roger Allard, "Le Salon des indépendants," *La Revue française*, February 17, 1924.

6 Roger Allard "Les Beaux-arts: Le Salon des indépendants," *La Revue universelle*, March 1, 1923.

7 André Warnod, *Les Berceaux de la jeune peinture: Montmartre-Montparnasse* (Paris: Albin Michel, 1925).

8 Barnes was also interested in Jacques Lipchitz, Maurice Utrillo, and Henri Rousseau (known as Le Douanier Rousseau, "the customs officer").

9 Waldemar George, "Un Musée-école d'art moderne aux États-Unis: La Fondation Barnes," in *L'Amour de l'art* (January 1923): "The museum of the Barnes Foundation represents the most beautiful homage paid in America to French art, of which it is the temple. At the next pilgrimage of university youths from across the Atlantic, it will reveal to them the highest expressions of our artistic genius. It will make the citizens of the United States understand that the strength of France, its universality, lies in the works produced by its artists."

10 There are several versions of Barnes's arrival on the scene. One is told by Paul Guillaume, who seems to have taken responsibility for the happy discovery himself. Another favors Zborowski. In both cases, Barnes met the artist personally, thus perhaps showing that he himself made his choice; and in *My Life in Sculpture* (1972), Lipchitz reports that it was he, along with Kisling and Pascin, who introduced Soutine to Barnes.

11 Letter from Maurice Loutreuil to Irène Champigny, February 1926, in *Maurice Loutreuil: L'Insoumis, 1885–1925*, exh. cat. Musée de Tessé and Abbaye de l'Épau, Le Mans 2006; Musée d'Art moderne de Céret 2006/07 (Paris: Somogy, 2006).

12 Paul Guillaume, "Soutine," *Les Arts à Paris* (January 1923): pp. 5–6. Guillaume and Barnes had already known each other for a few years and shared a passion for African sculpture.

13 Marcel Hiver, "Hello, Boys, Cheer Up! Monsieur Barnes est dans nos murs," *Montparnasse*, July 1, 1923, pp. 5–7: "A couplet about the painter [Soutine], off of whom the hustlers are trying to make a buck," and how Paul Guillaume has made himself "the shrewd mahout of this golden mammoth . . . to walk him through the studios of artists."

14 See Camille Mauclair, *La Farce de l'art vivant*, La Vie d'aujourd'hui 4 (Paris: La Nouvelle revue critique, 1929) and Camille Mauclair, *Les Métèques contre l'art français*, La Vie d'aujourd'hui 15 (Paris: La Nouvelle revue critique, 1930).

15 Adolf Loos, who arrived in France in 1924, was also attacked in the French press, notably by Louis Vauxcelles.

16 Louis Vauxcelles, "La Querelle des étrangers," *L'Ère nouvelle*, November 29, 1923: "No, I repeat, it is not a question here of men, of artists esteemed, respected by all, whose names I have already printed, living in France for a long time, who are assimilated, incorporated, and belong almost to the French School, like their glorious elders Sisley and Pissarro. . . . By contrast, when I learn that Monsieur Soutine (whom I do not know, and by whom I have seen nothing but bad paintings) represents the school of contemporary painting at the Barnes Foundation, and that Jean Marchand, for example, has been ousted to make room for him, I feel—if the fact is correct—that Monsieur Soutine and his associates are making a painful blunder."

17 Waldemar George wrote the catalog of Guillaume's collection: *La Grande Peinture contemporaine à la collection Paul Guillaume*, (Paris: Arts à Paris, [1929]).

18 To use the words of Louis Vauxcelles: *L'Ère nouvelle*, November 23, 1923.

19 Laurence Bertrand Dorléac, "L'Expressionnisme en point aveugle de l'histoire de l'art," in *Après la guerre* (Paris: Gallimard, 2010), pp. 137–155.

20 André Lhote, review of *L'Expressionnisme français*, Galerie Alice Manteau, in *La Nouvelle revue française* (December 1928): pp. 880–883.

21 Waldemar George, "Soutine," *L'Amour de l'art*, February 1926.

22 Oskar Kokoschka exhibited in Paris on March 18, 1931, at the Galerie Georges Petit.

23 Wilhelm Uhde, *Picasso et la tradition française: Notes sur la peinture actuelle* (Paris: Quatre Chemins, 1928), pp. 80–82. Uhde wrote an apologia for Jews in the artistic field as the only ones capable of establishing a European spirit; and it is against his claims that Camille Mauclair wrote the anti-Semitic pamphlets mentioned earlier.

24 In Paris, his work was shown in 1927 at the Galerie Samuel Bing and in 1937 at the exhibition *Les Maîtres de l'art independent* at the Petit Palais.

25 Ralph Dutli, *Soutine's Last Journey,* trans. Katharina Rout (Chicago: University of Chicago Press, 2019).

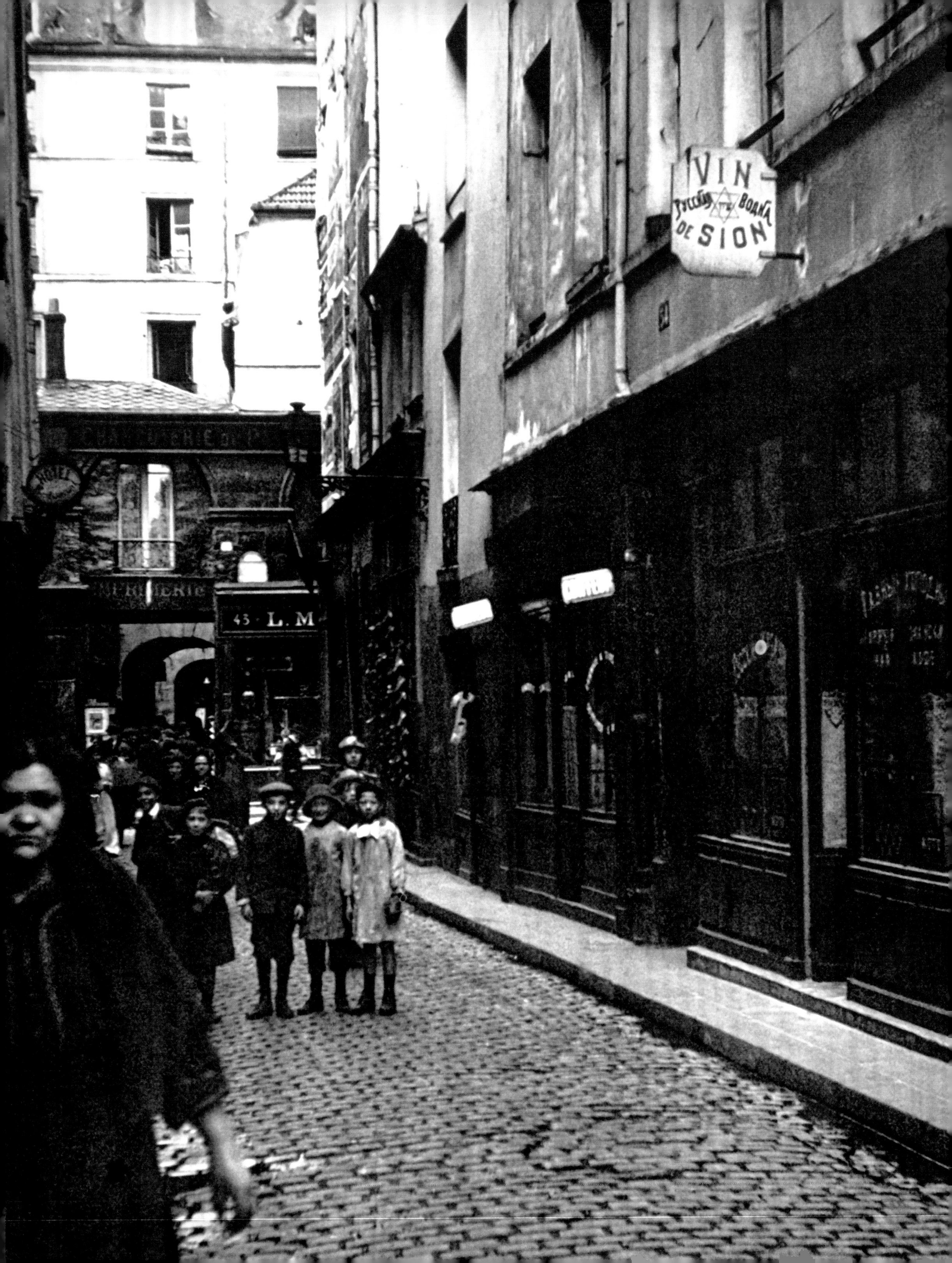

VIN
DE SION
43 L. M.

In Art's "Big Bowl of Soup"— Soutine's Legacy

Claire Bernardi

"Everything is already in art—like a big bowl of soup
Everything is in there already:
And you just stick your hand in, and find something for you.
But it was already there—like a stew."[1]

Willem de Kooning, 1959

A street in Pletzl with a shop sign advertising "Vin de Sion"
Paris, ca. 1920
Projections Molteni
Musée d'Art et d'histoire du Judaïsme, Paris

It has been a long process for Soutine's work to find its place in the history of painting. Indeed, it is his singularity that catches the eye at first. Not that critics are put off by that; from the outset his work has had fervent defenders, whose impassioned texts balance the virulent criticism that exhibitions have provoked.[2] His first commentators set the tone: by emphasizing the link between the painter's remarkable fate—his rapid assignment to the ranks of ill-fated, tortured artists, like Van Gogh before him or his fellow "peintres maudits" of the École de Paris (School of Paris)—and the tormented, expressionist character of his art, they made Soutine into both an exemplary figure and an unclassifiable painter. Because of its very originality, his work did not lend itself to tracing the breadth of its impact on the creations of other artists.

133

Perhaps it is this difficulty of definition that has opened his work to constant reinterpretation, and therefore constant examination. Until late in the first half of the twentieth century, Chaïm Soutine was sometimes considered a "primitive," a painter without roots, whose torment is at the origin of his genius, and who is sometimes seen as the worthy heir of a certain French tradition drawing from the painting of the Masters—of Jean Siméon Chardin or Gustave Courbet. Ultimately, it was as a true prophet of a new expressive abstraction that he was celebrated in postwar New York.[3] As we shall see, this radical turn in the reception of the artist's work is the result of an equally radical paradigm shift within the international art scene: for many artists and critics of the fifties, this figurative painter, adept at painting with a thick impasto and a form of existential expressionism, became an "unwitting abstract painter." That which, in his painting, could have condemned him to obscurity and oblivion, far from the great narrative of modernity, was to place him temporarily at its center.

In the postwar years, Soutine's work was widely accessible—to the general public, as well as to a generation of artists, in both Europe and the United States—through group exhibitions centering on what was then called the École de Paris, and also through monographic shows.[4] Although this may be seen as a misrepresentation of the very essence of his art, this exposure of his work enabled several generations of artists to discover it and find inspiration in it—from Francis Bacon and Willem de Kooning to Georg Baselitz today, a true kinship emerges.

In 1950, less than a decade after Soutine's death, New York's Museum of Modern Art (MoMA), a temple of modernity, dedicated a retrospective to him. The same curators and critics who at that moment were defending the new generation of New York painters were clearly trying to establish a link between contemporary art practice and prewar European painting. This attempt was double-edged: it was as much a matter of making the Abstract Expressionists the heirs of a certain pictorial tradition as it was of proposing an abstract re-reading of the great masters of figurative modernism, and in particular Henri Matisse, Pierre Bonnard, and Soutine.[5] The MoMA exhibition—by re-reading Soutine's work in terms of a linear art history, which would reach its apotheosis in abstraction, an autonomy of the medium, pictorial gesture, and two-dimensionality—made him a visionary, a pioneer of this new painting that was trying to define itself around a term: "Abstract Expressionism."[6]

But it is the artists themselves who have the most subtle and, perhaps, most accurate reading of Soutine's work: if they attempt to find in the work of their predecessor a presage, or even a legitimization, of their own painting, then they stress particularly the great freedom in the gesture, the very act of painting. The painter and art critic Jack Tworkov, in reviewing the exhibition for *ARTnews*, thus compares "certain attitudes toward paint" expressed in Soutine's compositions, which appear in common with those of Abstract Expressionists "like de Kooning and perhaps Pollock."[7]

Tworkov, who was close to Willem de Kooning—they shared a studio at the time—knew how fascinated de Kooning was by anecdotes about Soutine's particular working methods, which he recounted several times in his interviews.[8] De Kooning recognized his own practice in the way Soutine applied paint— Soutine's very physical relationship with his canvas and colors has always been emphasized by his biographers—and also the set of gestures and rituals that accompanied his work, which could be described as "gestural expressionism." So, Soutine's singular way of treating his canvases would have reinforced the idea, common to this rising generation of New York painters, that their reason for painting lay not just in the result of their work but in the very event that constitutes the creative process itself.

For de Kooning, resonances of Soutine's work are particularly detectable in the early fifties, a period that constituted a turning point in his artistic practice. It was then that he set about his major series of *Women* (fig. 1), those monumental female figures, primitive idols with bodies abused by the artist's brushstrokes. We have already shown in a previous exhibition and the accompanying catalog how Soutine's work constituted a real touchstone in Willem de Kooning's research into plasticity, helping him to free himself from the bipolarity between figuration and abstraction that had gradually crystallized in the postwar years.[9] He appreciates in the painter's work the fact that "Soutine distorted the pictures

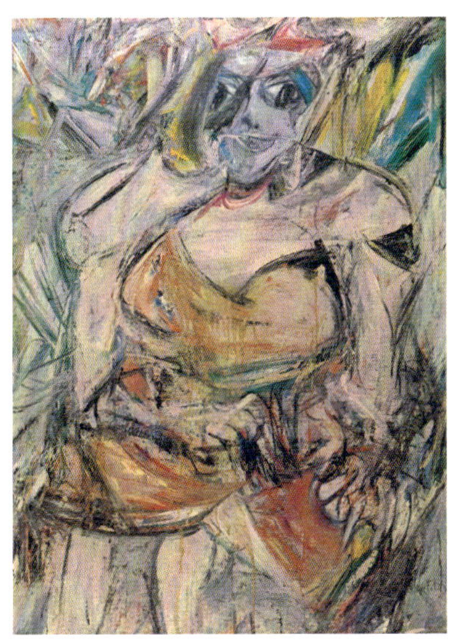

1
Willem de Kooning
Woman, II, 1952
The Museum of Modern Art, New York

but not the people. . . . If you would speak of distortions: for some mysterious reason he never distorted the people. Only the painting. You can somehow see the people. You know everything about the bellboy. . . . The painting is the painting, but he never destroyed the people."[10]

Deforming the pictures but not the people—is this not, in a nutshell, what Soutine's expressionism and the new expressive painting of the postwar period have in common, a painting that finds its balance in a relationship with the figure that is both free and intimate? British art critic David Sylvester was not mistaken when he was the first to see how Soutine's work could lead certain artists toward a sort of third, middle way between figuration and abstraction.[11] Because he studied both the works of de Kooning and his British compatriot Francis Bacon, and met them personally, Sylvester is the first to point out, on the one hand, their common obsession for a style of painting that escapes the dichotomy abstraction/figuration,[12] and on the other hand, how both borrowed from a common *Soutinian* vocabulary.

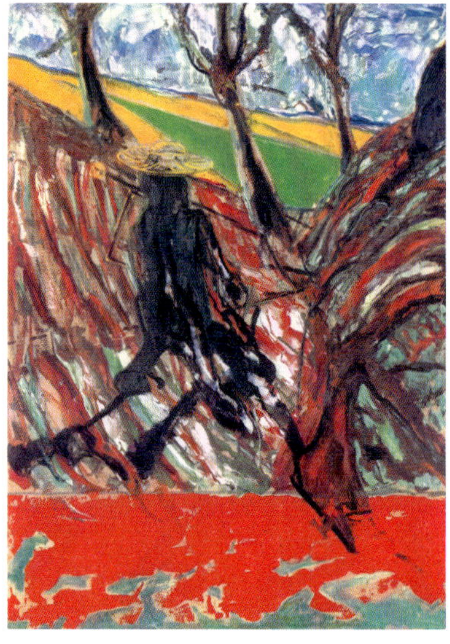

In the same way as we do for de Kooning, we know quite well the conditions in which Bacon had access to Soutine's paintings and the extent to which they may have influenced his work. In the fifties, Bacon often expressed his deep admiration for Soutine's way of painting.[13] It was the Soutine of the Céret period that first influenced his work; around 1953, Bacon suggested that Sylvester go with him to see the several Soutine canvases of this period that were then on display at the Redfern Gallery in London. Soutine's impact may be seen in Bacon's work of 1956/57—as he had on de Kooning in 1951. The series of paintings Bacon executed after a reproduction of Van Gogh's *The Painter on the Road to Tarascon* is, paradoxically, one of his first works in which we see the influence of Soutine. If we consider the 1957 *Study for Portrait of Van Gogh VI* (fig. 2), the vigorous and free brushstrokes and the luminous harmonies are close to Soutine's own manner.

But it was in the sixties that Soutine's impact on Bacon was most pronounced, and his work was revisited in light of the latter's own concerns. Thus, it is above all for his painting of the figure as living flesh, torn open, that Bacon takes up the Soutinian heritage. In *Three Studies for a Crucifixion* of 1962, (fig. 3), the human body in the central panel of this triptych seems to be seen from within, exposed as living flesh, similar to the carcass of the right side panel, which is strangely faithful to Soutine's *Side of Beef* (ca. 1922/23; fig. 4). Soutine's impact is thus experienced in Bacon's painting as a lesson in butchery, allowing him to express in all its pictorial violence a painting of the figure that asserts its presence as nothing less than living flesh.

When the German painter Georg Baselitz (fig. 5), then a student in Berlin, hitch-hiked in 1960 to Amsterdam to see Soutine's monumental *Beef* (ca. 1925) at the Stedelijk Museum, had he not come to confront the same lesson in butchery that had fascinated his elder, Bacon? Had he not come face to face with a singular painting that fascinated him, despite or because of his unwavering attachment to the figural, and whose filial connection he accepted—like Bacon or de Kooning before him?

This painter of the inverted, upside-down figure, of the shaken, wounded body, with his proclivity "for impasto, *alla prima*, expressive painting" which led the young man to make "Soutine and de Kooning [his] heroes," as he himself recently affirmed.[14] Bringing "painting experienced as a living, corporal presence" to its paroxysm,[15] Baselitz carries even further the fight against the tyranny of the disembodied image.

3
Francis Bacon
Three Studies for a Crucifixion, 1962
The Solomon R. Guggenheim Museum, New York

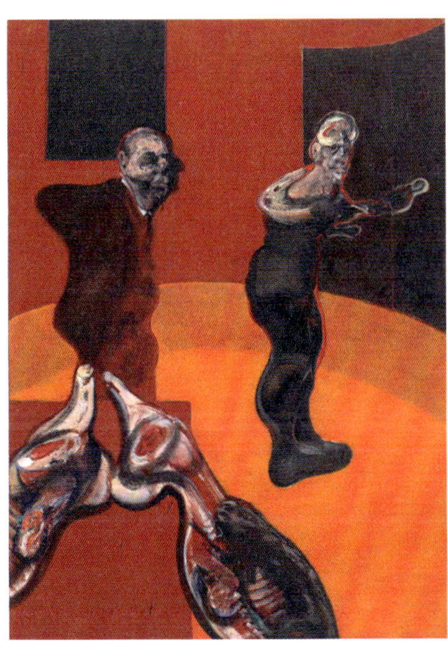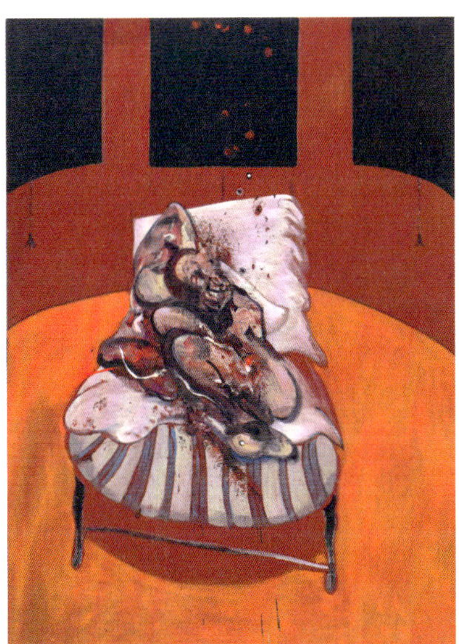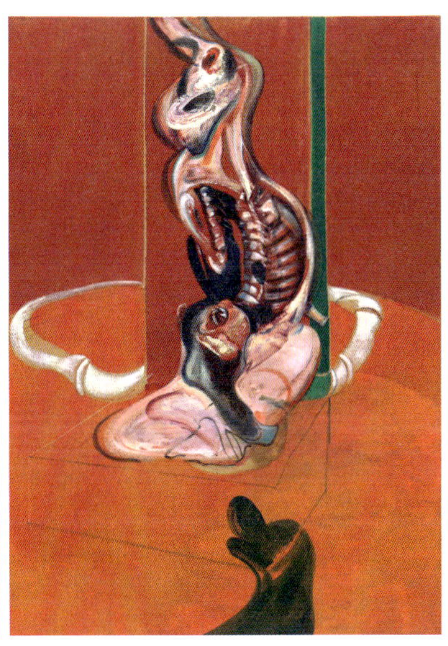

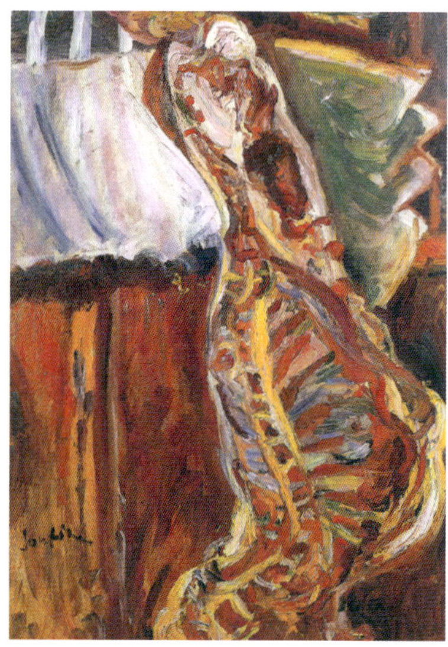

4
Pièce de bœuf, ca. 1922/23
(*Side of Beef*)
Private Collection

These painters, each of immense singularity, often considered unclassifiable, have in a way asserted their own genealogy: that of the "knacker-painters" (in Pierre Wat's striking formulation—*peintres équarrisseurs*),[16] artists playing with the brush as one would with a knife, maltreating the figure as they maltreat the medium.

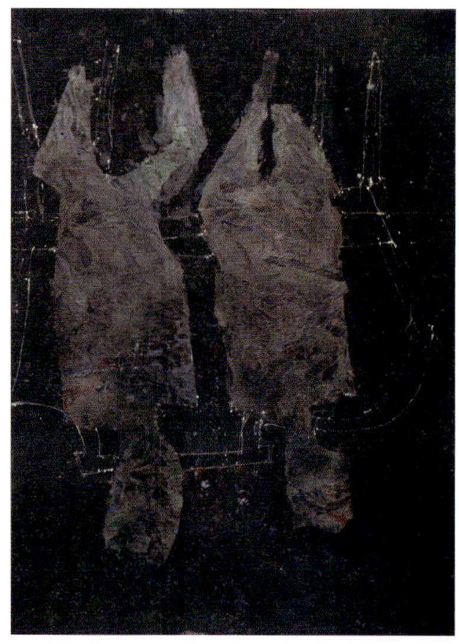

5
Georg Baselitz
Einer sieht dieses, der andere jenes, 2016
(*One Sees This, the Other That*)
Sprengel Museum Hannover,
On loan from the Warwick Collection

1 Willem de Kooning, "Inner Monologue," a conversation between de Kooning, Michael Sonnabend, and Kenneth Snelson, unpublished transcription by Marie-Anne Sichère, 1959, featured in *Sketchbook No. 1: Three Americans*, film by Robert Snyder, 1960, republished in *The Collected Writings of Willem de Kooning*, ed. George Scrivani (Madras and New York: Hanuman, 1988), p. 174; published in full, in French translation, in *Willem de Kooning: Écrits et propos*, ed. Marie-Anne Sichère (Paris: École nationale supérieure des Beaux-Arts, 1992), p. 50.

2 On this subject, see Sophie Krebs's contribution in *Soutine*, ed. Marc Restellini, exh. cat. Pinacothèque de Paris, 2007/08 (Paris: Pinacothèque de Paris, 2007): "Soutine lends himself to the excesses of writing, pompous, lyrical, and baroque, to bloody metaphors and morbid analogies."

3 These different layers of reading were taken as keys to the analysis of Soutine's work for the retrospective exhibition at the Jewish Museum, New York, and for its catalog: Norman L. Kleeblatt and Kenneth E. Silver, *An Expressionist in Paris: The Paintings of Chaim Soutine*, exh. cat. Jewish Museum, New York 1998; Los Angeles County Museum of Art 1998/99; Cincinnati Art Museum 1999 (Munich: Prestel, 1998).

4 See the preface to Maurice Tuchman and Esti Dunow, *The Impact of Chaim Soutine, 1893–1943: De Kooning, Pollock, Dubuffet, Bacon*, exh. cat. Galerie Gmurzynska, Cologne 2001 (Ostfildern-Ruit: Hatje Cantz, 2001).

5 This re-reading was as much the work of critics as of the artists themselves. On this, see Éric de Chassey, *La Peinture efficace: Une histoire de l'abstraction aux États-Unis (1910–1960)* (Paris: Gallimard, 2001), p. 171.

6 Here, the author relies on her previous research, in particular on two essays: Claire Bernardi, "Soutine et sa deuxième postérité," in *Chaïm Soutine: L'Ordre du chaos*, ed. Marie-Paule Vial and Claire Bernardi, exh. cat. Musée de l'Orangerie, Paris 2012/13 (Paris: Hazan, 2012), pp. 50–61; and Claire Bernardi, "De Kooning's Soutines: A Brief History of a Pictorial Encounter," in *Soutine/de Kooning: Conversations in Paint*, ed. Claire Bernardi and Simonetta Fraquelli, exh. cat. Barnes Foundation, Philadelphia 2021; Musée de l'Orangerie, Paris 2021/22 (London: Paul Hoberton, 2021), pp. 5–16.

7 Jack Tworkov, "The Wandering Soutine," *ARTnews*, November 1950, p. 32.

8 See Willem de Kooning, quoted in Diane Waldman, *Willem de Kooning in East Hampton* (New York: Solomon R. Guggenheim Museum, 1978), p. 21; cf. *Willem de Kooning: Écrits et propos*, pp. 261–262.

9 See *Soutine/de Kooning: Conversations in Paint* and *Soutine/de Kooning: La Peinture incarnée*, ed. Claire Bernardi and Simonetta Fraquelli, exh. cat. Barnes Foundation, Philadelphia 2021; Musée de l'Orangerie, Paris 2021/22 (Paris: Hazan, 2021).

10 Willem de Kooning, quoted in *The Impact of Chaim Soutine*, p. 102.

11 Sylvester suggests a direct influence of Soutine on de Kooning in his article "Americans Abroad," *New York Times*, April 12, 1959, p. 17. This affiliation was to be confirmed by the artist himself, when the two met in New York: David Sylvester, "Meeting de Kooning," *Modern Painters* (Winter 1997): p. 114.

12 Francis Bacon said that he wanted to produce images that are "a kind of tightrope walk between what is called figurative painting and abstraction," in an interview from 1962, in David Sylvester, *Interviews with Francis Bacon, 1962–1979* (London: Thames and Hudson, 1980), p. 12.

13 David Sylvester, *Looking Back at Francis Bacon* (London: Thames and Hudson, 2000), pp. 87–88.

14 Georg Baselitz, *art press*, no. 492 (October 2021), in an interview published at the time of the *Soutine/de Kooning* exhibition at the Musée de l'Orangerie.

15 Philippe Dagen, "Georg Baselitz, la peinture corps-à-corps," *La Boussole indique le Nord*, exh. cat. Galerie Thaddaeus Ropac, Paris Pantin 2023 (Paris: Thaddaeus Ropac, 2023), p. 15.

16 Pierre Wat, "Entrer dans l'histoire: Willem de Kooning, ou le plaisir d'être influencé," in *Soutine/de Kooning: La Peinture incarnée*, p. 49.

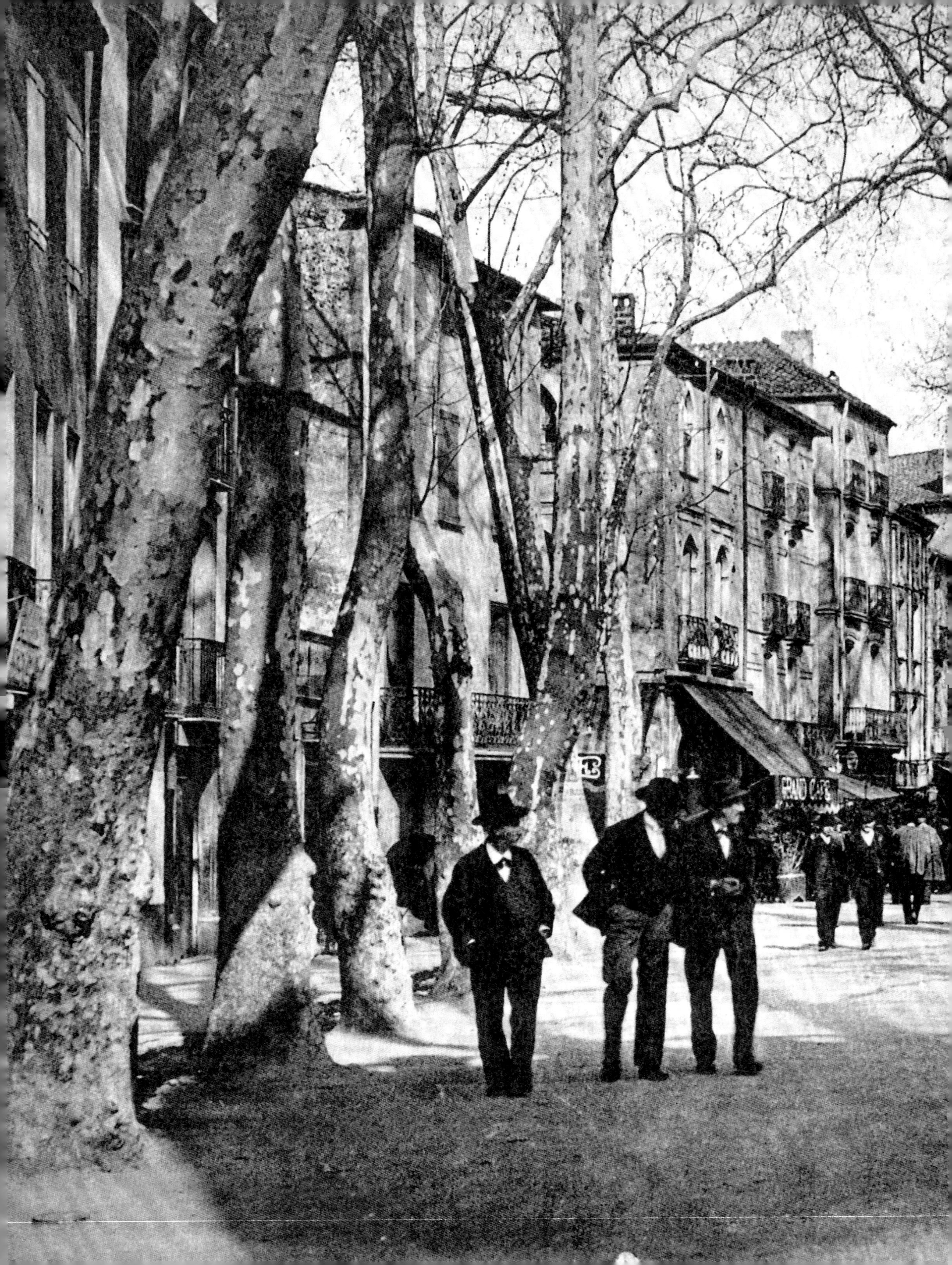
GRAND CAFÉ

The Fury of a Brushstroke

Marta Dziewańska

"You know what I am . . . I'm an expressionist . . . but I'm still aware of what reality is. Now who is that wonderful painter that does the *Side of Beef* and dead ducks? . . . Soutine . . . Now Soutine, I think he's a better artist than I am. But he is in the grip of his art. For instance, he does a landscape, the whole thing is falling downhill. It's mad, you know . . . well, I don't do a completely realistic thing. It has expressionist moments in it. But at the same time it's not that pure expressionism like Soutine does. I *love* what he does. He can't help himself, you know. He's completely taken over by his art."[1]

Alice Neel, 1984

Boulevard Saint-Roch in Céret, Roussillon, not dated
Musée national Picasso, Paris
Photo: Labouche Frères
phototypistes à Toulouse

As the subject of this text, if only partially, I would like to make Chaïm Soutine's swirling, "falling" and "mad" landscapes mentioned by Alice Neel in a fascinating interview from 1984. Before moving on to them, however, let me—following Neel herself—capture a few elements these two artists seem to have in common: artists who never met, who belong to completely different worlds, traditions, and contexts, while their sensibilities and chronologies were governed by radically different laws. What does this American painter and activist for women's and minority rights actually see in Chaïm Soutine's paintings? And can her brief statement about him be a way to grasp the risks taken by his work?

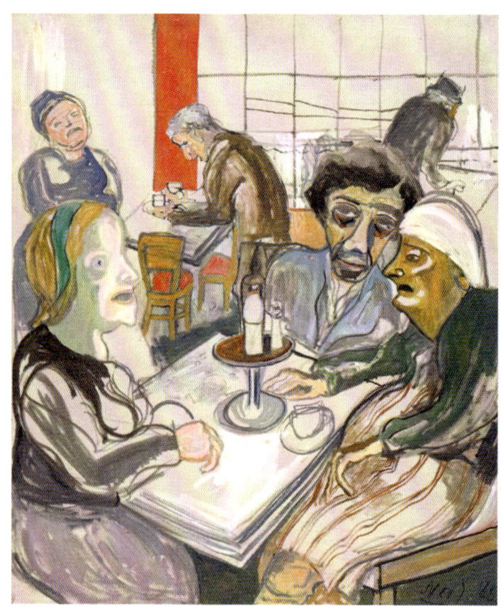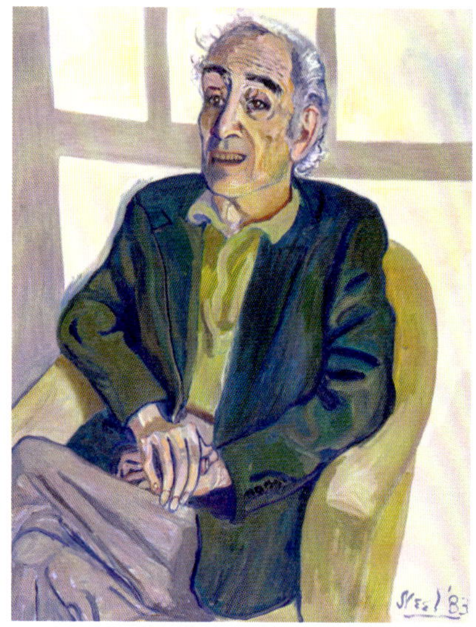

A major figure in North American art, Alice Neel (1900–1984) never stopped painting the marginalized throughout her life. "In politics," she once stated, "and in life I always liked the losers, the underdog."[2] A women in the male mainstream, she began by showing injustices and social conflicts. With a style that borders on expressionism and a somewhat naïve realism, she depicted segregation, isolation, as well as political protests in the streets. In Neel's portraits there are indeed many women represented without any idealization. They are shown with a frankness that was surprising at the time. But there are also many Black and mixed-race people, Jews, homosexuals, and transvestites. Friends. Relatives. Neighbors. People called upon in the street. Most often strangers. She said that she painted "the neurotic, the mad and the miserable."[3] She depicted without sensationalism the New York of minorities, of people who are victims or survivors of injustice, sexism, violence, racism, and capitalism (figs. 1 and 2). Her images are intense; she worked quickly, in only two or three sessions. Her touch remains visible as if she were seeking immediacy; in the seventies, this sort of painting would be called a "painting of urgency." The result aims at a frontal shock of the spectator—a shock tempered, however, by the visible empathy with the sitters. What is really striking is that the artist seems to be looking at things from the inside. She is definitely not a talker.

But what did she mean when she said that Soutine is "in the grip of his art"? Is Neel thinking about his highly intense portraiture, painted with strong gestural brushstrokes and filled with profound and palpable emotion? About his propensity to inject his own feeling into the subjects and figures of his paintings through radical deformations and, even more, through distortions of the space? Indeed, the American feminist states that Soutine's landscapes look as if they were *madly* "falling downhill." By saying this is she pointing at the intriguing tension palpable in his paintings between realism and expressionism, between the outside and the inside? In what sense, as she says, "can't [he] help himself" and is he "completely taken over by his art"? Is this a way to describe his art's sense of urgency—a brand so different from her own?

Dramatic atmosphere, insolent contrasts, sensual paste, these are what made the art critic Clement Greenberg (1909–1994) write in 1951 that Chaïm Soutine "was one of the most painterly painters there ever were."[4] But what is it that he painted as the abstract revolution was in full swing and while Surrealism was being invented? Nothing but dead animals, ordinary views of Paris, and rather banal self-portraits. Then, in the South of France, in Céret, where he settled in 1919 thanks to Modigliani's young dealer, Léopold Zborowski: floral bouquets, scenes of the countryside, and portraits of common people. However, all of these pictures are dominated by some basic distortion that is difficult to define.

It is important to underline that Soutine could not do without a model—he needed to be in front of his painting's subject. He "had to have the thing he was painting," writes David Sylvester, "out there in front of him. He couldn't invent. He couldn't paint from memory, even the memory of a motif he had worked from day after day. He couldn't paint from drawings or from photographs or from an earlier painting of the same subject. He had to have the real thing there."[5] It seems that he wanted to be, and was, a realist painter incapable of recreating his subjects from memory or imagination. In the same way that he painted his landscapes (always *en plein air*, "waiting for the wind" to agitate the leaves) or when he painted from Old Masters (he never worked directly from another artist's paintings but rather had to recreate the image in actuality, to work from life)[6]—Soutine needed present models to paint his figures. With a few exceptions, his portraits are anonymous and their titles designate them only as human types—*Woman in Red*, *The Old Actress*, *Village Idiot*—as social or professional types—*The Little Pastrycook*, *The Gypsy*—or simply pointing out a detail of dress or the color of clothing. The titles say as little as possible; he omits anything that might suggest an anecdote or a story.

His models were most often brought to him—by friends or by accident, on the street, in the village, in the corner bar—he needed to be surprised by them. And even if he authored many admirable portraits of eccentric or distinguished women, his favorite models—in a way comparable to those of Alice Neel—remain the servants, the beings of the common herd bound to a state, to a trade. What did he see in them? Like Soutine himself, they were young, living apart from their families, unsure of themselves, apprenticed to their craft. Why did they pose? Was it to find themselves, for once, at the center of someone's gaze? There is something intriguing about the relationship between a model and a painter: What if the pastry boy decided not to return? What if the chambermaid rejected the pose? Or the bellhop fell ill? Jeanine Warnod records a statement by Soutine when he said that he preferred "to paint a landscape than portraits. A model gets tired quickly and looks stupid so I have to hurry and I get angry. I grind my teeth, sometimes I start screaming . . . It's silly, I get the willies, when it's over, I'm exhausted like a woman who just gave birth. Eventually, it took him hours to recover and even talk after painting."[7] His woozily contoured, intimate, and borderline visceral portraits of random people force an oxymoron: empathetic caricatures seeming at once to mock and to cherish hapless humanity.

So, Soutine was working directly from nature. He was also known to draw very little and would attack his subject matter directly in his painting—no preparatory exercises, no mediation. However, it would be unfair to say that his art is immediate and spontaneous alone. We know that Soutine had his models pose for a very long time, waiting for them to tire, for his own gaze to become clearer, for the veils of habit and familiarity to fall away. Only then could he consider the person as if he or she were an *object* and then try to restore the individual particularities through expressive deformations. The testimonies provided by Soutine's models mention very stressful sessions where—by superimposing layers and strokes, walking around the models and cursing changes in the angles of light or becoming impatient with the models' own impatience (as we know, these also included children)—he worked under the greatest pressure.[8]

The same may be said about his landscapes. He waited for the right light, for the wind to blow, sometimes many hours. In one of his letters to a friend, Zborowski described Soutine's routine in Céret where the artist stayed between 1919 and 1922 thus: "He gets up at three in the morning, and walks twenty kilometres with his paints and canvas to find a site that pleases him, and at night returns to his sty to sleep, quite forgetting that he had nothing to eat. When he gets back, he takes the canvas out of the frame, puts it on top of the one he did the day before, and goes to sleep beside it."[9] It is as if he were in a constant search, simultaneously receiving sensations and projecting them onto his canvases. These two "almost antithetical timeframes," writes Sophie Krebs, are communicating not only what is seen and what is felt, but also *the urgency of its realization in paint*. Additionally, they seem to be "responsible for the destruction of works by the artist himself, who was continually dissatisfied with the results."[10] Not only did he regularly burn or rip up those paintings of which he said he was displeased and refused to attend the openings of his exhibitions (which were, in any case, few), but he also kept on buying back his own paintings in order to rework them (his outbursts of rage when someone refused to give him their property were infamous).

Could we then posit that, whatever the motive, the painter insufflates in the colored matter the impulses and the tensions of his own, ever unsettled, psychic energy? Let us then return to his landscapes, in which, as Alice Neel says, "the whole thing is falling downhill" (fig. 3). In 1918, with Paris under threat of German invasion, Soutine went to the Côte d'Azur, and in 1919, as we have said, he moved to Céret, near the Spanish border, and spent much of the next three years travelling in the South of France. At first, he was dazzled by the beauty of the light and nature there, but soon he was overcome by boredom and loneliness. His production at this time was very abundant (he later destroyed a large number of his works) and his inclination to inject his own affectivity into the subjects and figures of his paintings reached a sort of a climax.

Indeed, after distorting human figures, in Céret he additionally began to deform the surrounding spaces. It is as if he were painting both: what he saw and, at the same time, the internal energies, hidden under a very thin layer and ready to explode. The frenetic forms of the landscape and its structures seem to yield to the dynamics of internal pressures, which compress, twist, raise, and fall. In *View of Cagnes (La Gaude and the Baous)* (1922/23; see [29]), for instance, the town looks as if it were engulfed in a large, speedily rolling ball. In this avalanche of trees, hills, houses, and earth, one can see a human figure: out of scale, somehow incidental, a figure that seems to be flattened upon the ground rather than walking or even standing. In other paintings of the same motif, the figure is absent—as if it were already carried away, already buried under the pile of stones. The tumultuous off-balanced frenzy projected onto the canvas by Soutine becomes suffocating and sometimes leads to a complete saturation of the space. This is the case in *Landscape at Céret* (ca. 1920/21; see [16]), which may be considered an extremity of Soutine's oeuvre; it reaches the threshold beyond which the work tips into chaos. Or into abstraction.[11]

How are we to read these paintings in which the motif has almost entirely disappeared? The paintings in which swirling brushstrokes, thick pigments, and colored rhythms alone assume the expressive function? What does their dynamism, instability, and semi-visceral quality actually mean? Does Soutine really have the ability to look under the skin and peep at intimate energies, those of his models but also those pulsing in the cities and landscapes he observes? Or perhaps he is trying to capture his subjects with the whole mesh of their entanglements and dependencies? As if he could see their hidden fears, hopes, and desires. Or subterranean, pulsating sources, the hidden roots silently digging their way and the first rustlings of future avalanches? Maybe this is what he cannot stop seeing and the reason why his images are constantly pulsating, swaying, sliding, tumbling into one abyss or another? Or rather, is he constantly trying to give plastic expression to the ghosts tormenting him? Or both at the same time?

"What is the meaning of this art," asks Waldemar George, "whose origins are impossible to trace, which knows no law, no country, no principal directives, which is tied to no tradition? Is it the art of exiles or of Barbarians? I challenge anyone to discover Soutine's filiations."[12] It is interesting to note at this point that even in

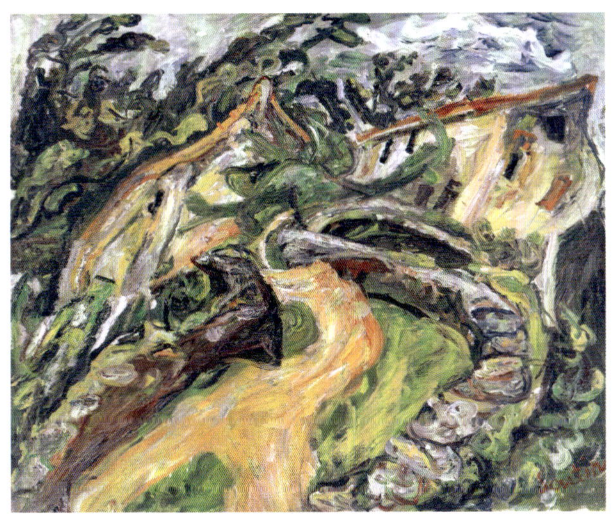

3
Mas à Céret (La Route montante), 1921
(*Mas to Céret [The Uphill Road]*)
Museum Sammlung Rosengart, Lucerne

Paris, where he arrived in 1913, after the trawl from the familial shtetl in Smilaviču, via Minsk and Vilnius, it was difficult for Soutine to settle down. He had many addresses. He left the storied La Ruche for the Cité Falguière, where he shared the studio of the sculptor Oscar Miestchaninoff, who had also come from what is now Belarus, and then that of Amedeo Modigliani, with whom he developed an intense friendship over the course of five years. In the thirties, Soutine was photographed in the studio of Chana Orloff, his neighbor at the Villa Seurat in Paris (fig. 4). His appearance is neat. He smiles. He is confident. But here, as well, he changed apartments regularly as if unable to get a foothold anywhere and only a few years later this Parisian life would be brutally destroyed by the war. Chaïm Soutine, a stateless man, was registered in October 1940 as a Russian refugee and was later listed in the registers of the Bureau des Affaires juives (Bureau of Jewish Affairs) under the number 35702. From then on, he was liable to be arrested at any moment and so embarked on a semi-clandestine life.

It is interesting to look at Soutine's paintings (portraits?) of trees within this context. He painted them throughout his career (cf. fig. 5). In Céret, he created many canvases of plane trees lined up in the square. When painting them he focused on their trunks to which he gave somewhat anthropomorphic silhouettes or the forms of flames twisting toward the sky. In *Landscape with Large Tree* (1920), it runs diagonally across the entire space of the picture as if it were caught, sucked in by an irresistible force that pulls it toward the upper right corner of the painting. It has neither a clear top nor a fixed bottom, no axis, no weight, no support.[13] . . . It is a tree reminiscent of a disheveled creature moved by every wind, without stability, rootless. Could Soutine's oeuvre be looked at as his continuous—tormented—self-portrait? Probably yes, but that would certainly be a reductive reading.

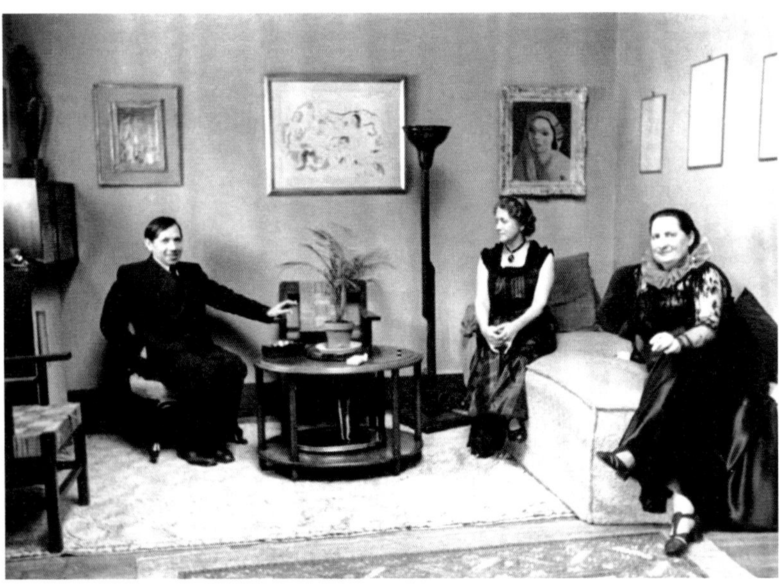

4
Chaïm Soutine, Olga Sacharoff, and Chana Orloff
Villa Seurat, Paris, ca. 1938
Musée d'Art et d'histoire du Judaïsme, Paris

Famously, Willem de Kooning once commented on Soutine portraits, saying that he "distorted the pictures but not the people."[14] What could that mean, and is it yet another contradiction in Soutine himself? I pointed multiple times at the emotional, borderline visceral intensity of his oeuvre and the ways in which he transcends his subjects not only by distorting them but also by exaggerating their parts, colors, or confusing forms. The real question is to know how it is possible that even if he were adding layers and colors, it feels as if, to the contrary, he were stripping his subjects of all their covering: of protective skin, of equilibrium, of gravity, of any rootedness. What is more *real* in this case? Clearly defined, self-contained, and classically painted stable figures or those pierced with fear, raging with furious color, or completely lost in a horizon that does not hold the level? Soutine's subjects—be they people, trees, (dead) animals, flowers, or entire landscapes—are *historical* and cannot be stabilized in any way. They escape either in their dreams or fantasies, or in memories and thoughts that keep on returning like an obsession. It is impossible to draw their clear contours and, as such, they appear on a shaky border between realism and abstraction, presence and projection, somewhere between their concreteness and this impossibility to hold the current of life, of constant mutation and change.

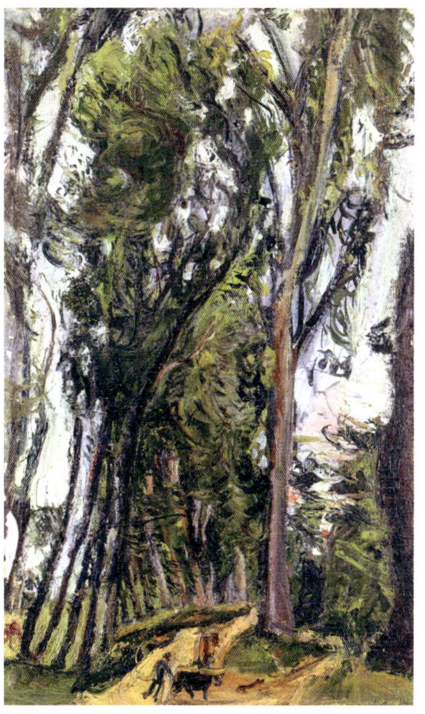

La Route des grands prés à Chartres, ca. 1935
(*Avenue of Trees at Chartres*)
Musée des Beaux-Arts de Chartres

To paint such dynamics, Soutine seems to be constantly measuring himself against the very medium of painting, which he loves. It is the medium itself that is, on the one hand, at the source of his artistic choices and his distinctive style; but, on the other hand, it is the main cause for the failure of his artistic enterprise. Indeed, the images that Soutine wished to paint cannot be painted. Clement Greenberg complained that Soutine's work was "more like life itself than like visual art."[15] Indeed, Soutine's best paintings convey nothing so much as a desperate exasperation with "visual art." And it seems that this is exactly what causes this multilayered explosion both on and *of* the canvas. "He can't help himself," says Alice Neel, "he's completely taken over by his art." Crisis after crisis, he tries to correct them, rejects them, destroys them. In this exact sense, Chaïm Soutine is an artist that prefigures not only expressionism but also leans in the direction of contemporary art. His wild and unstable paintings seem to point toward performance art, with its use of movement to express movement.

And what is that movement that escapes him? "You couldn't see him work," Chana Orloff noted.[16] "He was never happy with a painting he did, and the honesty of this painter is absolutely incredible. He would cut the painting he had done the day before into pieces, put them on the floor, and I would say to him, 'but how can you judge it since it is in pieces.' He would say, 'Oh, I know very well, I have to add something here,' and then, in small pieces, a foot or a hand, he would incorporate, he would glue it all back together. He would glue them onto another canvas. In any case, the real Soutines are all cut into pieces." It seems as if the world that Soutine sees is constantly falling into ruin, passing on irretrievably and, in his paintings, he already expects this passing, anticipates the collapse. It is worth noting that among his crotchets was an aversion to bare canvas: "He preferred to work over old paintings that he acquired cheaply from antique dealers and flea markets."[17] In his paintings, whether they were portraits, landscapes, or still lives, he tried to capture this dynamic of deterioration and loss. At the same time, he himself was part of such dynamics—a force that made him paint more and more new representations of the same subjects, the same streets and hills. It is all as if he were trying to paint them better or ostentatiously show that these *cannot* be painted. This is what prompted him to destroy his paintings again and again. Then he reassembled them, gluing them together: from previous waste, new wholes. Élie Faure convincingly described Soutine's impossible task: "To restore the matter in its palpitating depths, to rectify little by little this formal anarchy which gives to its fabric an aspect of chaos . . . monstrous faces, boiled, dented with bruises, gullied with holes, crooked houses as if crumpled by the storm, landscapes that seem to be painted during an earthquake, a world thrown without apparent order on the canvas but so rich and flamboyant that a great hope rises up from it, as from a newborn baby slimy with vernix and blood."[18] Is that really what Soutine is hiding under all these heavy and so nervously applied layers? Is that what gives his paintings, as Faure wrote, "a profound heat"?

In the narrower perspective of his own biography, one could say that no matter what Soutine was painting, he seemed to be constantly trying to capture his own unsettled, ever wandering condition. The condition of an eternal migrant, pariah, and stranger. Was this kind of painting of chaos within chaos so admired by Alice Neel? Or rather, was she impressed by the way Soutine's anxiety-ridden perspective on the world was translated into the emotional turmoil of his oeuvre? Or maybe how he was able to observe and capture the human circus parading in front of his eyes? And is it not precisely this unsettling psychological chaos that moves in Chaïm Soutine today? This remains an open question.

1   Alice Neel in a video interview with Marc H. Miller, Curator, Queens Museum, 1984.

2   Alice Neel, quoted in Henry Geldzahler, *Alice Neel in Spanish Harlem*, exh. cat. Dia Center for the Arts, Bridgehampton, NY 1991; Linda Cathcart Gallery, Santa Monica 1991/92 (Bridgehampton, NY: Dia Center for the Arts, 1991), p. 6.

3   Alice Neel in *The Hasty Papers: A One-Shot Review*, ed. Alfred Leslie (New York, 1960), p. 50.

4   Clement Greenberg, "Chaim Soutine," *Partisan Review* 18, no. 1 (January–February 1951), reprinted in *Clement Greenberg: The Collected Essays and Criticism*, ed. John O'Brian, vol. 3, *Affirmations and Refusals, 1950–1956* (Chicago: University of Chicago Press, 1986), pp. 72–78, here p. 73.

5   David Sylvester, introduction to *Chaim Soutine*, exh. cat. Edinburgh International Festival 1963; Tate Gallery, London 1963 (London: Arts Council of Great Britain, 1963), p. 4; a slightly revised version, "The Mysteries of Nature within the Mysteries of Paint," for the 1981/82 exhibitions in Münster and London, is reprinted in David Sylvester, *About Modern Art: Critical Essays 1948–2000*, rev. ed. (London: Pimlico, 2002), pp. 110–131.

6   Cf. Esti Dunow, "A 'Painter's Painter,'" in *The New Landscape, the New Still Life: Soutine and Modern Art*, by Maurice Tuchman and Esti Dunow, exh. cat. (New York: Cheim & Read, 2006), n.p.

7   Jeanine Warnod in *Chaïm Soutine*, film by Murielle Levy and Valérie Firla (Paris: Les Productions du Golem; Montpellier: France3 Sud; Paris: Réunion des Musées Nationaux, 2007.

8   See the recollections described in *Chaïm Soutine*, film by Levy and Firla.

9   Léopold Zborowski, quoted in Michel Georges-Michel, *From Renoir to Picasso: Artists in Action* (1954), trans. Dorothy Weaver and Randolph Weaver (Boston: Houghton Mifflin, 1957), p. 148.

10   Sophie Krebs, "Soutine – A Case Apart," in *Soutine und die Moderne / Soutine and Modernism*, exh. cat. Kunstmuseum Basel 2008 (Cologne: DuMont, 2008), pp. 39–62, here p. 54; cf. Esti Dunow, "The Late Works: Regression or Resolution?" in *An Expressionist in Paris: The Paintings of Chaim Soutine*, by Norman L. Kleeblatt and Kenneth E. Silver, exh. cat. Jewish Museum, New York 1998; Los Angeles County Museum of Art 1998/99; Cincinnati Art Museum 1999 (Munich: Prestel, 1998), pp. 136–149, here p. 138, and Dunow "A 'Painter's Painter,'" n.p.

11   Cf. Manuel Jover, "Matières sensibles," *Connaissance des Arts*, SFPA, special issue, no. 341 (2007).

12   Waldemar George, *Soutine*, Artistes juifs (Paris: Éditions Le Triangle, 1928), quoted in Sophie Krebs, "Soutine – A Case Apart," p. 49.

13   Cf. Jover, "Matières sensibles."

14   Willem de Kooning, quoted in *The Impact of Chaim Soutine, 1893–1943: De Kooning, Pollock, Dubuffet, Bacon*, by Maurice Tuchman and Esti Dunow, exh. cat. Galerie Gmurzynska, Cologne 2001 (Ostfildern-Ruit: Hatje Cantz, 2002), p. 54.

15   Clement Greenberg, "Soutine," in *Art and Culture: Critical Essay* (Boston: Beacon, 1961), pp. 115–119, here p. 115.

16   Chana Orloff, quoted in *Chaïm Soutine*, film by Levy and Firla.

17   Peter Schjeldahl, "The Vulnerable Ferocity of Chaim Soutine," *New Yorker*, May 7, 2018, https://www.newyorker.com/magazine/2018/05/14/the-vulnerable-ferocity-of-chaim-soutine.

18   Élie Faure, *Soutine* (Paris: Éditions G. Crès et Cie, 1929), p. 127.

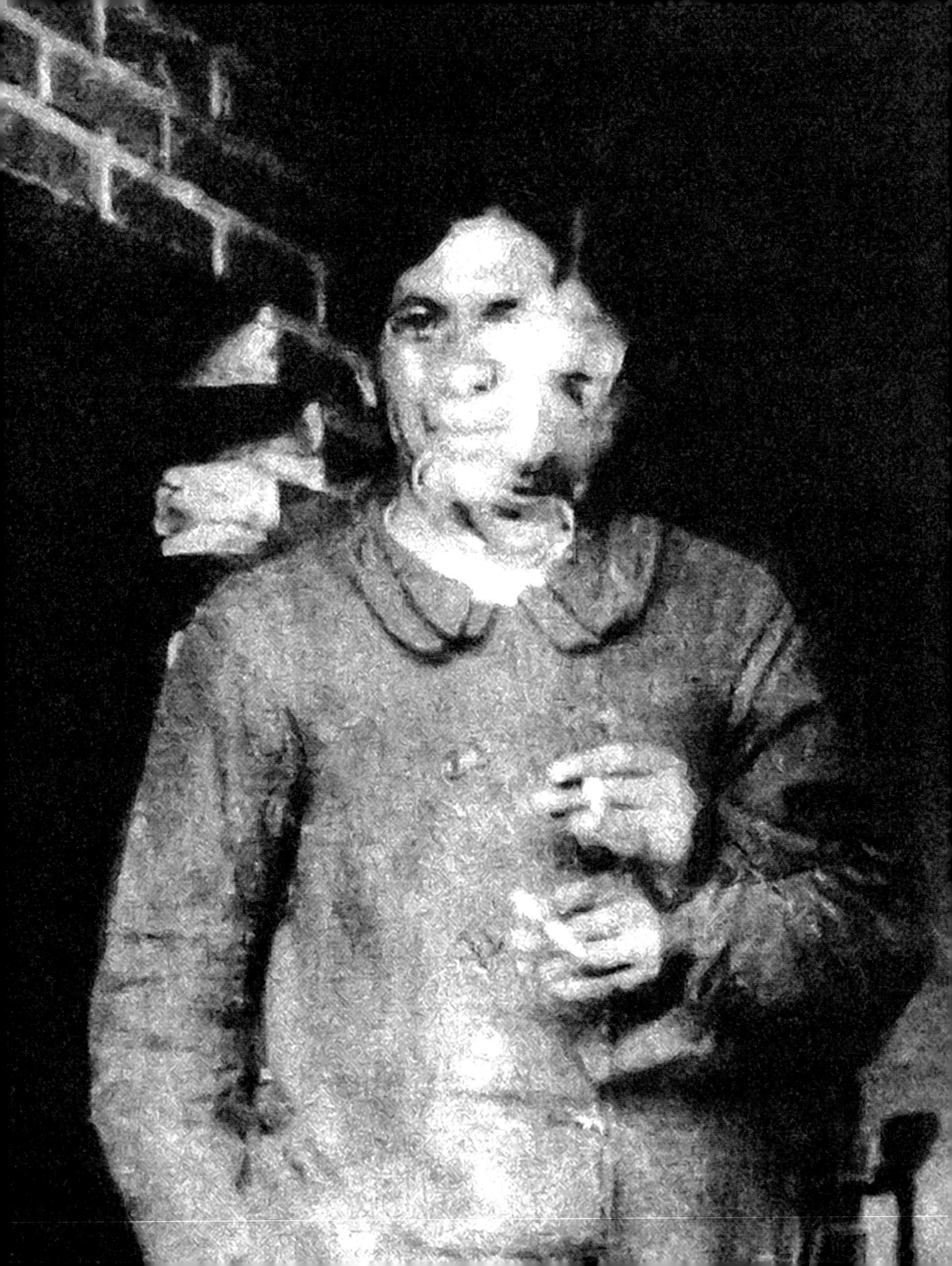

Biography

Catherine Frèrejean

1893

Chaïm Soutine is born in Smilaviçy, a small town of about four thousand inhabitants[1] near Minsk (then within the Russian Empire). Until the Russian Revolution of 1917, Smilaviçy belongs to Lithuanian territory of present-day Belarus. A shtetl (Yiddish for "small town"), Smilaviçy has a large Jewish population and is one of many settlements in Eastern Europe before the Second World War. Daily life there is characterized by existential hardships.

Soutine's first language is Yiddish, and his knowledge of Russian is rudimentary. He attends a Jewish school focused on the Talmud and grows up in a deeply religious and insular environment. The prohibition of pictorial representation, especially the depiction of people, is among the rules of Orthodox Judaism. In Smilaviçy, however, the folk art of anonymous craftsmen, carpenters, and woodcarvers is tolerated.[2] His father, Salomon, is a cobbler and wants his son to learn a trade as well. But Soutine instead decides to devote himself to painting.

In France, Alfred Dreyfus (1859–1935), a French army officer from a Jewish family in Alsace, is tried for treason in 1894. Despite his innocence, he is sentenced to life imprisonment in an offshore penal colony. The so-called Dreyfus Affair is a central event in the history of anti-Semitism in France.

Soutine in front of a gutted brick wall
Le Blanc, 1927
Photographer unknown

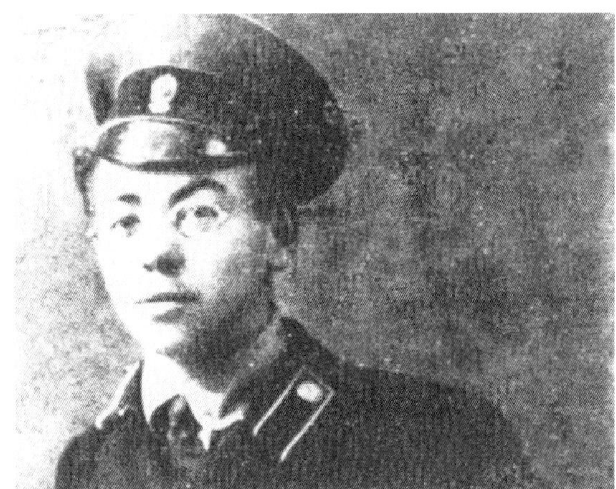

Michel Kikoïne as an art student, not dated
Photographer unknown

1903–1906

Despite his parents' misgivings, Soutine travels to Minsk to take art lessons. There, he meets Mikhail Kikóin, known as Michel Kikoïne (1892–1968), with whom he will share a lifelong friendship. Soutine works as a retoucher for a photographer.

In Russia, the first pogroms of the twentieth century claim some two thousand lives. The Kishinev massacre in 1903 (in what is now Chișinău, the capital of Moldova) leads to protests by artists and writers.

Also in 1903, the Salon d'Automne (also known as the Société du Salon d'Automne) is founded in Paris by avant-garde artists rejected by the jury of the official Salon.

In 1906, Alfred Dreyfus is exonerated and rehabilitated.

In 1908, Georges Braque (1882–1963) and Pablo Picasso (1881–1973) create the first Cubist works.

1910

Soutine paints the portrait of an Orthodox Jew in violation of the strict prohibition against the creation of images. He is badly beaten by the sons of the man he had depicted. Soutine's parents lodge charges against the assailants and receive financial restitution.

With this money, Soutine moves to Vilnius to enroll in the Academy of Fine Arts. He is joined by Kikoïne. Soutine is impressed by the dynamism and tolerance of the cosmopolitan university city. He befriends the painter Pinchus Krémègne (Pinhas Kremen; 1890–1981), who moves to Paris shortly thereafter.

1913

Thanks to the financial support of a private patron, Soutine is able to travel with Kikoïne to Paris, the artistic capital of Europe at the time. On June 9, he registers with the police prefecture of the French metropolis.

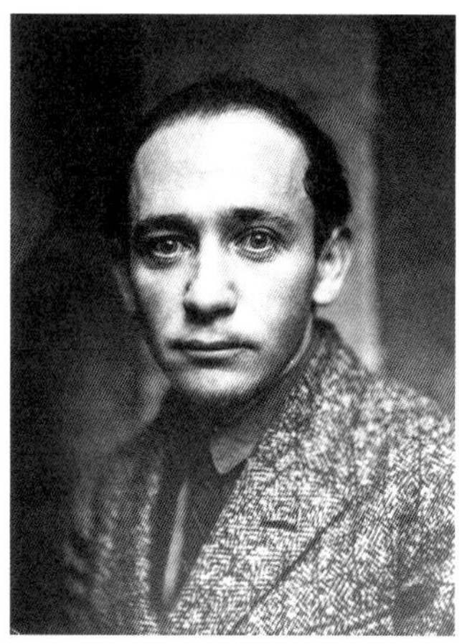

Portrait of Pinchus Krémègne,
Paris, beginning of the 20th century
Musée d'Art et d'histoire du Judaïsme, Paris

His first point of call is La Ruche ("The Beehive"), an artists' colony in the Montparnasse district. The studio complex is a three-story rotunda originally built by Gustave Eiffel (1832–1923) for the 1900 Paris Exposition. In 1902, the sculptor Alfred Boucher (1850–1934) transformed the edifice into living quarters and studios for artists. Among those who live and work here are Amedeo Modigliani (1884–1920), Marc Chagall (1887–1985), Jacques Lipchitz (1891–1973), Ossip Zadkine (1888–1967), Fernand Léger (1881–1955), and Pinchus Krémègne, who takes in Soutine.

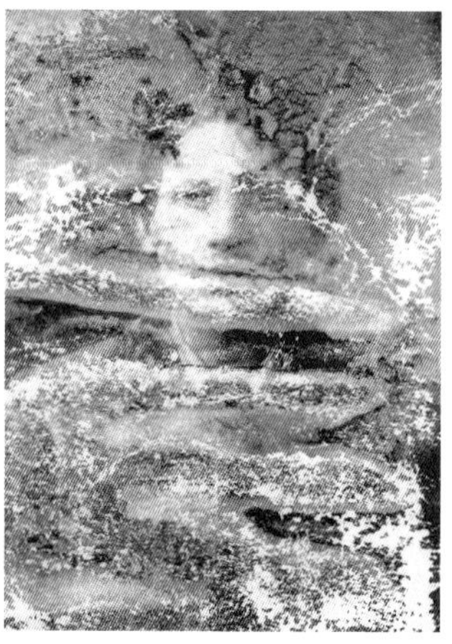

Identification photo of Soutine, ca. 1913
Photo: Archives de la Préfecture de Police de Paris

Kikoïne later remembers: *"On July 14, at four o'clock in the morning, the two of us were sitting on the pavement in front of the Opera . . . and Soutine seemed spellbound; everything delighted him: the square, the sculptures of this building, the décor, and the singing . . . and he declared that we would be truly inept if we could not achieve something in a city like Paris."*[3]

Soutine's beginnings in Paris are marked by hunger, cold, illness, and utter destitution. Already at this time, he suffers from stomach troubles. He takes on a series of odd jobs, working as, among other things, a bag carrier and a decorator at the Paris Motor Show at the Grand Palais.

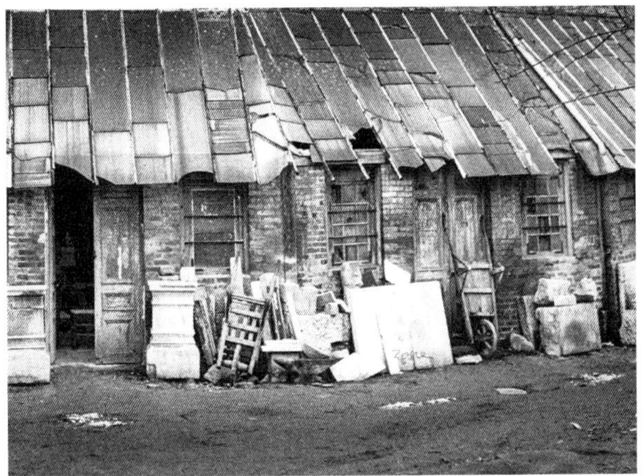

La Ruche, Paris, ca. 1968
Musée d'Art et d'histoire du Judaïsme, Paris
Photo: Walter Limot

In the summer of 1913, he enrolls at the École des Beaux-Arts de Paris and spends two years in the studio of the painter Fernand Cormon (1845–1924), who had previously taught Vincent van Gogh (1853–1890) and Henri de Toulouse-Lautrec (1864–1901).

Soutine is besotted by the openness of the metropolis; he is particularly impressed by the collections of the Louvre, especially by the works of Rembrandt van Rijn (1606–1669), Jean Fouquet (1420–1477/1481), Jean Siméon Chardin (1699–1779), Jean-Baptiste Camille Corot (1796–1875), and Gustave Courbet (1819–1877). Despite his difficulties with the French language, he also becomes enthusiastic about the poetry of Charles Baudelaire (1821–1867).

"Jacques Lipchitz recalls having met Soutine leaving the Louvre one Sunday afternoon. Soutine approached Lipchitz enthusiastically, brandishing a reproduction which he had bought in the museum. 'Here,' he said, 'is the greatest painting in the Louvre.' Lipchitz looked at the painting: it was Fouquet's Portrait of Charles VII.*"4*

1914

At the same time that the German Empire declares war on France, Soutine is granted a residence permit in the Saint-Lambert district on August 4. His status as a Russian immigrant allows him to avoid mobilization. Soutine and Kikoïne enlist as volunteers in the French army; however, due to his stomach problems, Soutine is quickly discharged. Like Picasso, Modigliani, and other foreign artists, he remains in Paris while artists and writers such as Léger, Braque, André Derain (1880–1954), and Guillaume Apollinaire (1880–1918) fight at the front.

Soutine moves to the Cité Falguière, yet another artists' residence in the 15th arrondissement, and shares a studio with the sculptor Oscar Miestchaninoff (1886–1956).

In France, after the outbreak of the First World War, the Parisian collections of the gallerists Wilhelm Uhde (1874–1947) and Daniel-Henry Kahnweiler (1884–1979) are confiscated as so-called "enemy assets."

On August 30, the first German air raid on Paris takes place.

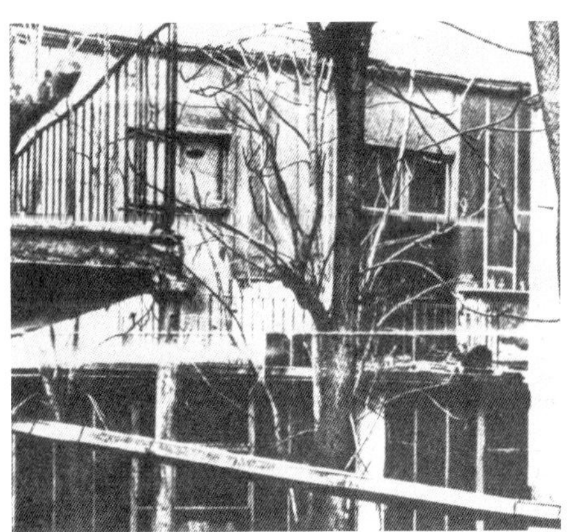

Cité Falguière, Paris, not dated
Photo: Archives Jacques Mauves

1915

Jacques Lipchitz introduces Soutine to Modigliani, who also lives in the Cité Falguière. Their Jewish origins and status as foreigners, as well as their various maladies, unite the two artists, who become close friends. Over the next five years, Modigliani paints four portraits of Soutine.

1916

During this period, Soutine mainly paints still lifes, of which, however, only a few have survived.

Modigliani, just recently represented by Léopold Zborowski (1889–1932), often takes Soutine to lunch at the gallerist's apartment. It is on one such occasion that the portrait on the door panel is painted (fig. 1, p. 127). Modigliani persuades the art dealer to take on Soutine as well, of whom Zborowski is initially not impressed. For the exclusive rights to his works, the latter offers him the meagre sum of five francs per day.

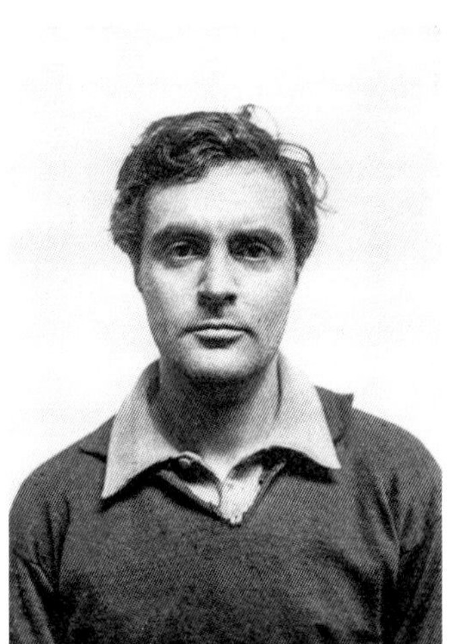

Portrait of Amedeo Modigliani, Paris,
beginning of the 20th century
Musée d'Art et d'histoire du Judaïsme, Paris
Photo: Marc Vaux

1918

In March, German forces bomb Paris. On Zborowski's recommendation, Soutine travels to the South of France together with Modigliani. Their stay in Vence and Cagnes-sur-Mer, on the Côte d'Azur, allows them to escape the wartime climate in the capital. Nevertheless, the atmosphere is still tense for foreigners, and Soutine is accused of making anti-French statements.

In this year, Zborowski sells works by Soutine to the Swedish collector Jonas Netter (1867–1946).

On November 11, the armistice is signed by Ferdinand Foch and Matthias Erzberger in a railway carriage in the Forest of Compiègne. It goes into effect immediately.

In the First World War, forty million people die and twenty million are wounded.

Apollinaire dies of the Spanish flu.

1919

Zborowski sends Soutine to paint in Céret, a small commune in the Pyrenees near the Spanish border and made famous by the Cubists Braque and Picasso. Over the next three years, Soutine paints mainly landscapes and several portraits of the few townspeople who sit for him.

Among the works created here are *Village Idiot* and *The Pastry Chef (Baker Boy)*.

In the fall, Soutine paints still lifes of flowers and the series of *Gladiolas*. However, life in the small town proves difficult, especially because of the Catalan dialect prevalent there. He travels frequently to Paris and Cagnes-sur-Mer.

On June 28, the Treaty of Versailles is signed in the Hall of Mirrors at the Palace of Versailles. The treaty sets down the terms of peace and the obligations required of the newly founded Weimar Republic as a defeated nation.

On November 16, the election of the French Chamber of Deputies takes place. The Bloc national, a coalition of right-wing and centrist parties, wins. It becomes known as the "Chambre bleu horizon" after the color of the uniforms worn by French servicemen in the First World War.

Following the First World War, the European art movement *Retour à l'ordre* (Return to Order) takes form, characterized by a predilection for classicism and a nationalist, conservative attitude. It seeks to respond to the traumas and destruction faced by postwar societies. Even avant-garde artists are attracted to the movement.

Tristan Tzara (1896–1963) launches Dada in Paris and maintains contact with Richard Huelsenbeck (1892–1974), Raoul Hausmann (1886–1971), Johannes Baader (1875–1955), and later Kurt Schwitters (1887–1948). The Bauhaus is founded in Weimar.

1920

During a stay in Cagnes, Soutine learns of the death in late January of his friend Modigliani. The news comes as a great shock to him.

In the summer, Léopold and Anna Zborowski visit Soutine in Céret, together with their employee, Paulette Jourdain (1904–1997). Beginning at the age of fourteen, the girl was one of Modigliani's favorite models, and she also sits for Soutine.

Soutine produces numerous landscape paintings with tilting lines and distorted forms.

The art dealer Léopold Zborowski later recounts: *"I paid him a monthly stipend for two years, without his giving me anything in return. When I finally went to stir him up about it, I found three hundred paintings piled one on top of the other in his wretched hole, which stank to heaven because he never opened the window for fear of 'damaging the canvases.' While I was out getting some food for him he set fire to them, giving as his excuse that he wasn't satisfied with them. However, I managed to save a few, but only after a knock-down fight with him."* [5]

The First International Dada Fair is held in Berlin. The *Dada Almanac* is published with texts by Tzara, André Breton (1896–1966), Francis Picabia (1879–1953), Philippe Soupault (1897–1990), and others.

The *Salon Dada, Exposition Internationale,* is held in Paris with, among others, Max Ernst (1891–1976), the first German artist to participate after the war.

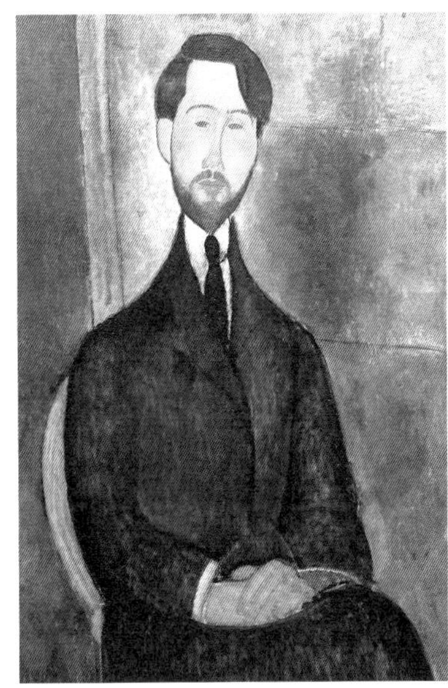

Amedeo Modigliani, *Léopold Zborowski*, 1916

1921

Soutine works on a series of old men in prayer.

Walter Gropius (1883–1969) corresponds with the journal *L'Esprit nouveau*, which, along with *Cahiers d'art*, founded later, becomes an important organ for the Bauhaus, new design, and the German abstract avant-garde.

1922

Soutine returns to Paris from Céret at the end of the year with more than two hundred canvases, many of which he destroys over the next few years. In the winter of 1922/23, his life takes a radical turn. The American millionaire and art collector Albert C. Barnes (1872–1951) is in Paris looking for suitable artworks for a collection he aims to establish in Merion, a suburb of Philadelphia. There are several variations on the story of how Barnes became aware of Soutine. In one, he happens to see Soutine's work *The Pastry Chef (Baker Boy)* in a café in Montparnasse. He is thrilled by it and purchases it along with fifty-one other paintings by Soutine from the artist's gallerist, Zborowski, at prices ranging from $15 to $30 apiece. In another variation, Barnes's agent, the art dealer Paul Guillaume (1891–1934), shows him *The Pastry Chef (Baker Boy)*, which he himself had purchased earlier.

155

The extraordinary story of Soutine's sale of numerous works to Barnes quickly spreads throughout Paris.

Max Ernst moves to Paris. The poet Paul Éluard (1895–1952) lends him his passport so that he can cross the border. He paints *Au rendez-vous des amis* (*Rendezvous of Friends*), depicting himself together with his Surrealist and Dadaist peers.

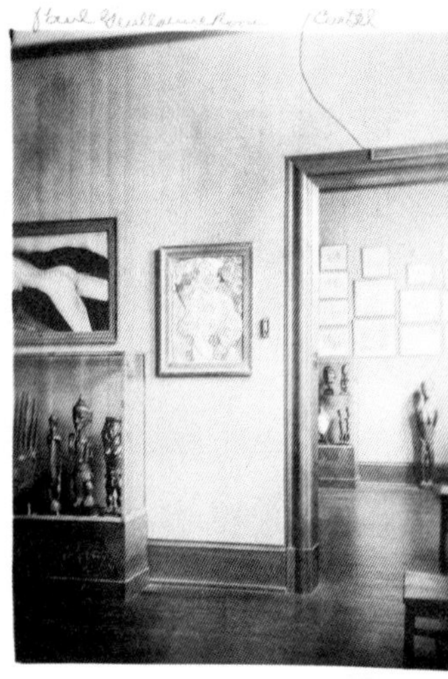

Entrance to the Paul Guillaume Gallery in the Barnes Foundation, Merion, Pennsylvania, not dated
Musée de l'Orangerie, Paris, Jean Walter and Paul Guillaume Collection, photo: Archives Alain Bouret / Dominique Couto

1923

In January, the first article about Soutine appears in *Les Arts à Paris*, a magazine founded by Guillaume in 1918.

On Zborowski's advice, Soutine returns again to Cagnes-sur-Mer, where he paints two more portraits of pastrycooks. He also produces numerous landscapes paintings, which, with their rounded, closed forms, reveal a certain amount of change from those created in Céret. Nevertheless, Soutine is increasingly unhappy in the South of France and writes to his gallerist, "It's the first time I haven't been able to do anything. I'm in a bad state of mind and demoralized and that affects me. . . . I'd like to leave Cagnes; I can't stand the landscape."[6]

Barnes organizes an exhibition of Soutine's works in Guillaume's gallery and presents his acquisitions in the *Exhibition of Contemporary European Painting and Sculpture* at the Pennsylvania Academy of the Fine Arts in Philadelphia.

The French critic Roger Allard (1885–1961) is the first to use the term "École de Paris" (School of Paris) as a kind of collective term for those foreign artists who, like Soutine, had lived in Paris for a long time and felt a close affinity with Parisian and French art and culture.

Léger's essay "L'Esthétique de la machine" (The Aesthetic of the Machine) is published in the Rhenish magazine *Der Querschnitt*.

In the winter of 1923/24, the French franc is in crisis.

1924

Barnes's large acquisition grants Soutine a certain amount of financial independence, as well as individual and artistic recognition. This "peintre maudit" now becomes an established artist who wears suits, goes to restaurants, and generally presents himself as now belonging to a wealthier, more sophisticated, smart set. He avoids the places where he used to live and his former painter colleagues. He maintains contact only with Kikoïne and Krémègne.

He creates a series of still lifes with marine skates, in which he refers to Chardin's 1728 *La Raie (The Ray)*. His interest in literature grows and he reads works by Honoré de Balzac (1799–1850), Arthur Rimbaud (1854–1891), and Maxim Gorky (1868–1936).

André Breton publishes the Surrealist manifesto, *Manifeste du Surréalisme*.

The Summer Olympics are held in Paris.

The dancer Josephine Baker (1906–1975) takes Paris by storm.

The journal *La Révolution surréaliste* is founded (twelve issues are published until 1929, edited by André Breton, Pierre Naville, and Benjamin Péret).

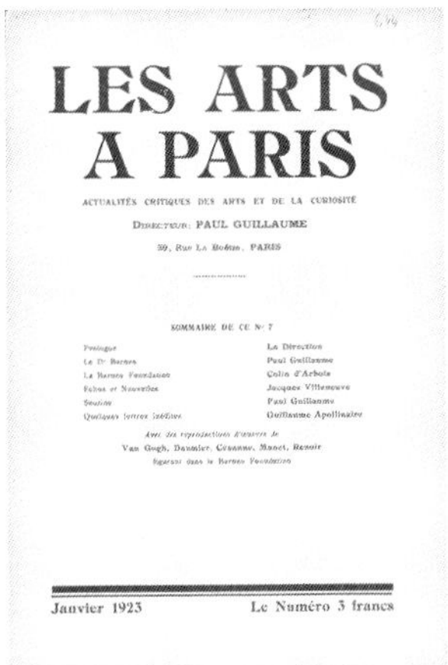

Paul Guillaume, *Les Arts à Paris: Actualités critiques des arts et de la curiosité*, no. 7 (January 1923)
Musée de l'Orangerie, Paris, Jean Walter and Paul Guillaume Collection

1925

Now able to afford his first apartment, Soutine moves into an elegant building on avenue du Parc-Montsouris. His large studio is located nearby on rue du Saint-Gothard. Over the next few years, Soutine often changes his residence, sometimes several times a year.

His partner Déborah Melnik, whom he has known since his studies in Vilnius, gives birth to their daughter Aimée. However, Soutine never recognizes the child as his own.

He travels to Amsterdam for the first time to study the works of Rembrandt van Rijn in the Rijksmuseum, and begins the series of slaughtered cattle, which comprises some ten works.

Chana Orloff later recalls: *"For a long time he had wanted to paint a picture in the spirit of Rembrandt's Carcass of Beef, without ever quite making up his mind to start. In the end he asked Zborowski to go with him to the abattoir and buy him a flayed beef carcass. The beef was brought back to the studio, and Soutine started painting. The beef carcass went black; it stank. The model had gone rotten, but Soutine could not afford another. He went to a butcher, bought a few litres of blood, splashed them over the carcass, and went on painting."* [7]

While the series of pastry chefs and cooks emphasized the color white, Soutine's painterly interest now focuses on the color red, which becomes a leitmotif in his ox paintings, as well as in the series of uniformed bellhops, elevator operators, and room service waiters. He then begins the series of choirboys.

Marcellin (1880–1966) and Madeleine Castaing (1894–1992) become avid collectors. At auctions, Soutine's works now fetch prices upward of three thousand francs.

The *Exposition internationale des arts décoratifs* is the first international exhibition to be held after the First World War. It takes place, however, without the participation of Germany.

Instead, German artists such as Willi Baumeister (1889–1955), Paul Klee (1879–1940), Walter Dexel (1890–1973), and Ida Kerkovius (1879–1970) concurrently show their works in the exhibition *L'Art d'aujourd'hui*.

1926

Soutine travels to Le Blanc (Centre-Val de Loire) to live and work in the house of the Zborowskis. He produces more paintings of slaughtered oxen and a series of still lifes with dead poultry.

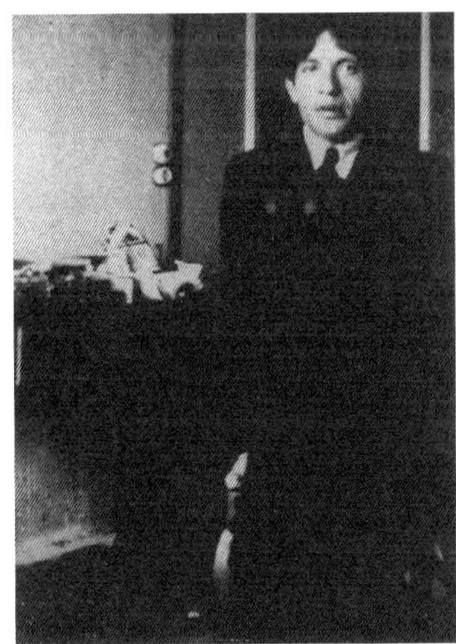

Soutine at Paris or Le Blanc, ca. 1927/28
Photographer unknown

Lunia Czechowska, a friend of the Zborowskis and a former model of Modigliani, will later report: *"Here, he painted large numbers of still lifes: ducks, guinea fowl, turkeys, pheasants, cockerels, chickens, to which he occasionally added a rabbit or a hare, as well as cabbages and tomatoes—all foodstuffs he brought from the market. He found the models for his portraits among the inhabitants of the village, especially among the young."* [8]

During this time, Zborowski puts his chauffeur, André Daneyrolles, at the artist's disposal. Daneyrolles drives the artist to Bordeaux, Le Blanc, and Paris.

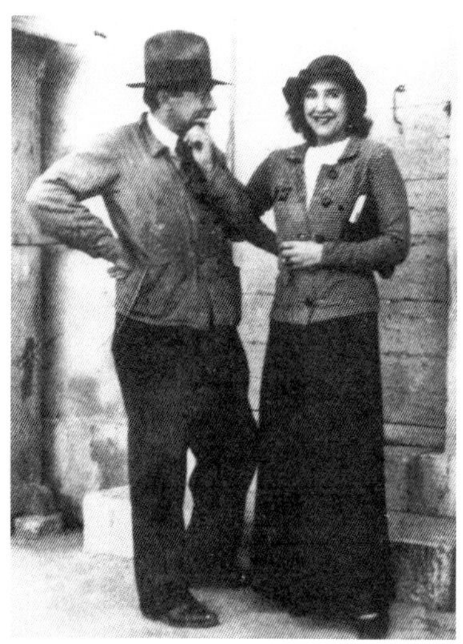

Soutine and Madeleine Castaing
Villefranche-sur-Mer, 1935
Photo: Archives Carlo Jansiti

He would say of the artist: *"Soutine made me read, imagine that! . . . He made me read Rimbaud. He made me read Seneca's letters to Lucilius. With him, you see, I wasn't a chauffeur. We would converse. We would talk about human evolution, the future of the world. He'd suffered so much, that Soutine!"* [9]

In *L'Amour de l'art*, the art critic Jerzy Waldemar Jarociński, known as Waldemar George (1893–1970), writes his first article on Soutine, who gains notoriety as a result and whose works now fetch twenty-two thousand francs at auction.

<hr>

The Dutch painter Kees van Dongen (1877–1968) meets with success in Paris.

Painters from the conservative École des Beaux-Arts, such as Paul-Albert Besnard (1849–1934) and Henri Gervex (1852–1929), are particularly popular.

1927

Soutine's first solo exhibition is held at the Galerie Henri Bing on rue La Boétie in Paris. He is generally uncomfortable around people and therefore does not attend the opening. [10]

In the United States—thanks to the commitment of Barnes—his works are shown in various group exhibitions, including in New York.

Soutine meets the art historian Élie Faure (1873–1937).

A close friendship develops between the Castaings and Soutine.

<hr>

In France, the extreme right-wing group Croix-de-Feu ("Cross of Fire"), composed mainly of war veterans, is founded. In 1931, this rightist league openly declares itself fascist, and by 1934/35, its membership rises to approximately 260,000.

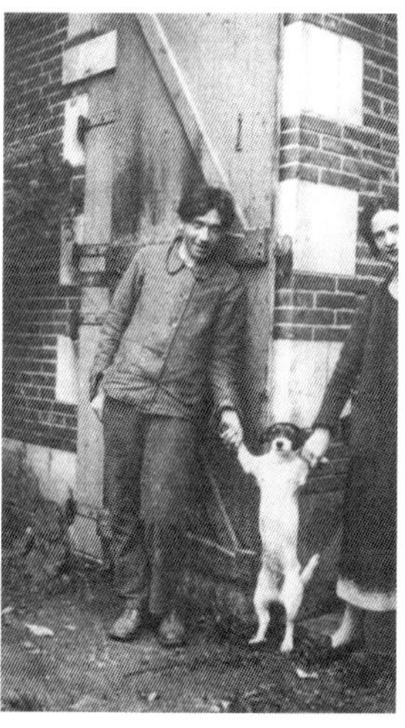

Soutine and Paulette Jourdain
Le Blanc, 1927
Photographer unknown

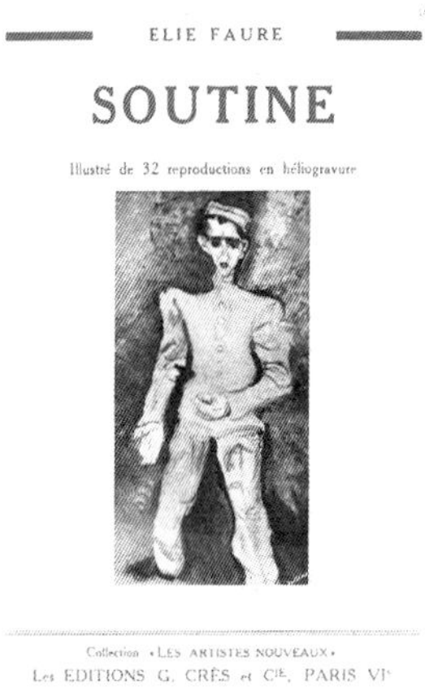

Élie Faure, *Soutine*
Les Éditions G. Crès et Cie, Paris 1929

1928

Waldemar George publishes the first monograph
on Soutine in a series on Jewish artists from Éditions
Le Triangle, *Artistes juifs*.

Soutine's works are shown in group exhibitions
in Paris and New York.

1929

Soutine spends time in Vence, where he paints
the series *Les Arbres de Vence*.

In Bordeaux, he visits Faure, who publishes a monograph on him. Because of a stomach ulcer, Soutine
takes the waters at Châtel-Guyon (Auvergne).

Sergei Diaghilev (1872–1929), who is planning
a ballet with a set painted by Soutine, dies before
the project comes to fruition.

In the fall, the collapse of the New York Stock
Exchange triggers the worldwide Great Depression.

1930–1932

The financial crisis weakens the Paris art market,
and with it Zborowski's business, which loses
its American clients. He can no longer represent
Soutine.

The Castaings become Soutine's patrons. They
support him financially, morally, and in everyday
matters. In return, they receive exclusive rights
to his works. Until the outbreak of the Second
World War in 1939, he lives intermittently with them
in Lèves (Centre-Val de Loire), where he meets the
art critic Maurice Sachs (1906–1945). The domestic
servants of the Castaing household sit for Soutine.

In 1932, Léopold Zborowski dies.

In 1930, the group Cercle et Carré is founded with
Willi Baumeister, Wassily Kandinsky (1866–1944), Piet
Mondrian (1872–1944), Fernand Léger, and Le Corbusier
(1887–1965).

The exhibition *Cent ans de peinture française* is held
in Paris, tracing a tradition in painting from Jean-
Auguste-Dominique Ingres (1780–1867) to Picasso.

A solo exhibition of Kandinsky is held at Galerie de
France in Paris.

In 1931, an exhibition of contemporary German painters
and sculptors is held, featuring works by Paul Klee,
Emil Nolde (1867–1956), Ernst Barlach (1870–1938),
Otto Mueller (1874–1930), and Paula Modersohn-Becker
(1876–1907).

The association Abstraction-Création is founded
by Josef Albers (1888–1976), Willi Baumeister,
Otto Freundlich (1878–1943), László Moholy-Nagy
(1895–1946), and Kurt Schwitters.

In 1931/32, the effects of the economic depression
become increasingly apparent in France.

1935

Soutine's first major exhibition in the United States is shown at the Arts Club of Chicago.

In Paris, he is represented with ten works in the exhibition *Peintres instinctifs: Naissance de l'expressionnisme*.

In 1933, French intellectuals, including André Gide (1869–1951), Paul Signac (1863–1935), Amédée Ozenfant (1886–1966), and Élie Faure sign a manifesto against fascism.

In 1934, the exposition of the *Comité francais pour la Protection des Intellectuels juifs persecutés* (French Committee for the Protection of Persecuted Jewish Intellectuals) is organized as part of the annual Salon d'Automne.

Salvador Dalí (1904–1989) is expelled in 1934 from the Surrealist group because of his work *L'Énigme Guillaume Tell* (*The Enigma of William Tell*).

The important exhibition of 1934/35, *Les Peintres de la réalité en France au XVIIe siècle*, draws on traditionalism (i.e., Nicolas Poussin, the brothers Le Nain, etc.) and supports the conservative tendency represented by the *Retour à l'ordre*.

The poet Louis Aragon (1897–1982) holds a lecture on "John Heartfield et la beauté révolutionaire."

The writers Georges Bataille (1897–1962) and André Breton speak out against National Socialism.

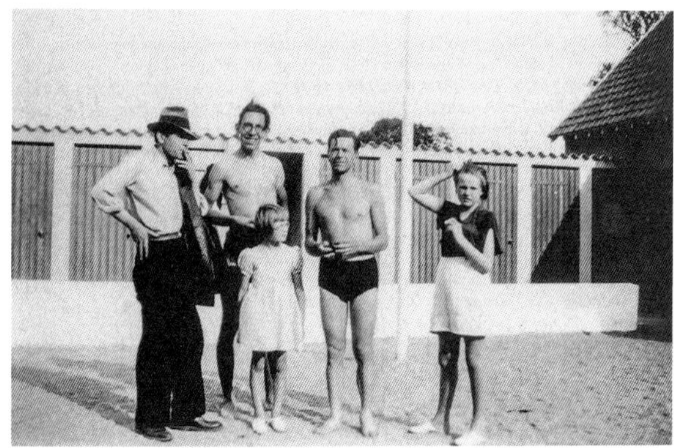

Soutine and the painter Constantin Terechkovitch at Pacy-sur-Eure, ca. 1936/37
Photographer unknown

1936

Soutine again moves several times within Paris. He finally settles in a small *hôtel particulier* on avenue d'Orléans.[11]

He reconnects with his family in Smilavičy for the first time.[12]

The Sullivan Gallery and the Valentine Gallery, which also represents Piet Mondrian, organize solo exhibitions of Soutine's work in New York.

In January, the French left agrees to a common program within the framework of the Front populaire (Popular Front).

In June, Léon Blum (1872–1950), a member of the Front populaire, becomes Prime Minister of France.

In Soutine's artistic circle, important debates on realism take place, led by, among others, Aragon, Le Corbusier, Léger, Ozenfant, André Lhote (1885–1962), and Édouard Goerg (1893–1969). The magazine *Commune* becomes the mouthpiece of their ideas.

1937

A retrospective of Soutine's work is held at the Leicester Galleries in London. Twelve of his works are shown in the exhibition *Les Maîtres de l'art indépendant, 1895–1937* at the Petit Palais in Paris.

Soutine meets Gerda Groth, née Michaelis, a German-Jewish exile. He calls her "Mademoiselle Garde." The couple moves into the Villa Seurat in the 14th arrondissement.

Gerda Groth later remembers: *"The atmosphere in the furnished apartment was very oppressive. There was nothing there to indicate the personality of the tenant. Later, I found out that Soutine was incapable of creating a personal ambience with his surroundings. He moved into an apartment without changing anything, as if he were just camping out there temporarily."*[13]

In the immediate neighborhood live, among others, Salvador Dalí, Henry Miller (1891–1980), and Chana Orloff (1888–1968), with whom he develops a close friendship.[14] The Ukrainian-Jewish sculptor is also friends with Chagall, Zadkine, and Max Jacob (1876–1944) and establishes close ties with Israel (then Palestine).

Increasingly severe pain, which a specialist diagnoses as a gastric ulcer, prevents Soutine from working. After adhering to a strict diet, his health gradually improves.

Léon Blum resigns due to the nation's financial difficulties.

Germany is represented at the 1937 Paris World's Fair by a pavilion designed by Albert Speer (1905–1981) with oversized nude sculptures by Josef Thorak (1889–1952).

Max Ernst and Paul Klee exhibit at the *Exposition internationale du surréalisme* in Paris.

1939

At the outbreak of the Second World War, Soutine lives with Gerda Groth in the village of Civry (Bourgogne-Franche-Comté). Both are registered as refugees and are not permitted to leave the small commune. Soutine again volunteers for the French army but is declared unfit to serve because of his health problems. He mainly paints poplars and landscapes with village children. Thanks to an exemption from his doctor, he is able to travel to Paris.[15]

Following the German invasion of Poland, France and Great Britain declare war on Germany on September 3.

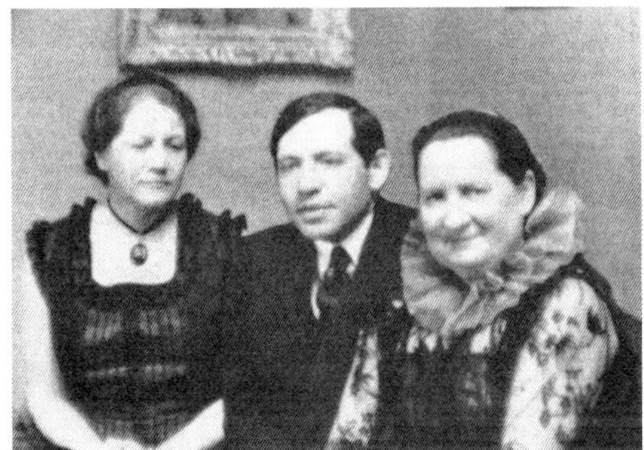

Olga Sacharoff, Soutine, and Chana Orloff, 1937
Photographer unknown

1940

Soutine is registered as a Jew. In May, Gerda Groth is deported by the German army to a camp at Gurs in the Pyrenees. She remains there for three months but, after being freed, never sees Soutine again, who nevertheless tries to help her financially.[16]

In Paris, the Castaings introduce Soutine to Marie-Berthe Aurenche (1905–1960), a painter and former wife of Max Ernst, and begins a relationship with her.

After the French defeat and armistice, German troops occupy Paris. France is divided into two zones, the north under German military occupation and the unoccupied south under the Vichy regime. Anti-Jewish restrictions and laws as well as anti-Semitic violence increase. Artists such as Chagall flee abroad and emigrate to the United States.

Charles de Gaulle founds the Comité national français (French National Committee) in London as the government in exile of Free France.

1941

Soutine returns to Paris. Despite the dangerous conditions, he refuses to leave the capital. He is afraid that he will not be able to find the milk he needs for his diet in the *zone libre* (free zone). He goes into hiding with Marie-Berthe Aurenche, and finds refuge with Fernand Moulin, a veterinarian well connected to the French Resistance. Forced to wear the yellow star, Soutine obtains false papers from Moulin. He now lives illegally and in constant fear of persecution. His stomach problems worsen and prevent him from painting.

Thanks to Moulin's support, the couple finds refuge in Champigny near Chinon (Centre-Val de Loire).

Under the new values of "Travail, Famille, Patrie" (work, family, fatherland) Philippe Pétain (1856–1951) promotes an ideological program of Révolution nationale (National Revolution).

Periodicals such as *Combat* and *Résistance* are founded.

The town of Smilaviči suffers the atrocities of the Holocaust. Almost all the inhabitants are murdered. It is assumed that Soutine's parents are among those killed.

1943

Soutine's health deteriorates dramatically, and he requires surgery. He is transferred from Chinon to a hospital in Paris.[17] The journey to the capital through several occupied departments is very risky for him. When he finally arrives in Paris, he is in critical condition. He undergoes surgery for a perforated ulcer and dies two days later, on August 9.

Picasso, Max Jacob, and Jean Cocteau (1889–1963) are among those who attend Soutine's funeral at Montparnasse Cemetery.

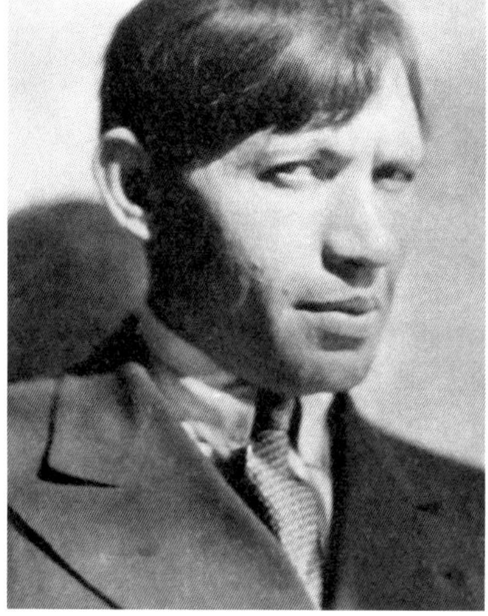

Chaïm Soutine, 1928
Musée d'Art et d'histoire du Judaïsme, Paris
Photographer unknown

In 1942, 65,000 Jews are deported from France to the East. Only 2,800 later return.

Hundreds of leftists and intellectuals are deported to Germany, including Aragon, Blum, Édouard Daladier (1884–1970), and Louis Madelin (1871–1956).

At the invitation of Joseph Goebbels, a group of French artists travels to Germany, including André Derain, Aristide Maillol (1861–1944), Maurice de Vlaminck (1876–1958), Kees van Dongen, and André Dunoyer de Segonzac (1884–1974).

Six thousand paintings, including works by André Masson (1896–1987), Picabia, Klee, Ernst, Léger, Joan Miró (1893–1983), Picasso, and Roger de La Fresnaye (1885–1925), are burned in the garden of the Jeu de Paume in Paris.

1 Henriette Zimmer, "Biography," in *Soutine und die Moderne/Soutine and Modernism*, exh. cat. Kunstmuseum Basel 2008 (Cologne: DuMont, 2008), pp. 199–233, here p. 199.

2 Michel Kikoïne, "Mes souvenirs sur mon camarade Soutine," in *Soutine*, ed. Maïthé Vallès-Bled, exh. cat. Musée des Beaux-Arts de Chartres 1989 (Chartres: Musée de Beaux-Arts de Chartres, 1989), p. 34.

3 Michel Kikoïne, quoted in "Repères biographiques," in *Chaïm Soutine: L'Ordre du chaos*, ed. Marie-Paule Vial and Claire Bernardi, exh. cat. Musée de l'Orangerie, Paris 2012/13 (Paris: Hazan, 2012), p. 158.

4 *Chaim Soutine*, ed. Maurice Tuchman, exh. cat. Los Angeles County Museum of Art 1968 (Los Angeles: Los Angeles County Museum of Art, 1968), p. 27.

5 Léopold Zborowski, quoted in Michel Georges-Michel, *From Renoir to Picasso: Artist in Action*, trans. Dorothy Weaver and Randolph Weaver (Boston: Houghton Mifflin, 1957), p. 148.

6 Soutine, quoted in Marcellin Castaing and Jean Leymarie, *Soutine* (New York: Harry N. Abrams, 1964), p. 23.

7 Chana Orloff, quoted in Esti Dunow and Ernst-Gerhard Güse, "Chronology," in C. *Soutine: 1893–1943*, ed. Ernst-Gerhard Güse, exh. cat. Westfälisches Landesmuseum, Münster 1981/82; Kunsthalle Tübingen 1982; Hayward Gallery, London (Arts Council of Great Britain) 1982; Kunstmuseum Luzern, Lucerne 1982 (London: Arts Council of Great Britain, 1982), p. 116.

8 Pierre Courthion, *Soutine: Peintre du déchirant* (Lausanne: Edita-Denoël, 1972), pp. 77–78.

9 André Daneyrolles, quoted in Courthion, *Soutine*, pp. 93–94; translation from Zimmer, "Biography," p. 212.

10 "Repères biographiques," p. 160.

11 Courthion, *Soutine*, p. 167.

12 This according to Sam Zarfin, a childhood friend of Soutine's from Smilaviçy: see Waldemar George, "Soutine," *Art et Style*, no. 52 (Paris, third quarter 1959), n.p.

13 George, "Soutine," n.p.

14 Zimmer, "Biography," p. 218.

15 Raymond Cogniat, *Soutine* (Geneva: Skira, 1952), p. 82.

16 Zimmer, "Biography," p. 222.

17 Cogniat, *Soutine*, p. 82.

Appendix

List of Works

[1]
Still Life with Herrings, 1915/16
Nature morte aux harengs
Oil on canvas
64.5 × 48.6 cm
Galerie Larock-Granoff, Paris

[2]
The Spotted Vase, 1918
Le Vase de fleurs
Oil on canvas
65 × 46 cm
Musée Unterlinden, Colmar
(Only in Humlebæk and Bern)

[3]
Bouquet of Flowers on a Balcony,
1916
*Bouquet de fleurs dans un vase
sur un balcon*
Oil on canvas
65.3 × 50.5 cm
Association des Amis du Petit
Palais, Geneva

[4]
Landscape with Houses, 1918
Paysage avec maisons
Oil on canvas
67.5 × 79 cm
Kunstmuseum Luzern, Lucerne

[5]
Self-Portrait, ca. 1918
Autoportrait
Oil on canvas
54.6 × 45.7 cm
Princeton University Art Museum
The Henry and Rose Pearlman
Foundation on loan since 1976
to the Princeton University Art
Museum
(Only in Humlebæk)

[6]
Le Mas Passe-Temps, Céret, 1920/21
Le Mas Passe-Temps, Céret
Oil on canvas
62.8 × 86.3 cm
Purchased 1981
National Galleries Scotland,
Edinburgh
(Only in Humlebæk and Bern)

[7]
Houses, 1920/21
Les Maisons
Oil on canvas
58 × 92 cm
Musée de l'Orangerie, Paris,
Jean Walter and Paul Guillaume
Collection

[8]
*The Plane Trees of Céret,
Place de la Liberté*, 1920/21
*Les Platanes à Céret,
Place de la Liberté*
Oil on canvas
60 × 73 cm
Von der Heydt-Museum,
Wuppertal

[9]
Village Square at Céret, 1920
La Place du village, Céret
Oil on canvas
76 × 94 cm
The Israel Museum, Jerusalem
Bequest of Sidney Bernstein,
London, on permanent loan from
The Jerusalem Foundation

[10]
Still Life with Pheasant, ca. 1919
Nature morte au faisan
Oil on canvas
92 × 60.5
Kunstsammlung Nordrhein-
Westfalen, Düsseldorf

[11]
Gladiolas, 1919
Glaïeuls
Oil on canvas
56 × 46 cm
Musée de l'Orangerie, Paris,
Jean Walter and Paul Guillaume
Collection

[12]
Child with a Toy, ca. 1919
L'Enfant au jouet
Oil on canvas
81 × 64.5 cm
Stiftung Im Obersteg, Depositum
im Kunstmuseum Basel 2004

[13]
The Old Girl, ca. 1920
La Vieille Fille
Oil on canvas
71.5 × 54 cm
MAH Musée d'Art et d'histoire,
Geneva, on loan from the
Fondation Jean-Louis Prevost,
Geneva, 1986

[14]
Peasant Boy, 1919/20
Le Paysan
Oil on canvas
64 × 55.2 cm
The Lewis Collection, London
(Only in Humlebæk and Bern)

[15]
Village Idiot, 1920
L'Idiot du village
Oil on canvas
92 × 65 cm
Musée Calvet, Avignon
Donation of Émile Joseph-Riqnault
to the Fondation Calvet, 1947

[16]
Landscape at Céret, ca. 1920/21
Paysage de Céret
Oil on canvas
55.9 × 83.8 cm
Tate

[17]
Hill at Céret, ca. 1921
La Colline de Céret
Oil on canvas
74.3 × 54.9 cm
Los Angeles County Museum of Art

[18]
The Little Pastrycook, 1922/23
Le Petit Pâtissier
Oil on canvas
73 × 54 cm
Musée de l'Orangerie, Paris,
Jean Walter and Paul Guillaume
Collection

[19]
Pastry Chef, ca. 1923
Chef pâtissier
Oil on canvas
64.5 × 48.3 cm
National Gallery of Art,
Washington, DC, Gift of the
Joseph H. Hazen Foundation,
Inc., 1971.2.2

[20]
Cook of Cagnes, ca. 1924
Le Cuisinier de Cagnes
Oil on canvas
61 × 51 cm
Kunstmuseum Bern, Bequest
Georges F. Keller, 1981

[21]
Landscape with Figures, ca. 1922
Paysage avec des personnages
Oil on canvas
64.1 × 38.1 cm
Private Collection
(Only in Bern)

[22]
*Still Life with Violin, Bread, and
Fish*, ca. 1922
*Nature morte au violon, pain et
poisson*
Oil on canvas
65 × 54 cm
Stiftung Im Obersteg, Depositum
im Kunstmuseum Basel 2004

[23]
The Rayfish, 1922
La Raie
Oil on canvas
81 × 47.5 cm
Musée Calvet, Avignon
Donation of Émile Joseph-Rignault
to the Fondation Calvet, 1947

[24]
Still Life with Rayfish, 1923
Nature morte à la raie
Oil on canvas
80.5 × 64.5 cm
The Cleveland Museum of Art,
Gift of the Hanna Fund

[25]
The Village, ca. 1923
Le Village
Oil on canvas
73.5 × 92 cm
Musée de l'Orangerie, Paris,
Jean Walter and Paul Guillaume
Collection

[26]
Landscape at Cagnes, ca. 1923
Paysage de Cagnes
Oil on canvas
60 × 73 cm
Kunstmuseum Bern, Bequest
Georges F. Keller, 1981

[27]
Landscape at Cagnes (La Gaude),
1923
Paysage à Cagnes (La Gaude)
Oil on canvas
81 × 100 cm
Gift of Pierre Larock and
his children, Pierre and Marc,
in memory of Katia Granoff, 1997
Centre Pompidou, Paris, Musée
national d'Art moderne / Centre de
création industrielle

[28]
Landscape at Cagnes, 1923/24
Paysage de Cagnes
Oil on canvas
60 × 73 cm
Courtesy Galerie Thomas, Munich

[29]
*View of Cagnes (La Gaude
and the Baous)*, 1922/23
*Vue de Cagnes (La Gaude
et les Baous)*
Oil on canvas
60.5 × 72.5 cm
Collection of the Musée des
Beaux-Arts, La Chaux-de-Fonds

[30]
The Road, ca. 1923/24
La Route (de Céret)
Oil on canvas
65.1 × 81 cm
SMB Staatliche Museen zu Berlin,
Nationalgalerie

[31]
The Road up the Hill, ca. 1924
La Route de la colline
Oil on canvas
72.4 × 60 cm
Tate, Bequeathed by Miss Helen
Drysdale, 1959

[32]
Stairway at Cagnes, ca. 1923/24
Escalier à Cagnes
Oil on canvas
60 × 73 cm
Courtesy David Lévy et associés,
Brussels

[33]
*The Uphill Road in Cagnes
(Landscape at Cagnes)*, ca. 1923/24
*Le Chemin montant à Cagnes
(Paysage de Cagnes)*
Oil on canvas
55.2 × 38.1 cm
Courtesy David Lévy et associés,
Brussels

[34]
The Old Actress, 1922
La Vieille Actrice
Oil on canvas
92.1 × 65.1 cm
Loaned from a Private Collection,
courtesy McClain Gallery, Houston

[35]
*Portrait of the Sculptor Oscar
Miestchaninoff*, 1923/24
*Portrait du sculpteur Oscar
Miestchaninoff*
Oil on canvas
83 × 65 cm
Bequest of Mme Miestchaninoff,
1972
Centre Pompidou, Paris, Musée
national d'Art moderne / Centre de
création industrielle

[36]
Woman in Red, 1923/24
La Femme en rouge
Oil on canvas
92 × 65 cm
Musée d'Art moderne de Paris

[37]
The Communicant (The Bride),
ca. 1924
La Communiante (La Mariée)
Oil on canvas
81.6 × 47.5 cm
The Lewis Collection, London
(Only in Humlebæk and Bern)

[38]
Woman in a Blue Dress, ca. 1924
La Femme à la robe bleue
Oil on canvas
81 × 60 cm
Musée d'Art moderne de Paris

[39]
Woman Knitting, ca. 1924/25
La Tricoteuse
Oil on canvas
82.55 × 59.69 cm
The Norton Simon Foundation,
Pasadena
(Only in Humlebæk and Bern)

[40]
The Gypsy, 1926
Le Tzigane
Oil on canvas
46 × 38 cm
SMK Statens Museum for Kunst,
Copenhagen

[41]
Hare against Green Shutter,
ca. 1924/25
Le Lièvre au volet vert
Oil on canvas
81.5 × 54.5 cm
Gifted in 1988
On loan since May 26, 1988, to
Musée d'Art moderne de Troyes
Centre Pompidou, Paris, Musée
national d'Art moderne / Centre de
création industrielle

[42]
*Chicken Hanging against Brick
Wall*, 1925
*Le Poulet pendu devant un mur
de briques*
Oil on canvas
65 × 46.5 cm
Kunstmuseum Bern, Bequest
Georges F. Keller, 1981

[43]
Chicken and Tomatoes, ca. 1924
Poulet et tomates
Oil on canvas
92.5 × 45 cm
Staatsgalerie Stuttgart

[44]
Two Pheasants, ca. 1924/25
Les Deux faisans
Oil on canvas
50 × 61 cm
Collection Emil Bührle, on long-
term loan to Kunsthaus Zürich

[45]
Pheasant, ca. 1924
Le Faisan
Oil on canvas
38.5 × 58.5 cm
ALBERTINA, Vienna

[46]
Dead Pheasant, ca. 1926/27
Le Faisan mort
Oil on canvas
52 × 72 cm
Stiftung Im Obersteg, Depositum
im Kunstmuseum Basel 2004

[47]
Turkey and Tomatoes, 1923/24
Dindon et tomates
Oil on canvas
81 × 49 cm
Musée de l'Orangerie, Paris,
Jean Walter and Paul Guillaume
Collection

[48]
Carcass of Beef, 1925
Le Bœuf écorché
Oil on canvas
116.21 × 80.65 cm
Lent by the Minneapolis Institute
of Art, Gift of Mr. and Mrs. Donald
Winston and an anonymous donor

[49]
Flayed Beef, 1925
Le Bœuf écorché
Oil on canvas
202 × 114 cm
Musée de Grenoble

[50]
Woman in Pink, ca. 1924
La Femme en rose
Oil on canvas
73 × 54.3 cm
Given by Sam J. Levin and Audrey
L. Levin
Saint Louis Art Museum

[51]
Grotesque, 1922–1925
Grotesque
Oil on canvas
81 × 45 cm
Musée d'Art moderne de Paris

[52]
Flayed Beef, ca. 1925
Le Bœuf écorché
Oil on canvas
72.5 × 49.9 cm
Kunstmuseum Bern, Bequest
Georges F. Keller, 1981

[53]
Side of Beef and Calf's Head,
ca. 1925
Bœuf et tête de veau
Oil on canvas
92 × 73 cm
Musée de l'Orangerie, Paris,
Jean Walter and Paul Guillaume
Collection

[54]
Hanging Fowl, 1925
La Volaille pendue
Oil on wood
125 × 80 cm
Former collection of Baron Kojiro
Matsukata allocated in 1959 to
the Musée national d'Art moderne
under the terms of the peace
treaty with Japan of 1952
Centre Pompidou, Paris, Musée
national d'Art moderne / Centre de
création industrielle

[55]
Hanging Turkey, 1925
La Dinde pendue
Oil on canvas
91.4 × 72.4 cm
Loaned from a Private Collection,
courtesy McClain Gallery, Houston

[56]
Dead Fowl, ca. 1924
La Volaille morte
Oil on canvas
110.4 × 81.1 cm
The Museum of Modern Art,
New York, Gift of Mr. and Mrs.
Justin K. Thannhauser, 1958

[57]
Bellboy (also known as *The
Groom*), 1925
Le Groom
Oil on canvas
98 × 80.5 cm
Former collection of Baron Kojiro
Matsukata allocated in 1959 to
the Musée national d'Art moderne
under the terms of the peace
treaty with Japan of 1952
Centre Pompidou, Paris, Musée
national d'Art moderne / Centre de
création industrielle

[58]
Page Boy at Maxim's, ca. 1927
Le Chasseur de chez Maxim's
Oil on canvas
129.5 × 66 cm
Collection Buffalo AKG Art
Museum
Edmund Hayes Fund, 1953

[59]
The Valet, ca. 1927
Le Valet de chambre
Oil on canvas
68.9 × 46 cm
The Lewis Collection, London
(Only in Humlebæk and Bern)

[60]
Head Waiter, ca. 1927
Le Maître d'hôtel
Oil on canvas
60 × 49.5 cm
Private Collection, Berlin,
on long-term loan to the
Museum Folkwang, Essen

[61]
Large Choirboy, 1925
Le Grand Enfant de chœur
Oil on canvas
100 × 55.9 cm
Gifted in 1995
On loan since June 19, 1995, to
Musée des Beaux-Arts de Chartres
Centre Pompidou, Paris, Musée
national d'Art moderne / Centre de
création industrielle

[62]
The Choirboy, ca. 1927
L'Enfant de chœur
Oil on canvas
77.5 × 39 cm
Stiftung Im Obersteg, Depositum
im Kunstmuseum Basel 2004

[63]
The Choirboy, 1925
L'Enfant de chœur
Oil on canvas
35.6 × 27.9 cm
Princeton University Art Museum
The Henry and Rose Pearlman
Foundation on loan since 1976
to the Princeton University Art
Museum
(Only in Humlebæk)

[64]
The Choirboy, 1927/28
L'Enfant de chœur
Oil on canvas
63.5 × 50 cm
Musée de l'Orangerie, Paris,
Jean Walter and Paul Guillaume
Collection

[65]
Cook with Blue Apron, ca. 1930
La Cuisinière en tablier bleu
Oil on canvas
128 × 50.5 cm
Stiftung Im Obersteg, Depositum
im Kunstmuseum Basel 2004

[66]
The Chambermaid, ca. 1930
La Femme de chambre
Oil on canvas
110.3 × 34 cm
Kunstmuseum Luzern, Lucerne

[67]
The Young Englishwoman, ca. 1934
La Jeune Anglaise
Oil on panel
56 × 34 cm
Stiftung Im Obersteg, Depositum
im Kunstmuseum Basel 2004

[68]
Little Girl in Blue, ca. 1934/35
La Petite Fille en bleu
Oil on wood
73 × 31.5 cm
Kunstmuseum Bern, Bequest
Georges F. Keller, 1981

[69]
Portrait of a Lady, ca. 1928
Portrait d'une dame
Oil on canvas
73 × 60 cm
Collection Emil Bührle, on long-
term loan to Kunsthaus Zürich
(Only in Bern)

[70]
Young Girl in Red, 1928
La Robe rouge
Oil on canvas
81.3 × 34.3 cm
The Israel Museum, Jerusalem
Bequest of Richard S. Zeisler,
New York, to American Friends of
the Israel Museum

[71]
White House, ca. 1933
La Maison blanche
Oil on canvas
65 × 50 cm
Musée de l'Orangerie, Paris,
Jean Walter and Paul Guillaume
Collection

[72]
Great Tree of Vence, ca. 1929
Le Grand Arbre de Vence
Oil on cardboard on plywood
61 × 44.5 cm
Kunstmuseum Bern, Bequest
Georges F. Keller, 1981

[73]
Tree in Vence, ca. 1929
L'Arbre de Vence
Oil on canvas
90 × 70 cm
The Israel Museum, Jerusalem
Gift of Jeanne Chasseguet Smirgel
and Bela Grunberger to the State
of Israel, by the Administrator
General, on permanent loan to the
Israel Museum, in memory of their
relatives from Poland, Hungary,
and France who perished in the
Holocaust

[74]
Woman Reading, ca. 1940
La Liseuse
Oil on canvas
65 × 80.5 cm
Gifted in 1995
Centre Pompidou, Paris, Musée
national d'Art moderne / Centre de
création industrielle

The paintings listed are included
in *Chaim Soutine (1893–1943):
Catalogue Raisonné – Werkverzeichnis*, ed. Maurice Tuchman,
Esti Dunow, and Klaus Perls, vols
1 and 2 (Cologne: Taschen, 1993).
The above catalog numbers 13,
19, 29, 32, 51, 63, 69, and 73 are
not listed therein. Vol. 3 of the
catalogue raisonné is currently in
preparation.

Authors' Biographies

Claire Bernardi is Senior Curator and Director of the Musée de l'Orangerie in Paris. She is a specialist in painting from the early twentieth century.

Among the exhibitions that she most recently curated are *Edvard Munch. A Poem of Life, Love and Death* (2022/23), *Picasso. Blue and Rose* (2018/1019), *Gauguin. The Alchemist* (2017/18), *Le Douanier Rousseau. Archaic Innocence* (2016), and *Allegro Barbaro. Béla Bartók and Hungarian Modernity, 1905–1920* (2013/14). In 2021/22, she co-curated *Soutine/de Kooning: Conversations in Paint* at the Barnes Foundation in Philadelphia and the Musée de l'Orangerie in Paris.

Marta Dziewańska is Curator at Kunstmuseum Bern. Between 2007 and 2018, she was Curator and Head of Research at the Museum of Modern Art in Warsaw, and in 2017, she was also a curatorial advisor for documenta 14, Athens and Kassel.

She has curated and co-curated various exhibition projects including *Anecdotes of Destiny. Selected Works from the Collection of Kunstmuseum Bern* (2023), *miriam cahn: MA PENSÉE SÉRIELLE* (2023), *Feliza Bursztyn: Welding Madness* (2021/22), *Things Fall Apart. Swiss Art from Boecklin to Vallotton* (2020), *MIRIAM CAHN: I AS HUMAN* (2019), and *Alina Szapocznikow: Human Landscapes* (2017).

She has also been the editor or co-editor of numerous exhibition catalogs. These include *Miriam Cahn: Ma pensée sérielle* (2023), *Tools for Utopia: Selected Works from the Daros Latinamerica Collection* (2020), *Points of Convergence: Alternative Views on Performance* (2017), *Maria Bartuszová: Provisional Forms* (2015), *1968–1989. Political Upheaval and Artistic Change* (2009). She has contributed to numerous other catalogs and art periodicals.

Catherine Frèrejean is an art historian and research assistant at the Kunstsammlung Nordrhein-Westfalen, Düsseldorf, where she most recently collaborated on the exhibitions *Etel Adnan. Poetry of Colors* (2023) and *Der Mucha – An Initial Suspicion* (2021/22).

She completed her Master's Degree in Curatorial Studies for 20th- and 21st-Century Art at Paul Valéry University of Montpellier. She wrote her interdisciplinary German-French doctoral thesis on the representation of the mechanical body in the avant-garde.

Her areas of interest in art history are corporeality, concepts of masculinity, and cultural transfer.

Sophie Krebs has been Chief Heritage Curator at the Musée d'Art moderne de Paris since 1989 and was responsible for the collections between 2011 and 2019. From 2001 to 2003, she was Curator of the Maison de Victor Hugo.

She has curated numerous exhibitions and was also responsible for editing the accompanying catalogs. These include *Victor Brauner: Je suis le rêve. Je suis l'inspiration* (2020), *Léonard Foujita: Œuvres d'une vie* (2019), *Albert Marquet: Peintre du temps suspendu* (2016), *Van Dongen: Fauve, anarchiste et mondain* (2011), *Raoul Dufy: Le Plaisir* (2008/09), *L'École de Paris, 1904–1929, la part de l'autre* (2001), *Le Temps menaçant, les années Trente en Europe* (1997), *Sima et le Grand Jeu* (1992).

She completed her doctoral thesis in 2009 under the supervision of Laurence Bertrand-Dorléac on the history and art of the "School of Paris" ("L'École de Paris, une invention de la critique d'art des années vingt"). She has published extensively, especially on subjects related to the École de Paris.

Susanne Meyer-Büser has been Curator for Contemporary Art and Classical Modernism at the Kunstsammlung Nordrhein-Westfalen, Düsseldorf, since 2009. Between 2006 and 2009 she was Director of Collections for the Painting and Sculpture Department at the Sprengel Museum Hannover.

She has curated numerous exhibitions, including *Mondrian. Evolution* (2022/23), *Georges Braque. Inventor of Cubism* (2021/22), *Carmen Herrera – Lines of Sight* (2017/18), *Otto Dix – The Evil Eye* (2017), *Alexander Calder – Avant-Garde in Motion* (2013/14), *Tomás Saraceno – in orbit* (2013), and *Marc, Macke and Delaunay. The Beauty of a Fragile World (1910–1914)* (2009).

She has taught at the Academy of Fine Arts (AdBK) in Munich, the University of Hildesheim, and the Karlsruhe University of Arts and Design (HfG). From 2010 to 2015, she was a member of the Expert Commission for the Support of Annual Programs of Art Associations in Lower Saxony. She is a member of the Expert Committee on Cultural Property of National Significance of North Rhine-Westphalia.

Pascale Samuel is Curator for Modern and Contemporary Art at the Musée d'Art et d'distoire du Judaïsme (mahJ), the Museum of Jewish Art and History in Paris.

She recently curated the exhibitions *Paris Magnétique. 1905–1940* in Berlin (2023, with Shelley Harten), *Chagall, Modigliani, Soutine. . . Paris as a School, 1905–1940* (2021), *Hersh Fenster and the Lost Shtetl of Montparnasse* (2021), *Si Lewen, The Parade* (Paris, 2021/22), and *Maya Zack, Acting Memory. Video works, 2007–2017* (2020/21).

She was previously Heritage Curator at the French Ministry of Culture. She completed her doctoral thesis at the Institut national du patrimoine and the École du Louvre, and she holds a Master's Degree in Law and Cultural Management. She is Associate Professor at Paul Valéry University of Montpellier.

Picture Credits

Francis Bacon © The Estate of Francis Bacon. All rights reserved / VG Bild-Kunst, Bonn 2023
Georg Baselitz © Georg Baselitz 2023
Oskar Kokoschka © Fondation Oskar Kokoschka / VG Bild-Kunst, Bonn 2023
Willem de Kooning © The Willem de Kooning Foundation, New York / VG Bild-Kunst, Bonn 2023
Alice Neel © Estate of Alice Neel, Courtesy Aurel Scheibler
Jean Fautrier, Jean Hélion, Abel Pann, and Georges Rouault © VG Bild-Kunst, Bonn 2023
Claims pursuant to §60 UrhG for the reproduction of images of works or works in the collection are asserted by VG Bild-Kunst.

© ADAGP, Paris 2010, pp. 57, 66.
Alamy Stock / Photo: Peter Horree, p. 54.
ALBERTINA, Vienna – Sammlung Batliner, p. 90.
akg-images, p. 64.
© Artists Rights Society (ARS), New York, p. 67.
bpk / Buffalo AKG Art Museum / Art Resource, NY, p. 107.
bpk / CNAC-MNAM / Jacques Faujour, p. 123.
bpk / CNAC-MNAM / Philippe Migeat, pp. 32, 80, 86, 101, 105.
bpk / CNAC-MNAM / Bertrand Prévost, p. 110.
bpk / CNAC-MNAM / Adam Rzepka, p. 69.
bpk / Los Angeles County Museum of Art / Art Resource, NY, pp. 12, 59.
bpk / Nationalgalerie, SMB, Eigentum des Landes Berlin / Jörg P. Anders, p. 74.
bpk / RMN-Grand Palais / Jean-Gilles Berizzi, p. 113.
bpk / RMN-Grand Palais / Agence Bulloz, pp. 83, 97.
bpk / RMN-Grand Palais / Yvan Galerne, p. 42.
bpk / RMN-Grand Palais / Thierry Le Mage, p. 61.
bpk / RMN-Grand Palais / Hervé Lewandowski, pp. 47, 51, 71, 99, 120.
bpk / RMN-Grand Palais / Franck Raux, p. 93.
bpk / Staatsgalerie Stuttgart, p. 89.
CC∅ Paris Musées / Musée d'Art moderne de Paris, p. 81.
Collection: Association des amis du Petit Palais, Genève / Photo: Studio Monique Bernaz, Geneva, p. 42.
© Courtesy Galerie Thomas, Munich, p. 72.
Courtesy Hastings Contemporary, p. 55.
Courtesy National Gallery of Art, Washington, DC, p. 62.
© David Levy & associés, Brussels, pp. 76, 77.
DIGITAL IMAGE © 2023, The Museum of Modern Art / Scala, Florence, p. 103.
Galerie Larock-Granoff, Paris, p. 41.
GRANGER, p. 94.
Paul Hester; Private Collection, courtesy McClain Gallery, pp. 79, 102.
© The Israel Museum, Jerusalem by Avshalom Avital, pp. 49, 119, 122.
Kunstmuseum Basel / Photo: Martin P. Bühler, pp. 53, 65, 91, 111, 114, 116.
© Kunstmuseum Bern, pp. 63, 70, 87, 98, 117, 121.
Kunstmuseum Luzern / Photo: Robert Baumann, p. 115.
Kunstmuseum Luzern / Photo: Andri Stadler, p. 43.
Kunstmuseum Zürich, Sammlung Emil Bührle, pp. 90, 118.
Kunstsammlung Nordrhein-Westfalen, Düsseldorf / Photo: Walter Klein, Düsseldorf, p. 50.
Musée des Beaux-Arts, La Chaux-de Fonds, Collection René et Madeleine Junod / Photo: Pierre Bohrer, Le Locle, p. 73.
© Museum Folkwang Essen – ARTOTHEK, p. 109.
National Galleries of Scotland / Photo: Antonia Reeve, p. 46.
Princeton University Art Museum, Princeton / Photo: Bruce M. White, pp. 45, 112.
Photo: Courtesy The Lewis Collection, pp. 82, 108.
Photo: Courtesy The Norton Simon Foundation, p. 84.
Photo: Hugo Maertens (F. Bacon CR 62-04), p. 136.
Photo: Tate, p. 58, 75.
SMK, National Gallery of Denmark, p. 85.
Vidimages / Alamy Stock Photo, p. 94, 96.
Ville de Grenoble / Musée de Grenoble – J. L. Lacroix, p. 95.
Von der Heydt-Museum Wuppertal / Photo: Von der Heydt-Museum Wuppertal, p. 48.

Copyright and Picture Credits for the Figures and Illustrations:

Archive PL / Alamy Stock Photo, p. 22.
Artepics / Alamy Stock Photo, p. 25.
bpk / adoc-photos, p. 21.
bpk / DeAgostini / New Picture Library / M. Carrieri, p. 147.
bpk / DeAgostini / New Picture Library / G. Dagli Orti, p. 155.
bpk / The Jewish Museum of New York / Art Resource, NY, p. 142r.
bpk / The Metropolitan Museum of Art, p. 19.
bpk / Ministère de la Culture – Médiathèque du Patrimoine, Dist. RMN-Grand Palais / Jules Seeberger / Louis Seeberger / Henri Seeberger, p. 16.
bpk / Paris Musées, Dist. RMN-Grand Palais / Photo: Ville de Paris, pp. 128, 130.
bpk / RMN-Grand Palais / Archives Alain Bouret / Dominique Couto, pp. 127, 156, 157.
bpk / RMN-Grand Palais / Labouche Frères phototypistes à Toulouse, p. 140.
bpk / Scala, p. 145.
bpk / The Solomon R. Guggenheim Foundation / Art Resource, p. 137.
bpk / Sprengel Museum Hannover, Leihgabe Warwick Collection / Herling / Herling / Werner, p. 138.
Courtesy Galerie Alain Margaron, p. 130.
culture-images / fai, p. 128.
Digital image, The Museum of Modern Art, New York / Scala, Florence, p. 135.
GRANGER – Historical Picture Archive / Alamy Stock Photo, p. 26.
Gravure Francaise / Alamy Stock Photo, p. 34.
IMAGO / KHARBINE-TAPABOR, p. 124.
Michel LeBrun-Franzaroli, pp. 2–3, 8.
Matteo Omied / Alamy Stock Photo, p. 127.
Photo: © mahJ / Christophe Fouin, p. 31.
Photo: © mahJ, pp. 28, 35, 132, 152, 153, 154, 156, 162.
Vidimages / Alamy Stock Photo, p. 18.
World History Archive / Alamy Stock Photo, p. 24.

The Following Figures and Illustrations Were Taken from the Below Mentioned Publications

Image citation from: *Chaim Soutine (1893–1943): Catalogue Raisonné – Werkverzeichnis,* ed. Maurice Tuchman, Esti Dunow, and Klaus Perls (Cologne: Taschen, 1993), pp. 561, 567, 471; here pp. 19, 22, 138.
Image citation from: Michel LeBrun-Franzaroli, *Soutine photographié* (Concremiers: Michel Lebrun-Franzaroli, 2018), pp. 71, 40, 21, 62, 21, 95; here pp. 36, 150, 152, 153, 157, 160, 161.
Image citation from: *Soutine und die Moderne / Soutine and Modernism*, ed. Nina Zimmer, exh. cat. Kunstmuseum Basel 2008 (Cologne: DuMont, 2008), pp. 24, 201, 51, 225; here pp. 151, 158.
Image citation from: Élie Faure, *Soutine* (Paris: Éditions G. Crès et Cie, 1929), cover; here p. 159.

We have made every effort to list all copyright notices. Copyright holders that are not correctly identified are kindly asked to contact the editors. Compensation will be made according to standard practice.

Colophon

This catalog is published on the occasion
of the exhibition

Chaïm Soutine. Against the Current
K20 Kunstsammlung Nordrhein-Westfalen, Düsseldorf
September 02, 2023, to January 14, 2024
Louisiana Museum of Modern Art, Humlebæk
February 9 to July 14, 2024
Kunstmuseum Bern
August 16 to December 01, 2024

The exhibition is a collaboration between
Kunstsammlung Nordrhein-Westfalen,
Louisiana Museum of Modern Art, Humlebæk,
and Kunstmuseum Bern.

CATALOG

Edited by Susanne Gaensheimer and
Susanne Meyer-Büser

Editing: Susanne Meyer-Büser

Image Editing: Catherine Frèrejean

Publication Management: Cordula Frevel

Editorial Direction: Angelika Thill

Production: Kati Klaeske

Copyediting: José Enrique Macián

Translation: Gérard Goodrow (German–English),
R. J. Wheelwright (French–English)

Design: Bureau Mathias Beyer, Cologne

Typeface: LL Brown

Paper: Arctic Volume White, 150 g/m^2

Reproductions: Schwabenrepro, Fellbach

Printing and Binding: Westermann Druck Zwickau
GmbH, Zwickau

Published by
Hatje Cantz Verlag GmbH
Mommsenstrasse 27
10629 Berlin
Germany

www.hatjecantz.com

A Ganske Publishing Group company

ISBN 978-3-7757-5541-2 (English)
ISBN 978-3-7757-5540-5 (German)

Printed in Germany

Bibliographic information published by the Deutsche
Nationalbibliothek
The Deutsche Nationalbibliothek lists this publication in
the Deutsche Nationalbibliografie; detailed bibliographic
data are available online at http://www.dnb.de

All rights reserved. No part of this publication may be
reproduced, translated, stored in a retrieval system, or
transmitted in any form or by any means (electronic and
mechanical, including photocopying or recording) without prior written permission from the copyright holders.

© 2023 Hatje Cantz Verlag, Berlin, Kunstsammlung
Nordrhein-Westfalen, Düsseldorf, and the authors

Front Cover:
Chaïm Soutine, *La Vieille actrice* (*The Old Actress*), 1922
Oil on canvas, 92.1 × 65.1 cm, Loaned from a Private
Collection, courtesy McClain Gallery, Houston

Back Cover:
Chaïm Soutine, 1928
Musée d'Art et d'histoire du Judaïsme, Paris
Photographer unknown
Photo © mahJ

EXHIBITION

Director: Susanne Gaensheimer

Commercial Manager: Bianca Knall

Curator: Susanne Meyer-Büser

Assistant curator: Catherine Frèrejean

Exhibition Management: Dagmar Kurtz

Registrar: Katharina Nettekoven

Conservation: Elena Fernandéz-Vegue,
Rea Grammatikopoulou, Sven Kamp, Tzu-Chuan Lin,
Nina Quabeck, Anne Skaliks, Jessica Völkert-Lunk

Architecture, Media, and Light: Thomas Hoppe,
Ingo Lanninger, Bernd Schliephake, Bernd Strauchmann

Media Technology: Jens Meller, Oswin Schmidt

Education: Anika Plank, Peter Schüller, Nesrin Tanç

Publishing: Cordula Frevel

Library and Research: Christine Breitschopf

Press and Public Relations: Susanne Fernandes Silva,
Jan Schillmöller

Marketing and Digital Marketing: Meike Lotz-Kowal,
Marita Rowlands, Aras San

Public Procurement: Christina Rock

Funding: Isabella Wild

TEAM STIFTUNG KUNSTSAMMLUNG NORDRHEIN-WESTFALEN

Board: Susanne Gaensheimer, Bianca Knall

Director: Susanne Gaensheimer

Commercial Manager: Bianca Knall

Curatorial Assistent to the Director: Leonore Spemann

Assistent to the Commercial Manager: Isabella Wild

Secretarial Assistants to the Directors: Miriam Pohle, Arpi Sarkissian

Curatorial Department: Patrizia Dander, Kathrin Beßen, Catherine Frèrejean, Victoria Haas, Doris Krystof, Isabelle Malz, Susanne Meyer-Büser, Vivien Trommer, Katja Winterpagt, Falk Wolf, Victor Zaiden

Library: Christine Breitschopf, Michelle Borrey, Gesa Krauss, Gabriele Lauser

Education: Julia Hagenberg, Zoe Benien, Irina Bernt, Anna Döbbelin, Anjouna Novak, Annika Plank, Peter Schüller, Nesrin Tanç

Visitor Service: Nikolaos Kessopoulos, Markus Vogt

Exhibition Management: Stefanie Jansen, Dagmar Kurtz, Karoline Sieg

Registrar: Katharina Nettekoven, Jennifer Buchholz, Daphne Kramer

Conservation: Nina Quabeck, Elena Fernández-Vegue, Lennart Foppe, Rea Grammatikopoulou, Sven Kamp, Tzu-Chuan Lin, Anne Skaliks, Jessica Völkert-Lunk

Press and Public Relations: Susanne Fernandes Silva

Marketing and Digital Marketing: Meike Lotz-Kowal, Sophie Krause, Marita Rowlands, Aras San, Maike Teubner

Administration and Human Resources: Christina Rock

Administration: Klaus-Peter Allenstein, Ingo Lanninger, Frank Mankel, Stefan Müller-Stapper, Daniel Vetter

Public Procurement, Purchasing, Legal: Christina Rock, Claudia Fischer-Jaworsky, Dorothea Heitfeld

Human Resources: Nadine Cura, Georgia Coutri, Monika Fischer

Finances: Caroline Krump, Désirée Berendonk, Kerstin Thielo

Sales and Publishing: Cordula Frevel, Martin Heyer, Alexia Krauthäuser, Roman Majewski, Marion Vogt

Technical Department: Bernd Schliephake, Andreas Grella, Thomas Hoppe, Birger Labinsch, Jens Meller, Britta Pfeiffer, Oswin Schmidt, Bernd Strauchmann, Zoltan Ternai

Security: Ramon Karbach, Davoud Afrasiabi, Tobias Becker, Dietmar Bütau, Artur Burgner, Dirk Fittkau, Andreas Grund, Philipp Grund, Hans Peter Hönig, Michael Jaschzyk, Nicholas Robert Johnson, Carsten Laaser, Torsten Machtans, Mario Metz, Dominik Nowak, Bülent Özer, Elvis Selim, Katrin Sondermeier, Michael Stanaszek, Vassilios Vassiliou

ArtPartner Relations GmbH
Lilli von Bodman, Anne Clever

Freunde der Kunstsammlung Nordrhein-Westfalen e.V.
Chairman: Leopold Freiherr von Diergardt
Jutta Müller, Bianca Böhm, Linda Inconi-Jansen

Stiftung Kunstsammlung Nordrhein-Westfalen
Grabbeplatz 5
40213 Düsseldorf
www.kunstsammlung.de

**Kunstsammlung
Nordrhein-Westfalen**

LOUISIANA MUSEUM OF MODERN ART

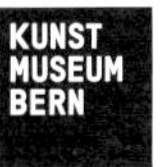

Supported by

**Freunde der
Kunstsammlung
Nordrhein-Westfalen**

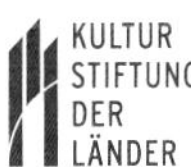
KULTUR
STIFTUNG
DER
LÄNDER

Ministerium für
Kultur und Wissenschaft
des Landes Nordrhein-Westfalen

Media partner

Frankfurter Allgemeine